Exoticisation undressed

MANCHEStER
1824

Manchester University Press

New
Ethnographies

Series editor
Alexander Thomas T. Smith

Already published

The British in rural France:
Lifestyle migration and the ongoing quest for a better way of life Michaela Benson

Ageing selves and everyday life in the North of England:
Years in the making Catherine Degnen

Chagos islanders in Mauritius and the UK:
Forced displacement and onward migration Laura Jeffery

South Korean civil movement organisations:
Hope, crisis and pragmatism in democratic transition Amy Levine

Integration, locality and everyday life:
After asylum Mark Maguire and Fiona Murphy

An ethnography of English football fans:
Cans, cops and carnivals Geoff Pearson

Loud and proud:
Passion and politics in the English Defence League Hilary Pilkington

Literature and agency in English fiction reading:
A study of the Henry Williamson Society... Adam Reed

International seafarers and the possibilities for transnationalism in
the twenty-first century Helen Sampson

Devolution and the Scottish Conservatives:
Banal activism, electioneering and the politics of irrelevance Alexander Smith

Performing Englishness:
Identity and politics in a contemporary folk resurgence
Trish Winter and Simon Keegan-Phipps

Exoticisation undressed

Ethnographic nostalgia and authenticity in Emberá clothes

Dimitrios Theodossopoulos

Manchester University Press

Published by Manchester University Press
Altrincham Street, Manchester M1 7JA, UK
www.manchesteruniversitypress.co.uk

British Library Cataloguing-in-Publication Data is available

ISBN 978 1 5261 0083 2 *hardback*
ISBN 978 1 5261 3458 5 *paperback*

First published by Manchester University Press in hardback 2016

This edition first published 2018

Typeset by Out of House Publishing

Contents

Figures

All images and figures © Dimitrios Theodossopoulos unless otherwise stated

Boxes

Preface to the paperback edition

The first edition of this book positioned my account of the Emberá of Chagres in time. It provided a narrative—a record of some sort—that can play a part in shaping the self-representation of these people as it unravels in contemporary debates. Such is the power of ethnographic monographs: they freeze ethnographic realities in time, setting up standards of authenticity to compare the present with the past. In this respect, ethnographic monographs generate nostalgia, but also authority. They constrain the ways we think about the present and the past—by generating authenticating descriptions locked in the past—but they also inspire comparison, providing a pivotal foundation for the self-reflexive subversion of authoritative, authenticating descriptions.

This book is—and has been, during the first two years of its existence—a provocation to re-examine the ethnographic project: in particular, the influence of earlier scholars (or that of our own previous work) on what we write in the present. I refer to the influence (of past-writing on current-writing) as 'ethnographic nostalgia', an analytical concept that I use to make visible the exoticising filters of Western imagination in shaping parallel views of indigeneity. As such, the book is as much about the Emberá of Chagres, as about the manner in which others see them.

Another innovation introduced in this book relates to a representational tactic: the split of authorship in to two; here, between a younger empiricist author and an older deconstructive analyst. The resulting tension provides a dynamic avenue for reflexivity. It makes visible, more explicitly, the simple truth that the ethnographic project is not singular, but involves a struggle of different voices in the author's mind: these may address different views of social reality and more than one local opinions. Reflexivity also exposes the exotic bias, making obvious that ethnographic nostalgia is not a single battle that can be fought and won, but a formidable bias that continuously re-emerges as a phoenix rising out of its ashes.

So, I now look with nostalgia at the moment when I completed this book: the possibilities that this moment of completion has made available for the study of the Emberá, or for ethnographic representation more generally. I am worried that I may fall, once more, in the trap of exoticising nostalgia; that my own view of the Emberá will be distorted by the authoritative effect of my writing. But I am also excited about the possibilities of using the knowledge in the book for the benefit of the Emberá. I see with pleasure that NGO practitioners and indigenous leaders use the histories (I traced through my writing) to solidify their struggle for land rights and recognition. And I recognise, with some ambivalence, that a certain degree of ethnographic authority can help indigenous groups in their political battles. Here my young empiricist authorial Self—and his 'evidence'—can be, at a practical level, more useful than the more nuanced, de-essentialising voice in my head. Time will tell.

On the theoretical side, my decision to use concepts developed through research in other parts of the world—for example, Herzfeld's notion of *disemia*—in an Amerindian context, speaks to my belief that this cross-fertilisation should be a primary objective in social analysis, despite the contemporary tendency to confine particular academic literatures within specific regional fields. And I find the claim of the Emberá that they are (and can be) indigenous *and* modern a fascinating enticement to embark in new cross-cultural comparisons.

My final reflection in this foreword concerns the use of digital- and hand-drawing in the book, a medium I employed to make visible the exoticising filters and distortions of the ethnographic project; in particular, the view that the present is a shadow of the past emerging from the pages of a previous, older ethnography. Since the publication of the book, drawing and sketching have received renewed acknowledgement by ethnographers. Graphic ethnography is now emerging as an acclaimed medium, enabling analytic interventions that expand beyond the descriptive use of drawing as illustration. I am delighted to see these developments and I admit that my own sketches—those in the pages of the book, and those I omitted—have shaped my analytical thinking and my understanding of authenticity, exoticisation and nostalgia.

With these thoughts in mind, I welcome the paperback edition of *Exoticisation Undressed*, and I am looking forward to seeing how the book will inspire or enable the work and arguments of others: academics, NGO practitioners and indigenous leaders.

Dimitrios Theodossopoulos
Canterbury, June 29, 2018

Preface to the original

I should start by making myself more visible to the reader; I see this as a responsibility and duty, more so in the preface of a monograph that is deeply concerned with the style of ethnographic exposition. My journey through the world of Emberá clothes has been haunted by the spectres of nostalgia and exoticisation, and in particular the persistent tension brought about by the recognition of my limitations as an analyst and the liberating analytic possibilities engendered by this very recognition. My internal struggle to balance my idealisation and deconstruction has produced in its wake creative disagreement. On the one hand I battle with my proclivity to idealise, over-interpret and identify with indigenous tradition while overlooking non-indigenous influences. On the other hand I take great effort to identify the nostalgic, exoticising inclinations of the anthropological endeavour. Importantly, I approach such liabilities without guilt, treating them instead as opportunities for the production of knowledge, committed to my argument that through reflexive treatment, ethnographic nostalgia can lead to thicker anthropological analysis.

In the box below you see the caricatures of my two authorial voices, presented to capture idealisation and deconstruction. Such caricatures are comfortably situated in the artificial environment of exoticisation; with their comic simplicity, they embrace the very source of embarrassment. Used here, they point sharply to the contradictions that engender the futile and essentialist search for a singular authenticity in social life, the illusion of singular narrative. My self-caricaturing here attempts to defy singularity:

Box 1

THE
AUTHOR,
YOUNG

There is one particular niggling voice in my mind that I have never managed to dismiss, that of myself as a young ethnographer. His contagious enthusiasm for fieldwork comes partly from the training he received in the United Kingdom. He believes that recording the details of local social life is an end goal in itself, and that ethnography is more important than theory. Yet, despite his firm belief in the empirical project of anthropology, he is not a positivist, but is fully dedicated to the study of the particular. Ethnographic detail is magical and beautiful, he advocates.

My younger anthropological Self is a champion of ethnographic nostalgia. He is fascinated by indigenous-*cum*-traditional structure and form, which he encounters both in anthropological literature and in everyday life. And he searches for the past in the present – a past formed by a previous ethnological record. This is why he spends significant time collecting other ethnographic accounts, published and unpublished, about the people he studies.

He values the systematic comparison of the ethnographic past with the present, and calls this endeavour 'scholarly work'. He dismays when he realises that his scholarly work is considered by many boring, or outdated. Hence, he persists in writing for a small readership of specialists.

THE
AUTHOR,
OLD

The other voice that prevails in my mind challenges, like a sophist, everything that my younger Self has accomplished. This is an identity I acquired after reading widely, teaching and embracing more than one type of anthropology. This part of me appreciates ethnography in depth, but does not believe that the anthropological project is ethnographic. Aware that non-specialists are bored with ethnographic details, he experiments with new mediums of representation. Anthropology should address broader and more timely questions, he advocates.

This older anthropological Self of mine attempts to problematise ethnographic nostalgia. He is likely to acknowledge that indigeneity is not confined to pre-modern structure and form, and that indigenous people embrace modernity. He does not see the technologies of globalisation as corruptive or alienating, and he hastily embraces change. Rather than dismissing the exotic form, he attempts to learn from the process of exoticisation.

He approaches his own writing and scholarly comparisons with a critical spirit, aware that what he finds fascinating may only concern a privileged readership of specialists. Hence, he keeps on reminding himself that anthropology should be communicable to the wider public.

The struggle between those two ideal-*cum*-stereotypical anthropological types has shaped the presentation of this book. Although my older authorial Self has obviously the upper hand in managing the plot, my younger Self has negotiated some concessions in relation to content. A concern with close ethnographic comparison and corroboration – however wearisome some readers may find it – is still evident in the main body of the book, confined to particular chapters or text boxes. Such detail is valuable to area and subject specialists, making its contribution to a slowly expanding ethnographic literature about the Emberá. Yet, by becoming part of this literature – a standard of academic authenticity of a sort – the book signals its complicity with the production of ethnographic nostalgia.[1]

Ethnographic nostalgia, I argue, is at play in the way that previous ethnographic writings – in this case, about the Emberá – structure, perhaps even preempt, the ethnographer's comprehension of the ethnographic reality in the present. However irredeemable, ethnographic nostalgia has played a crucial role in the furthering of academic knowledge. It has motivated a persistent scholarly endeavour that attempts to compare the ethnographic past with the present, often in an effort to grasp the secrets of social change. Everything, including our knowledge about society, is subject to change. Our struggle to depart from the knowledge we have acquired – often with some nostalgic reluctance – engenders the discovery of what is new. It is in this sense that the tension between these two positions, empiricist and deconstructive, shapes the form of this book.

I started my fieldwork in the rainforest of Chagres as an established academic, renowned for my research on the anthropology of Europe. I thus carried with me the lessons acquired in my previous research and training, including a sceptical inclination towards the exaggeration of difference. But coming to a new field, I felt also the desire of my younger anthropological Self to 'rediscover' the Emberá in a manner that bore resemblance to previous ethnographic accounts. In other words, this part of me hoped to see the Emberá as they had been recorded before, as if they had emerged from the pages of a book. Admittedly, such exoticising and nostalgic predilections were accentuated by the particular ethnographic setting. In Chagres, where I conducted my fieldwork, the Emberá put on traditional attire to entertain foreign tourists. Their daily dress codes shift during the day and include modern, indigenous and indigenous-*and*-modern clothes. These varied – formal, informal and spontaneous – dress combinations encouraged me to compare the Emberá of Chagres with the ethnographic accounts of previous eras: the Emberá conceived as people outside modernity (Nordenskiold 1928; Torres de Araúz 1966; Reverte Coma 2002), and the Emberá as a rapidly modernising people (Kane 1994; Herlihy 1986).

I traced these two separate ethnographic views of the Emberá in the everyday reality of my fieldwork at Chagres. And as I found elements of both in the present, I gradually acquired the nostalgic impression that reality was in part constructed through the ethnographies I had read. As if images from different eras – the 1920s, 1960s, 1980s – were superimposed on each other, generating a contradictory complexity and a number of 'authentic discontinuities', an expression I borrow from

Kane (1994) to address the rifts between an idealising past and a modernising encroaching present, where the past persists and re-emerges in the present.

The illustrations that support this book attempt to capture this sense of simultaneity. By filtering (digitally) and altering (by hand) my photographic record, I have produced a series of black-and-white sketches. They make visible precisely the nostalgic sensation I had during fieldwork, the feeling that the present comes to light filtered through the pages of an older book. And by presenting my visual aids as artistic reconstructions of my ethnographic nostalgia – as incomplete, open-ended depictions (Taussig 2011; Ingold 2012), not absolute records of a singular authenticity – I expose the subjectivity of my account and its proclivity to fuel – by freezing ethnographic time (see Fabian 1983) – the ethnographic nostalgia of the future.

As I mentioned above, I have approached the parallel, coexisting and complicating authenticities I experienced in the field through the lens of my previous training, writing and career. This partly involved introducing analytical tools that are not rooted in the anthropology of Latin America, resulting in some cross-fertilisation across otherwise discrete fields. An example of this is *disemia*, a concept that I borrow from Herzfeld (2005) to address the ambivalence between official self-representation and informal self-recognition. The originality of Herzfeld's conception allows to us appreciate how ambivalence – and the tensions it propagates – does not necessarily generate an unresolvable split in the identities of local actors. My adaption of *disemia* to analyse indigenous representation attempts to illustrate the simultaneity of modernity and indigeneity in everyday narratives and experiences. *Indigenous disemia* captures the ambivalence between a formal view of modernity and indigeneity, and a fluid, subversive experience of being simultaneously modern-*and*-indigenous. Some of the dress codes of the Emberá in Chagres, despite clothes-shifts and contradictions, are simultaneously indigenous-*and*-modern.

In being simultaneously indigenous-*and*-modern, the shifting dress codes of the Emberá in Chagres – the westernmost edge of the Emberá distribution in Panama – offered me an opportunity to think anthropologically about modernity and indigeneity; not as two forces in opposition, but as two sides of the same coin. Chagres, as a location for my fieldwork, encouraged me to think in broader terms, not merely about the representational awareness of the Emberá, but also about authenticity as representativeness. It is precisely because Parara Puru, my field site, is located so close to the Panama Canal and Panama City that it has attracted accusations of inauthenticity, as if the community is, somehow, less Emberá than other Emberá communities:[2] a community only an hour and half away from Panama City, yet approachable only by dugout canoe; a community in the rainforest, so far away but so close to the crossroads of international capitalism and commerce. Contradictions of this type stimulate the allure of the exotic, but also its very denial: the Emberá in Parara Puru do not live in a museum, but in a politically organised community, as so many other Emberá in Eastern Panama.

I could have written many different accounts of the Emberá in Parara Puru. The one I present in this book intentionally adopts more than one style of ethnographic description. Taken alongside the visual aids that support this book, these styles represent different elements of analysis, different degrees of tinkering with the ethnographic moment. They are incomplete depictions of a reality that is so complex that it defies comprehensive explanation. However, by putting these different styles of writing side by side I attempt to shed light on more than one – incomplete – aspect of the same theme. Indeed, at times I deliberately refer to the same story, but narrated from a different point of view. For example, early in the book (Chapter 2) I provide a 'static' description of the traditional Emberá attire, which represents a prescribed authenticity denied by all other chapters in the book. And I have chosen to present a linear story of the Emberá clothes (Chapter 3), drawing attention to processes and inter-connections in time and space, which is further complicated by the bottom-up ethnographic style adopted in the second half of the book. Similarly, the historical ethnography in Chapter 4, where I examine the exoticising narratives of two Western explorers, is complemented by a more synchronic analysis – the voices of here and now – in the chapters that follow.

I would have liked to write many different accounts about the Emberá in Chagres. Not only are there different styles of ethnographic presentation, but also countless aspects of the life of the Emberá that I do not tackle in this book, although I hope to in the future. Many colleagues who are Amazonian specialists will be disappointed to find only a small amount of information about kinship, ontology and symbolism, themes that remain fertile grounds for investigation in the Emberá world. Similarly, many colleagues who write about Panama might expect a comprehensive ethnography about the Emberá of Chagres, with more emphasis on the economy of tourism and the representational peculiarities that make this ethnographic context so distinctive.[3] And there are also several themes I examine in the book that invite further exploration. For example, the topics of Emberá body painting in particular, and the distinctive fashion of the Emberá-Wounaan *paruma*-skirts deserve monograph-length analysis in their own right.

As for the account I provide in this book, I want to issue a disclaimer. My ethnographic experience addresses the Emberá of Panama, and in particular those of Chagres. My generalising statements with respect to certain sartorial aspects of the Emberá culture often extend beyond Chagres, to address the Emberá of Eastern Panama – that is, the Emberá living on the lands east of the Canal and up to the Colombian border. My generalisations are corroborated by close comparison with previous ethnographic work,[4] my extensive travel, but also the comparative reflections of my Emberá interlocutors at Chagres, who are intimately interconnected with wider Emberá society. Nevertheless, and in most respects, my partial and incomplete references to the Emberá as a generic ethnic category closely reflects a Chagres perspective, and does not, by any means, aspire to represent the Emberá in Colombia.[5]

In all these respects my account remains incomplete. But this is a creative sort of incompleteness that invites future investigation, and makes visible the complex and partial nature of ethnographic engagement. In my own journey with the

Emberá, I have used ethnographic nostalgia as an analytical device to discover and disseminate knowledge, a way of navigating the countless errors and misperceptions that emerged from my ethnographic experience. I continue to learn from these errors, and I continue to feel nostalgic sentiments about my time with the Emberá at Chagres. In fact, every sentence I write, every attempt I make to organise my description of the Emberá, generates the possibility for further nostalgia; and alongside this, further opportunities to learn from it, as much about myself as an ethnographer as the Emberá.

* * *

I would like to end the preface by acknowledging the numerous people who have provided me with help throughout the ten-year cycle that has informed the production of this monograph. First and foremost my gratitude goes to the residents of Parara Puru at river Chagres, to whom I dedicate the book. I visited the community after completing a first manuscript draft in January 2015, and I am now worried that I will not be able to return to the community every year, as I did between 2007 and 2012. Among my many friends in Parara, special thanks go to Claudio Chami and Ubertina Cabrera, Antonito Sarco, Anel Sarco, Francisco Chami and Escolatica Flaco, Alberto Tocamo, Gorge Martinez and Crecencia Caisamo, Brenio Dogirama and, finally, Claudio Junior Chami. I refer to them in my text with their first name in appreciation of their views, but the overall responsibility of my analysis, and any potential mistakes, are all mine to bear. Among my friends in Panama City I would like to thank George, Lambros, Mary and Sofia Efthimiopulos, Danae Brugiati and Nicasio de León; their consistent support for my research – material, psychological and academic – has been invaluable over the years. Keith Alpaugh, Kim Rowell, Lisa Carter, Mark Horton, Carlos Fitzgerald and Claudio Junior Chami travelled with me to Darién, while Tomás Mendizábal accompanied me in the exploration of Venta de Chagres; I am grateful for their companionship and friendship. I would also like to thank Jim Howe for sharing with me visual material from the Marsh expedition, and Cay Tsilimigra for translating for me Nordenskiold's (1928) book from Swedish to Greek. And closer to home, I would like to thank Tasia Kolokotsa for drawing four sketches especially for this book, Melissa Benson for proofreading the first draft and, finally, Michaela Benson, my wife, for her support and advice over the years – she has borne my long periods of absence in the field without complaint. I should also acknowledge the support of the ESRC (research grant RES-000-22-3733) upon which the lengthier part of this research was based. The British Academy (small grants SG-49635 and SG-54214), the University of Bristol and the University of Kent provided me with small research funds, which allowed me to travel to Chagres on an annual basis. Finally, I should express my gratitude to the two anonymous reviewers who read the manuscript of this book, and my colleagues at the University of Kent who read some of its chapters: their suggestions and inspiration has been invaluable.

Notes

1 To avoid misunderstanding, I use 'complicity' here in its less known meaning, to denote complexity and involvement (Marcus 1998: 107).
2 For the authenticity traps associated with the dichotomy of authenticity and inauthenticity, see Theodossopoulos 2013a.
3 In previous and forthcoming work I focus extensively on indigenous tourism and challenges introduced by tourism at Chagres (see Theodossopoulos 2007, 2010a, 2011, 2013c, 2014). But this body of work is by no means comprehensive, and relies only on a small fraction of the data I have collected on Emberá tourism.
4 Apart from ethnographic work about the Emberá written in English, I have paid special attention to refer closely to the ethnographic literature written in Spanish, especially that of Reina Torres de Araúz (1966) and Reverte Coma (2002), but also that of some of the former's students. I have searched meticulously for unpublished BA and MA dissertations in the library of the University of Panama, and some of this work – which largely descriptive – has informed directly or indirectly my text or my fieldwork. I have also shared some of this descriptive information with my interlocutors at Parara Puru. In most cases where I refer to this Spanish literature on the Emberá of Panama I have tried to focus on its descriptive strengths, usually to corroborate comparisons, instead of dwelling on or criticising its theoretical weakness.
5 I do aspire in the future to extend my close ethnographic comparisons of the literature on the Emberá of Panama to include more systematic reference to the literature on the Emberá in Colombia. This task will undoubtedly involve another long-term cycle of dedicated work, and, ideally, travelling to parts of Colombia that are, at the moment, not fully secure.

Series editor's foreword

At its best, ethnography has provided a valuable tool for apprehending a world in flux. A couple of years after the Second World War, Max Gluckman founded the Department of Social Anthropology at the University of Manchester. In the years that followed, he and his colleagues built a programme of ethnographic research that drew eclectically on the work of leading anthropologists, economists and sociologists to explore issues of conflict, reconciliation and social justice 'at home' and abroad. Often placing emphasis on detailed analysis of case studies drawn from small-scale societies and organisations, the famous 'Manchester School' in social anthropology built an enviable reputation for methodological innovation in its attempts to explore the pressing political questions of the second half of the twentieth century. Looking back, that era is often thought to constitute a 'gold standard' for how ethnographers might grapple with new challenges and issues in the contemporary world.

The *New Ethnographies* series aims to build on that ethnographic legacy at Manchester. It will publish the best new ethnographic monographs that promote interdisciplinary debate and methodological innovation in the qualitative social sciences. This includes the growing number of books that seek to apprehend the 'new' ethnographic objects of a seemingly brave new world, some recent examples of which have included auditing, democracy and elections, documents, financial markets, human rights, assisted reproductive technologies and political activism. Analysing such objects has often demanded new skills and techniques from the ethnographer. As a result, this series will give voice to those using ethnographic methods across disciplines to innovate, such as through the application of multi-sited fieldwork and the extended comparative case study method. Such innovations have often challenged more traditional ethnographic approaches. *New Ethnographies* therefore seeks to provide a platform for emerging scholars and their more established counterparts engaging with ethnographic methods in new and imaginative ways.

Dr Alexander Thomas T. Smith

1

Nostalgia, invisible clothes and hidden motivations

I first met the Emberá dressed in full traditional attire. Emerging from the rainforest of Panama with their painted bodies, decorated with beads and adornments, reminiscent of pictures from old anthropology texts, icons of quintessential indigeneity. At first sight I was filled with exhilarating enthusiasm; this gaze brought to mind myriad questions. Had these people turned their back on the enticing temptations of modernity? I wondered … were they resisting what I had failed to resist, the lure of consumerism, the comfort of Western commodities? And yes, I knew very well that the Emberá lived in an interconnected world: 'isolated communities exist only in our imagination,' I told my students again and again. But for a brief moment, a Rousseauian vision of primordial authenticity – noble, uncompromised – crossed my mind: a fleeting, exoticising shadow.

As I was about to discover, the Emberá do not resist all those marvellous Western things that I could not resist. They do use Western clothes after all, and mobile phones, and see themselves as indigenous people of our contemporary world, modern and indigenous at once: an intriguingly ambivalent possibility. In Emberá social life ambivalence is engendered in 'authentic discontinuities' (Kane 1994), rooted in contradictions, 'disjunctures' between modernity 'at large' and locally realised (Appadurai 1996): the Emberá with or without Western clothes; the Emberá citizens of a modern nation; the Emberá as icons of indigeneity; the Emberá in the eyes of Others and the Emberá for themselves.

Ambivalence, the nuanced view, comes after nostalgia, the uncomplicated view. My first glance was nostalgic – with all the biases this generates – and led me to the dilemmas that lie at the heart of this book. So, I should start by introducing 'ethnographic nostalgia', a concept that I use as a deconstructive tool, but also as a liberating remedy for my ceaseless inclination to exoticise, only to feel embarrassed by my own exoticising prejudice. Revelations of this kind are not exactly what anthropologists talk openly about, despite the fact that reflexivity – the art of revealing one's subjectivity and research motivations – is the discipline's best chance for methodological redemption. The nostalgia from which I try to repent was not unusual. It was the type that many authors (academics or not) feel in their confrontation with Otherness: when they secretly hope to encounter some type of cultural difference uncontaminated by modernity, representative of a hidden

1.1 A first gaze of the Emberá

authenticity. This is a romanticising nostalgia, crypto-colonialist and naïve, and more importantly, impossible to redeem. I was guilty of it, and I still am. The more I try to get rid of it, the more nostalgia I uncover within myself.

The nostalgia that emerges from the ethnographic endeavour shares similar properties – and exoticising proclivities – with broader types of nostalgia identified by colleagues. Rosaldo's (1989, 1993) 'imperialist nostalgia', for example, unmasks the tendency of the coloniser to mourn what colonisation has previously destroyed. The Westerner – colonial officer, missionary (in the original formulation), and I should add, traveller, philanthropist, anthropologist – yearns for what the Western civilising mission has transformed, a paradox that exposes anthropology's indirect implication with wider processes of domination. Herzfeld (2005) unravels a different kind of nostalgic evocation – independent of colonial discrepancies – but common in many official and vernacular discourses: each successive generation yearns for an idealised irrecoverable age of reciprocal sociality (cf. Angé 2015: 178). This particular type of yearning Herzfeld calls 'structural nostalgia': the longing for an imagined time of 'balanced perfection' in social relations, which is now 'slipping from our fingers' (2005: 64, 147). In most communities – including the anthropological community – we can find those who deploy the nostalgic evocation of a former Golden Age 'as a stick to beat the present' (R. Williams 1973: 12).

The particular nostalgia that led me to write this book shares elements of the essentialisms Rosaldo and Herzfeld try to expose. 'Imperialist nostalgia' unravels a static, 'allochronic' view of cultural difference (Fabian 1983), which substantiates sentimental pessimism (Sahlins 2000) or motivates a desire to salvage 'ethnography's disappearing object' (Clifford 1986: 112; see also Bissell 2005; Berliner 2015). This is, after all, 'a foolish and self-contradictory attempt to reconstruct a vanished and largely imaginary past' (Howe 2009: 249). 'Structural nostalgia', in turn, can help us see the failings of a singular view of authenticity hidden deep in oneself (Bendix 1997; Lindholm 2008; 2013; Fillitz and Saris 2013) or beyond the surface of social reality (Miller 2005; Theodossopoulos 2013c). This is an imagined, unspoiled authenticity, impervious to the blight of human imperfection and time itself (Herzfeld 2005), deemed to be uncompromised by modernizing change.

'Ethnographic nostalgia', a perspective inherent in anthropological representations of social reality, is constituted by elements of both 'imperialist' and 'structural' nostalgia. It motivates the detailed recording of a people's social experience framed by the record of what has been written or said about these people before. Ethnographic nostalgia emerges from the comparison of the ethnographic object as encountered in the present with previous scripted or oral descriptions, e.g. the ethnographic literature or local lore. And it is exactly here that the temptation to develop a nostalgic perspective lies: since society is constantly undergoing transformation, the ethnographer is destined to encounter a picture that contrasts – slightly or dramatically – with the idealised, refined and structured depiction of a previous standard of social life, often presented as a measure of authenticity. The longing to salvage what is perceived to be disappearing – that is so characteristic of 'imperialist nostalgia' – is framed by an idealised picture of how society was in the past, which is likely to contrast unfavorably with the present, an inconsistency representative of 'structural nostalgia'.

But let's return to the point when my awareness of what others had written and said about the Emberá set the foundation for my own ethnographic nostalgia. Equipped with ethnographic works that had already dealt with the Emberá – in static terms (Torres de Araúz 1966; Isacsson 1993), but also in more politically aware analyses (Kane 1994) – I set off to meet the Emberá holding in my mind puzzles from the images recorded by previous ethnographers; looking for the missing pieces of a picture constructed before my time. Was I arriving too late – to become another regretful exponent of ethnography as 'the art of being late' (Sarró 2009)? How could I withstand this paralysing sense of 'too-latism' (Berliner 2015: 25)? And the silliest question of all: would I recognise the Emberá as the people others described? How much cultural difference – resisting, uncompromising – would I encounter and eagerly record? How much ceaseless change would I be able to commit to paper, to make concrete and unchangeable through the written form? Ethnographic nostalgia stems from such an outdated frame of thought, but as I will gradually outline in this book, it can also motivate its own demise by unravelling – through its persistent urge for comparison – a more complicated view.

Indigenous *disemia*

The fact that I first saw the Emberá dressed in traditional attire, wearing crowns of flowers and multicoloured beads, played a trick on my exoticising imagination, blurring the boundaries between indigenous representation and everyday life. This blurring of perspectives was, in fact, a gift. It helped me destabilise the Goffmanesque distinction between the 'staged' and the 'everyday'. The indigenous clothes in which I first saw the Emberá were used to welcome and honor visitors from faraway places around the world, international tourists. After the tourists departed, the Emberá replaced the adornments of their formal costume with 'Western', mass-produced items of clothing. However, as I soon came to realise, the separation between traditional and modern codes of dress was not rigid, absolute and complete: there was no unyielding distinction between 'tradition' and 'modernity'; no absolute rift, trauma or vanishing culture. The Emberá were (and are) Emberá, whether they don 'Western' or indigenous attire. In fact, some of their 'Western' (mass-produced or market-bought) clothes also have an indigenous aesthetic, when combined with those considered traditional.

1.2 Between representation and everyday life: an ambivalent view of Emberá clothes

It is this practice of combining the old and new – what the Emberá see as 'traditional' and what they see as 'modern' – that is constantly changing. It is this fine act of balancing that provides us with a view of how the Emberá create their own particular and culturally meaningful modernities. 'The micromodernities that are so locally and culturally situated and they become practically a synonym for current custom or personal performance' (Knauft 2002a: 20). And by wearing Western clothes or obtaining other 'modern things', the Emberá I know have reassured me that they do not intend to distance themselves from their familiar older practices. 'To gain the new', while 'packing the innovative into the familiar', argues Miller, does not necessarily predicate a loss of the familiar (Miller 2008: 124). The new and the old, the unfamiliar and familiar, what comes from outside and what can be combined with that which is recognisably 'ours' are issues under negotiation among the Emberá, and, I believe, in most other societies. This is a comforting idea that may potentially help us escape – even if temporarily – from the temptation of referring to modernity and tradition as fixed and immutable concepts. Their content, instead, is a matter of constant negotiation, and manifests itself ambivalently in different contexts of social life.

All of this brings me to another concept introduced by Herzfeld to address identity dilemmas emerging (originally) from a different context, my native country

Greece. The versatile term *disemia* is used by Herzfeld (1987, 2005) to describe the tensions between the official representation of the Self (defined in formalistic and essentialist terms) and the informal, intimate view of the Self, which can be fluid, imperfect and not necessarily articulated in precise terms. *Disemia* does not outline a rigid distinction between formal and everyday life. On the contrary, it directs analytic attention to the ambivalence and contradictions experienced by local actors when their formal and intimate identities do not fully overlap – e.g. the European-*but*-anti-western Greek, the indigenous-*but*-modern Emberá. So, *disemia* is itself a form of ambivalence, a concept I will adapt in this book to refer to a particular predicament that involves the interface of indigeneity with tradition and modernity (however ill-defined 'indigeneity', 'tradition' and 'modernity' may be).

My adaptation of *disemia* here intends to elucidate the contradictions that emerge from the politics of indigenous representation, as these are experienced by local actors who self-identify as 'indigenous'. They may choose to identify with 'modernity', conceived of as the acceptance of new practices or consumerist opportunities, including appearances that Others – the state, non-indigenous neighbours – expect them to adopt. Or they may choose to simultaneously carry out everyday practices that relate to (or contain) elements from previous traditions, conceived as what earlier generations did, let's say 'the grandparents'. I refer to this emerging overlap (between what is locally seen as modern *and* indigenous) as 'indigenous *disemia*'. It encapsulates an ambivalence between *established* ways of being, either modern or indigenous, and *negotiated* ways of being oneself, which may be fluid, hybrid, subversive and incomplete. The contradictions that emerge from this type of ambivalence are tackled by local actors, such as for example the Emberá, in dilemmas of transformative change that stretch from public representation to the intimate contexts of everyday life. In fact, indigenous *disemia* – as perpetual ambivalence about change in everyday life – blurs the artificial boundary between representation and lived experience.

An Emberá woman, for example, may decide to take off her t-shirt and body-paint the upper part of her body to participate in cultural presentations for tourists. Later in the same day she may put on purely 'modern clothes' ('Western', industrially manufactured) to attend an Evangelical worship along with non-indigenous neighbours. These two established, well-defined dress codes – seen as purely 'modern' or purely indigenous – are most likely to diverge from her usual, everyday dress choices, which include mixed combinations of clothes seen as of both indigenous and non-indigenous. The contrast between 'pure' (uncomplicated) practices – conceived as either modern or traditional – and the non-normative fluidity of everyday social life – which can be seen as both modern-*and*-indigenous – are constitutive of indigenous *disemia*: an ambiguity that sets dilemmas for situated actors, but also – as Herzfeld (2005: 37) would stress – inspires the corruption of social conventions in the informality of intimate contexts. The resulting contradictions between established social codes engender the negotiation of unexpected indigenous authenticities, fluid combinations of previously prescribed views of authentic indigenous life.

Under the spell of authenticity and nostalgia

My references to the illusive concept of authenticity so far are not made in a light and unexamined spirit, but with full awareness of the political and controversial dimension of the concept (see Theodossopoulos 2013a, 2013c), which becomes accentuated when authenticity is paired with the adjective 'indigenous'. My interest in the multiple manifestations and evaluations of the authentic emerged from my very first sight of the Emberá dressed in traditional full attire. As other anthropologists have identified (Conklin 1997, 2007; Ramos 1991, 1998; Gow 2007; Santos-Granero 2009), non-indigenous observers (tourists, politicians, non-indigenous neighbours of indigenous groups) contest the authenticity of Amerindians dressed in either 'Western' or 'traditional' clothes. Wearing traditional costume is often associated with staged performances, while wearing market-bought clothes with identity loss. In either case, Amerindians are tainted by a shadow of inauthenticity based on the assumption that a true authentic identity hides beyond the surface of social interaction.

To offset such a dichotomous, essentialist view – which sets the presumed inauthentic against its opposite – I have proposed in a recent essay that it would be much better to conceptualise the simultaneous coexistence of more than one authenticity at any given negotiation of the authentic (Theodossopoulos 2013c). This leads us to the acknowledgement of plural, multidimensional authenticities (see Bruner 1994; Field 2009; Banks 2013a, 2013b), particular experiences of the authentic with their distinctive, authenticating meaning. The articulation of such multilayered, plural authenticities – and their multiple, often conflicting criteria – provides opportunities, but also contradictions in the representation of indigenous actors, which, in turn, generate ambivalence – a further example of indigenous *disemia*.

Ambivalence about the authenticity of indigenous cultural practices emerges nostalgically from the dialectic of what is seen today as representatively modern with what is seen as representative of social life a generation or two ago. Here, we can see more clearly how *disemia* is rooted in structural nostalgia: every generation of parents burdens their children with the evocation of a previous social time (Herzfeld 2005: 149). Indigenous actors, such as the Emberá, often deal with more than one set of authenticity as representative of the past (Theodossopoulos 2013a): the authentic social life of two or three generations ago – when men and women lived scattered in the forest dressed with minimal clothing – and the authentic social life of a later, now aging generation – when clusters of families formed politically organised communities and started to rely more heavily on Western clothes. In local discourses, each view of authenticity has its merits, which are stressed, as we shall see, in different arguments.

The same parallel measures of authenticity – the Emberá represented with more or less clothes – excite the nostalgia of non-indigenous observers. Those from Europe or North America are more likely to define indigenous authenticity in terms of the dress codes and practices of older generations, the idealised and simultaneously infantilised Indians (Ramos 1998) of a vanishing social world (Clifford 1988). Any signs of Western modernity that spoil this exoticised image are received with ambivalence, rooted in 'imperialist nostalgia'. Here the nostalgic perspective, with its misleading innocence (Rosaldo 1989; Herzfeld 2005; Angé and Berliner 2015), may obscure our view of the authenticating politics, which in the case of indigenous representation can be informed by dissimilar, not always overlapping, criteria: the presuppositions of the 'authenticators' who determine the authentic (Warren and Jackson 2002), the indexing of authenticity by Western audiences (Conklin 1997), the local views of indigenous actors who may see authenticity as representative of more than one past (Theodossopoulos 2013a), and in some cases, a previous literature (ethnographic or not) about Others (which sets the benchmark of how particular Others should be).

These considerations about the interface between nostalgia and authenticity bring me back to where I started: the essentialising proclivities of an exotic view of Otherness nostalgically conceived; an 'imagined essence that is irretrievably lost' (Bryant 2015: 156). But at this point I would like to issue a disclaimer. Despite my critical perspective, I am obliged to acknowledge that the nostalgic mood that stems from contemplating an ideal past (conceived of as forever lost) can also encourage a reflexive or deconstructive perspective. If we see nostalgia only as racism and ethnocentrism – which is undeniably a possibility – we risk blinding ourselves to its 'plasticity and mutability' (Howe 2009: 250). Pnina Werbner has argued in a recent article that the over-critical angle towards salvage ethnography 'risks deflecting criticism away from the real destruction which capitalism, religious proselytizing and modern education may inflict on small, vulnerable communities' (Werbner n.d.: 4). The nostalgia experienced by situated local actors, for example, may inspire innovative avenues of self-representation, or even creativity. From this point of view it can be seen as 'a vehicle of knowledge, rather than only a yearning for something lost', and knowledge about one's own past can inspire resistance towards the 'disempowering conditions of postcolonial life' (Battaglia 1995: 77).

As a result, when indigenous actors become interested in recording their own past, their nostalgia can be turned into a political argument (see Angé and Berliner 2015; Bryant 2015). When the present is compared with an idealised past, the vernacular nostalgic view may lead to a reconfiguration of knowledge, a synthesis of diverse elements – 'a restructuring' (C. Stewart 2007) – which, at the moment of its conception, contains bursts of spontaneity and creativity (see Bruner 1993; Ingold and Hallam 2007). As such, nostalgia may constitute an 'expressive and creative activity grounded in the dynamics of everyday life' (Bissell 2005), a possibility that entails an element of 'hope' (Berliner 2015: 30). Therefore, some nostalgic engagements may be potentially imaginative and resourceful, even analytical, in their comparative logic, for example when they juxtapose one social reality to another. A self-critical nostalgia may even 'engender its own ironies' (Battaglia 1995: 78), a subversive attitude inherent in social poetics (Herzfeld 2005). Or, when confronted by a self-reflexive ethnographer, nostalgia can encourage the systematic pursuit of contradictions that complicate the simplicity of the conventional ethnographic presentation (or expose its incompleteness) – as I will try to demonstrate in this book.

And indeed, a confrontation with nostalgia, as I admitted above, instigated my interest in the Emberá dress codes – modern, indigenous and mixed. Every collapsing layer of my nostalgic imagination, every illusionary static world that I realised did not exist, transformed my encounter with Emberá culture: every time I returned to Panama, after a break of a year or a few months, I battled with a new 'first gaze' of the Emberá, nostalgically compared with my previous experience, and the new information I had collected and read from older ethnographies in the meantime. By the time I erroneously believed that I had contained my exoticising admiration for the Emberá dressed in indigenous clothes, my ethnographic nostalgia was stirred once again: this time, by my recognition of mixed combinations of indigenous and Western clothes, in which I saw as a subversive indigenisation of modernity. In fact, the more time I spent reading older descriptions of the Emberá, and the more follow-up visits I made to the same Emberá community, the greater my proclivity to search for continuities in Emberá social life became: a nostalgic quest for a lost Emberá authenticity. As with ethnocentrism, nostalgia – 'imperialist', 'structural' or 'ethnographic' – comes in many layers. Once you free yourself from one – a singular, nostalgic authenticity – another presents itself before your eyes.

Bruce Kapferer (2013) has recently attempted to refigure the anthropological use of the exotic, focusing on the moment of the exotic recognition: 'the exotic as a challenge to understanding', the discovery of new possibilities 'at the edge of knowledge' (Kapferer 2013). The problem, for Kapferer, is not the exotic per se, but the dualisms it propagates. This is the same quality that makes authenticity and nostalgia so obsolete: their dependence upon authentic, ideal referents of an imagined world of being at once yourself and Other. In this respect, nostalgia and authenticity have been the spectres that stir up my exoticising view: setting up obstacles, ethnocentric barriers and static social realities. But, at the same time, they also sparked what Kapferer describes as exotic recognition, a challenge that undermined my nostalgia for authenticity – destabilising, opening a door to invite complexity in. The ethnography presented in this book is structured so as to demonstrate how this happened. In the final chapter, I will continue the discussion I have started here, which for now I leave deliberately open.

They are wearing clothes. Can't you see?

My original idea was to take advantage of the theme of Emberá clothes and use it as an excuse for writing a book about the authentic and the exotic in Emberá culture. As I came to spend more and more time observing Emberá codes of dress, which combined indigenous and non-indigenous elements, I became increasingly interested in the clothes themselves and their role in the processes that constitute the authentic and the exotic. My younger anthropological Self encouraged me to pay painstaking attention to detail, taking careful clothes-notes, or comparing Emberá clothes diachronically. My older anthropological Self, in his struggle

with ethnographic nostalgia, reluctantly opened his eyes and began to appreciate how the Emberá used *non*-indigenous clothes. Meanwhile, back in the United
Kingdom, and at a distance from the field, a broader anthropological concern with
materiality, which intensified during the first decade of the twenty-first century,
called into question the old-fashioned academic denigration of clothing as superficial (Miller 2005a, 2005b, 2010).

The first source of inspiration that provided me with a model of how to exploit
the theme of clothes – though maybe 'exploit' is too harsh a term – comes from
the late twentieth century: it is an anthropological literature that focuses on body
art and decoration among indigenous societies, primarily in Oceania, Africa and
Amazonia (see, for example, Strathern and Strathern 1971; M. Strathern 1979;
A. Strathern 1987; Faris 1972; Gell 1975; T. Turner 1980; Knauft 1989; Seeger 1975;
Sillitoe 1988; O'Hanlon 1989). It engages primarily with ethnic groups perceived
by the Western public as quintessentially exotic, a coincidence that may lead the
rushed critic to assert that anthropologists reproduce exoticising stereotypes by
concentrating on 'colourful', 'tribal', 'semi-naked' Others. Nevertheless, the persistent, those who take heed of the details of this dense body of work, are likely to
reach the opposite conclusion. The ethnographic contextualisation of indigenous
body decoration conveys a de-exoticising message, as it elucidates the meaningfulness of dress practices in local social life. Anthropological particularism here
provides an antidote to unconstrained exoticism.

The literature outlined above, as O'Hanlon (2007: 4) acknowledges, made a serious contribution in foregrounding the topic of body decoration as a legitimate
object for study to complement other more established anthropological topics,
such as kinship, gender, economic exchange and art (cf. Hansen 2004; Schildkrout
2004). Although attention to indigenous dress was framed in terms of such classic topics, ethnographic engagement signalled the social relevance of dress codes
and their relationship with myth, symbolism or personhood. In this manner, rich
anthropological interpretations of indigenous dress and adornment opened the
way for appreciating how body decoration reflected the relationship of the individual with society, where the decorated body was seen as representing 'a celebration
of social and cultural vitality in its myriad local dimensions' (Knauft 1989: 254), or
'a microcosm' of the social 'body politic' (T. Turner 1980: 121).

However enticing and anthropologically rich it is, this 'first wave'[1] of literature
on body arts and decoration uses the theme of indigenous clothes and adornments primarily as a vehicle to talk about other dimensions of social life. 'In the
social sciences, to be objectively serious about clothes', notes Colchester, 'came
to mean studying how they reflected other domains of experience' (Colchester
2003: 7). From the point of view of scholars specialising in dress, this particular
academic treatment of clothes – as a stepping-stone for reaching something else –
can be seen as reducing clothes to the 'accessories' of broader analyses (Hansen
2004: 370).[2] Yet a more important problem with this earlier anthropological literature on indigenous body arts and decoration was its relative neglect of the
mass-manufactured clothes worn by the very same people who decorated themselves in artful, exotic styles. As O'Hanlon aptly observes, Western clothes 'were

often treated as 'the "noise" against which the indigenous system of body arts had to be delineated' (2007: 5; see also Veber 1992: 51–2).

The widespread use of mass-produced clothes by local communities on the periphery of world economic power draws attention to the interface between clothes made locally and clothes introduced from outside. To the degree that the former are seen as old or 'traditional' and the latter as new or 'modern', we can consider the possibility that today's tradition may very well be yesterday's modernity; a realisation that opens the way to consider the gradual indigenisation of exogenous fashions or factory-made clothes. Sometimes, and as H. Hendrickson observes, our significant Others may use 'our products to create *their* identities' (1996: 2). Potentialities related to the materiality of certain mass-produced clothes – e.g. the way they combine with previous styles of clothing, the embodied experience of wearing them, their suitability for the various different requirements of everyday life – encourage the generation of local fashions, some of which may take a distinctive local character. In the Pacific, for example, imported textiles or previously 'Western' styles of dress have acquired in time their own local resonance or post-colonial authenticity (see, for example, Colchester 2003; Thomas 2003; Küchler 2003; Küchler and Were 2005; Bolton 2003, 2007).

In Panama, the Guna have historically relied on imported textiles to create a unique – and distinctively indigenous – dress code, a component of which, the *molas*, are now recognised as internationally acclaimed indigenous art (see Salvador 1976, 1997b; Sherzer and Sherzer 1976; Hirschfeld 1977a, 1977b; Swain 1989; Tice 1995; Martínez Mauri 2012). The making, reuse and exchange of clothes by Guna women using non-indigenous fabrics, as Margiotti (2013) highlights, are indispensable elements of Guna sociality. Observations like this lead us to appreciate a parallel and anthropologically intriguing process: apart from the spread of inexpensive factory-made clothes around the globe, we may encounter the modification of certain types of 'Western' clothes and their re-identification as indigenous. We may even discover, as I did during my fieldwork in Panama, that exogenous clothes are matched with indigenous ones to produce mixed (indigenised) combinations. As we will see later in this book, the *paruma*-skirts of the Emberá and the Wounaan are mass-produced, yet they are considered indigenous articles of dress. In everyday life, they are easily matched with non-indigenous clothes to produce clothing combinations with an indigenous ambience.

Although it seems that 'Western' (mass-produced) clothes go everywhere, often replacing on their way pre-existing local styles of dress, 'many non-western cultures have shown remarkable resilience and ingenuity at … modifying indigenous codes, and developing their own versions of "western" clothes' (Craik 1994: 26). In this respect, textiles that have been manufactured industrially provided 'a resource for, rather than a threat to, indigenous stylistic development' (Schneider 1987: 440). In fact it is often difficult to tell when mass-produced Western clothes stop being considered alien or alienable, and instead become representative of local styles or mixed indigenous-'Western' combinations; and, from the point of view of their wearers, 'inalienable' (Weiner 1989, 1992). The very possibility that mass-produced clothes can be re-appreciated in locally relevant terms encourages us to reconceptualise the interface of endogenous and exogenous clothes as having no definite boundary. Non-indigenous clothes may acquire indigenous referents at any given point in time.

The recognition that many so-called 'tribal' people do in fact wear 'Western', mass-produced clothes – most of which are made, after all, in Asia – has inspired a second wave of anthropological literature that engages with clothes-related dilemmas initiated by modernity or globalisation. In fact, some of the authors who provided us with classic earlier accounts on body arts and decoration[3] have subsequently addressed the role of indigenous dress in a world of international flows and connections. As these anthropologists kept returning to their previous field sites, they came face-to-face with accelerated social change that made directly visible or invisible indigenous costuming (see Knauft 2002a, 2007), including, in some cases, the violent destabilisation of the previous dress codes (see Faris 1988, 2007). Shifting from a more synchronic focus on the symbolic language of body decoration,[4] anthropologists started to embrace the wider politics of indigenous clothing. The latter included the use of body decoration to support indigenous resurgence and their struggle for recognition (see, for example, T. Turner 1992b, 1992c, 2002; Turner and Fajans-Turner 2006), which indicates the ingenuity of local actors in reaching out to a globalising world (Strathern and Stewart 2010).

The second wave of anthropological accounts on indigenous dress and body decoration also includes a good number of articles that address Latin American clothing dilemmas (Veber 1992, 1996; Conklin 1997; Gow 2007; Ewart 2007; Santos-Granero 2009; Margiotti 2013). They constitute an anthropological literature that has directly influenced my analysis of Emberá clothing practices. Veber's (1992, 1996) and Conklin's (1997, 2007) contributions in particular signal a profound acknowledgement of the strategic decisions of Amerindians and their agency in using the visual exoticism (Conklin 1997) of their traditional attire to communicate with wider audiences of potential sympathisers. The revival of native dress provides opportunities for redefining local identities in a world where, from the Amerindian point of view, 'modernisation and change' are not 'incompatible with being indigenous' (Conklin 2007: 25). Such perceptive theoretical observations have paved the way to accept, as I argue in the conclusion of this book, that indigenous clothes could be also seen as modern, and the modern ones as indigenous.

In a more recent article, Santos-Granero (2009) attempts to enrich this emerging politically aware perspective by stressing the importance of native ontological conceptualisations, such as, for example, a long-standing Amerindian openness to the Other. Yet, in the end, what makes Santos-Granero's article so vibrant and theoretically exciting is his recognition that hybrid clothes combinations engender creative strategies. As Gow highlights, and Santos-Granero acknowledges, Amerindians do not want to become white people (Gow 2007: 58): they want to adopt the perspective and clothes of the whites to engage with them in social relations. Thus, by dressing in the clothes of the whites, they can be seen as 'acquiring certain attributes and capabilities' that make it easier 'to operate in the social world of those who produce and wear these clothes'

(Ewart 2007: 44, 45). In other words, clothes can be seen as enabling perspectives, a point that beautifully links the discussion on indigenous clothes with Viveiros de Castro's (1998) influential 'perspectivist' approach. In this manner, Gow (2007), Ewart (2007) and Santos-Granero (2009) ground Viveiros de Castro's (1998) rather intellectualist position in the reality and strategic dilemmas of indigenous clothing.

Now, if we are ready to recognise that the traditional – previously exoticised as 'tribal' – anthropological subjects do wear Western clothes for part (or most) of their lives, then we come closer to challenging another silent distinction in the anthropology of clothes: that between (i) dress codes that leave a great part of their body uncovered (and/or rely on painting mediums, tattoo inscriptions, or adornments of a non-textile nature), and (ii) those dress codes that cover the body more closely and rely on fabric-based garments – or 'woven cloth' (Schneider 1987: 410). Interestingly, different anthropological literatures tend to focus on one dress code or the other, but only partially converse with each other. For example, my experience with the 'traditional' Emberá dress, which fits primarily description (i), led me initially to ignore the broader anthropological literature on textiles (see, for example, Theodossopoulos 2012). My acknowledgement of the latter grew slowly after I opened my anthropological eyes to accept the obvious fact that the Emberá use commercial, mass-produced clothes, and combine them with clothes conceived as indigenous (e.g. their *paruma*-skirts).

The division of anthropological attention between body decoration and woven clothes may very well reflect traditional areas of study, rather than a deliberate attempt to exoticise certain styles of dress; after all, fabric-woven clothes can be as exotic, sensualising – or 'indigenous' – as body painting, masks and feathers. In this respect, the rather isolated anthropological treatment of dress codes that do not heavily use textile garments is clearly misleading, and indirectly perpetuates the Western illusion that lack of fabric garments equals nakedness. 'Adornment is an aspect – even a major aspect – of clothing', notes Delaney (2004: 326). Body painting, many Emberá would agree, is 'like dress', while 'tattooing can also be thought of as a specific technique of dressing the body' (Craik 1994: 24), and in some parts of the world it is conceived as such. Therefore, there is no obvious reason to keep the analysis of different codes of dress separate.[5]

I have so far made an implicit call for increasing the conversation between anthropological approaches that study clothes. I should admit, however, that my own work does not fully converse with all. As I confessed above, my initial interest in Emberá clothes was superficial. It reflected what Miller (2005a, 2005b) had identified as a widespread anthropological trend to denigrate the material world or use it instrumentally as a gateway to a deeper realm of authentic sociality. It was this privileging of the 'social' over the 'material' that explained 'the sartorial silence' of many 'ethnographic accounts' (Tarlo 1996: 4, 7), and mine came very close to remaining silent. So, when I saw the Emberá wearing clothes – modern, traditional or mixed – I looked, with a considerable degree of ethnographic nostalgia, for clues about social structure and cultural continuities. My misadventures with the illusive notion of authenticity were rooted, as I will explain later, in a predisposition to treat clothes as 'trivial and fleeting expressions of a seriousness that resides elsewhere' (Küchler 2005: 211).

Inspired by a growing theoretical appreciation of materiality, I came to realise that Emberá clothes are 'not just a superficial cover' or the surface manifestation of some hidden identities; on the contrary, clothes constituted and shaped identities (Miller 2005b: 32; see also Keane 2005; Küchler 2005). Thus, I was reformed – at least partially. In the pages that follow, the younger anthropological voice within me will continue wavering – nostalgically – towards the mysterious, over-valued world of social structure, while my older, pragmatist self will attempt to keep the younger one at bay. As with ethnocentrism, or ethnographic nostalgia, the tendency to overlook materiality is deeply ingrained in social scientific analysis. Overcoming it is often a matter of degree, and usually the product of continuous self-deconstruction. At least one of the anthropological voices that battle within me will attempt to confront the anthropological proclivity of locating the Emberá in non-material exotic worlds of Otherness.

Inspiration from closer to Panama

To help the reader to understand how previous anthropological studies on the Emberá have influenced the production of this book – and predicated my ethnographic nostalgia – I would like to say a few words about some of the books and authors that accompanied me on my long journey of learning about Emberá culture. Some of these books I carried with me in the field and made available to my Emberá friends, who searched their pages with curiosity, looking for photographs of other Emberá – the contemporaries of their parents and grandparents – or ethnographic sketches of objects that elicited memories of people and practices. As I will stress in the following section, the dialogue between ethnographic literature and fieldwork practice can be inseparable. Beyond fieldwork, however, and while teaching or reading about the Emberá back in the UK, a previous literature shaped my comparative understanding of Emberá transformations in time.

The writings of two anthropologists in particular, James Howe and Michael Taussig, have been constant sources of inspiration throughout the writing of this book. In my mind their works represent two different ways of engaging with anthropology, one more conceptual (Taussig), the other more concrete (Howe). In this respect, their distinct perspectives resonate with my internal conflict about the focus of this book and the balance between the conceptual and the concrete. James Howe has maintained a commitment to Guna society and ethnography – and more broadly to the anthropology of Panama – that spans many decades. His long-term dedication to the study of one particular ethnic group represents for me an ideal model to guide my relationship with the Emberá. My interest in exoticisation and exoticising explorers – such as Richard Marsh, for example – originated after reading Howe's *A People Who Would Not Kneel* (1998), while his later book, *Chiefs, Scribes, and Ethnographers* (2009) has structured and stimulated my thoughts about indigenous self-representation in Panama. Howe's analysis of the indigenous politics of identity brings to the fore the complexity of social reality, providing an antidote to exoticisation and my proclivity – as much as any author – to caricature by generalising.

In comparison to Howe, Michael Taussig's work can be seen as representing a somewhat more intellectualist and top-down approach to interpretation. As far as exploring new avenues of anthropological representation is concerned, Taussig's resourcefulness in writing – and drawing (see Taussig 2011) – has freed me from my own reservations regarding ethnographic form and style, and I owe him an intellectual debt in this respect. His engagement with exoticisation in *Shamanism, Colonialism, and the Wild Man* (1987) provided me with the initial inspiration to launch my own critique. More directly, his influential theoretical analysis in *Mimesis and Alterity* (1993) addresses the concerns of this book; not only because he refers to the Emberá and the Guna, but primarily because a particular reading of his writing about the mimetic faculty can help us untangle the relationship of exoticising imagination with alterity. Notwithstanding these important contributions to the deconstruction of the exotic, and despite Taussig's best intentions, his use of the Guna and the Emberá as examples of an indigenous proclivity to emulate Western colonialism is not fully substantiated, and may potentially offend the reader who identifies more closely with these ethnic groups. For this reason, Howe has criticised Taussig for belittling the Guna as subservient mimics of foreign explorers and ethnographers (Howe 1998: 303–4, 2009: 17, 98), while Fortis's criticism stresses how Taussig underestimates Guna agency in evaluating foreign colonialists (Fortis 2012a: 12–13).

My understanding of Emberá society and culture has been shaped to a great extent – and beyond my own fieldwork – by regularly referring to the work of three authors: two anthropologists (Isacsson, Kane) and one geographer (Herlihy). They have produced long ethnographic accounts that if read in conjunction – or in juxtaposition – can open parallel windows through which to see the Emberá from different angles. The first of these three authors, Sven-Erik Isacsson, provides us with a structuralist perspective. He does not refer to Levi-Strauss, but his interest in the deep structures of Emberá thought, conceptions of personhood and cosmology – themes that he interprets by relying heavily on Emberá linguistic elements – resonate with the French structuralism of the 1960s. Isacsson's monograph, *Transformations of Eternity* (1993) is the publication of his doctoral thesis at the University of Göteborg. It represents a continuation of Swedish interest in the Emberá and the Wounaan, established by Erland Nordenskiöld (1927, 1928) and Henry Wassén (1935, 1955) in the early and middle part of the twentieth century respectively. Yet Isacsson's writing style diverges from the rather dry descriptions of his Swedish predecessors: his is poetic and captivating, and deeply concerned with meaning.

Transformations of Eternity is the outcome of Isacsson's many years studying colonial archives and recorded myths, and conducting original field research among the Emberá of the department of Chocó in Colombia. His personal experience with the Emberá emerged from at least four different field trips, spread from 1969 to 1988. Despite Isacsson's profound understanding of historical processes, a result of his thorough study of colonial archives (see Isacsson 1976, 1987), *Transformations of Eternity* is a rather synchronic study. Its depth does not stretch in time, but within the uncharted inward world of cosmology. If this book were to be published today, it would have received a very warm welcome by many contemporary anthropologists of Amazonia who share Viveiros de Castro's interest in Amerindian ontological perspectives. As with Viveiros de Castro, Isacsson's ethnography takes attention 'away from the nitty-gritty of indigenous real life' and political reality (Ramos 2012: 482), instead prioritising a world of meaning emerging from a timeless indigeneity. Very few Emberá I know in Panama have much to say about several of Isacsson's over-interpreted explanations, and those few who do are shamans (*jaibanás*).

If Isacsson's structuralism exoticises, Stephanie Kane's ethnography de-exoticises. Her theoretical reflections about Emberá society in *The Phantom Gringo Boat* remain to this day as timely and relevant as when the book was first published in 1994. Kane's perspective makes visible the inequalities and contradictions that the Emberá confronted in the 1980s. She allows us a stimulating glimpse of how the Emberá navigate through these contradictions, placed within a world of opportunities and limitations. Throughout her account, Kane retains an astute awareness of the wider political processes that unravelled while she shaped her narrative. It is in this specific respect that her account of the Emberá is so different from Isacsson's synchronic and over-interpreted approach. Like Isacsson she is interested in shamans, symbols and cosmological features, but her political consciousness keeps her connected with reality.[6] Although she spent less time than Isacsson studying colonial archives, and despite her limited interest in the past, Kane relocates the Emberá in history: in a particular phase of Panamanian politics (Torrijos' populism, Noriega's regime), and in a particular moment of indigenous mobilisation (the transition from dispersed settlement to nucleated communities, the first years of the Emberá-Wounaan reservation in Darién).

One limitation of *The Phantom Gringo Boat* prevents Kane's perceptive insights on the Emberá from being more widely disseminated. Although the ethnography is extremely vibrant – in conceptual terms – it is written in purposeful disorder. In her effort to depart from orthodox and static modes of anthropological representation, Kane's narrative-based approach does not provide the standard – more static typological – description that one expects to read in an ethnographic monograph. The uninitiated reader[7] – overpowered by Kane's sophisticated but non-descriptive writing style – struggles to come to grips with the complexity she intends to convey. Nevertheless, it is this challenging complexity that de-exoticises the Emberá experience, as I came to realise after overcoming my initial frustration with the style of this book's presentation. Kane seems to have been challenged by the same trouble that has haunted the writing of my book: how to communicate the Emberá experience without freezing the dynamism of Emberá life in motionless, generalising descriptions: as if the Emberá are 'like this' or 'like that'. She confronted this problem by presenting fragments of her experience with the Emberá in a non-linear plot. In contrast, I chose to maintain linearity for the benefit of the general reader, while I simultaneously challenge the exoticising simplicity and nostalgia generated by my narrative.

Conveniently, Peter Herlihy's (1986) ethnographically inspired doctoral dissertation on the Emberá of Eastern Panama fills most of the small gaps that Kane does not directly address writing at approximately the same period. Although Herlihy is a geographer, his thesis – based on long-term fieldwork – represents an intense engagement with local processes (of the kind one expects from an anthropological monograph). Surprisingly, this work remains unpublished, despite its completeness and thoroughness in breadth and exposition. Once more, Herlihy provides an account of the great transformation of Emberá life – the 'quiet revolution', as he calls it (1988) – that resulted in the foundation of concentrated communities with political representation. He describes this transition in terms of changes in social organisation and structure, yet without exoticising the Emberá by placing them in a synchronic motionless depiction. In fact, the Emberá structures in his description are new and emerge from a transformative period – the 1980s – that reshaped the relationship of the Emberá with space, the productive resources of their land, and the national society.

If Kane (1994) and Herlihy (1986) – when read together – provide a fairly comprehensive view of the Emberá of Eastern Panama in the 1980s, another pairing of ethnographers, Reina Torres de Araúz and José Manuel Reverte Coma, open a window on indigenous Panama in the 1960s. Until that time, we are told, the Emberá – or according to the ethnographic convention of that time, 'the Chocó' (the Emberá and Wounaan addressed with one term) – followed the old code of dress and lived in dispersed settlement. Ethnographic descriptions from this era present the Chocó as maintaining an ancient tribal way of life with minimal adjustment, escaping from modernising trends at the margins of Western society. In spite of such moderately exoticising inclinations, Torres de Araúz attempts to chart Emberá culture by adopting a broad descriptive perspective, following the old-time model of the comprehensive ethnography. Her writing conveys the following simplified message: here are the Chocó, these people who live at the margins of our society, and here is what you need to know about them.

Torres de Araúz visited Darién and Bayano in numerous field trips in the 1950s and 1960s, at a time when the Chocó were undergoing significant geographic and demographic expansion in Eastern Panama. She and her students (see, for example, Caballero and Araúz 1962; Guzman 1966) attempted to chart this expansion with descriptive accuracy. One monograph by Reina Torres, *Darién: etnología de una región histórica* (1975), provides a good overview of the ethnic and cultural diversity in Eastern Panama, but as Howe observes, it reads 'as a kind of scientific inventory or survey' (Howe 2009: 195). An earlier book, *La cultura Chocó* (Araúz 1966), focuses exclusively on the Emberá. It addresses an impressive variety of themes that range from geography, technology and material culture to social organisation, shamanism and colonial history – including a detailed account of the Emberá attire, partly reproduced in an earlier article (Araúz 1961). In terms of exposition, *La cultura Chocó* constitutes an indicative example of Torres de Araúz's systematic, measured and authoritative style.

Beyond her ethnographic contribution, Torres de Araúz (1932–1982) is widely recognised for setting the foundations of anthropology as a discipline in the

Republic of Panama. During her career she devoted her time and scholarly efforts to the study of most Panamanian ethnic and cultural groups, a combination of interests that gave her close control of most fields of investigation, which in turn constrained the opportunities available for subsequent generations of Panamanian researchers (Howe 2009: 197). Despite her contribution and personal involvement – as an academic expert – in the political processes that let to the recognition of the 'Chocó' as one of Panama's indigenous groups, Torres de Araúz's interest in indigenous history is strictly ethnological, and her analysis deliberately apolitical. Although she refers extensively to colonial history – in *La cultura Chocó*, and in her later book, *Panama indigena* (1980) – her ethnographic accounts of Emberá remain surprisingly ahistorical. In fact, her references to contemporary social change, including the relationship of indigenous groups with the state, do not engage with contentious themes, of which she had first-hand experience (see Howe 2009: 193–8). Notwithstanding such limitations, it is undeniable that her ethnographic observations of the Emberá – detailed, descriptive, self-assured and somewhat detached – represent a priceless contribution to the anthropology of Panama and, more importantly, a reliable foundation for comparisons with previous and later accounts.

At about the same time,[8] José Manuel Reverte Coma, a medical doctor from Spain with a strong interest in more than one anthropological field, visited nearly all Panamanian indigenous groups in field trips 'lasting days or weeks' (Howe 2009: 192). His experience with the Emberá informs a 624-page-long monograph, *Tormenta en el Darién*, published many years later, in 2002.[9] Reverte Coma's writing style is opinionated, personalised and autobiographical, in sharp contrast with the reserved and impartial outlook of Reina Torres. At times, his account of the Emberá even resembles an ethnographically informed traveller's account aiming to provide a Western audience with an insight into how it is to be with these fascinating people, the Emberá, in that inapproachable part of the world, the Darién. Yet, despite this exoticising perspective, Reverte Coma does not sensationalise the Emberá. With remarkable self-discipline he sticks to the project of recording – without departing from the rigid and awkward role of the Western observer – the *imponderabilia* of Emberá life. He presents detailed descriptions of cultural practices, undeveloped diary entries from his fieldnotes, sketches of material culture, scientific facts about biology and indigenous medicine (that appealed to his medical background), and a lengthy glossary of Emberá terms. In its entirety, this avalanche of information complements the work of Torres de Araúz by providing another corroborating voice.

If Torres de Araúz and Reverte Coma locate their description of Chocó culture in the wider region of Eastern Panama, a couple of Colombian anthropologists, Pineda and Gutiérrez de Pineda, adopt a much wider geographical angle. Instead of focusing on one community or region – ideally studied by protracted fieldwork – they provide a broad ethnographic manual of Chocó customs and practices. Their monograph, *Criaturas de Caragabí* (1999) is based on data collected from 1949 to 1950, and makes available thematically organised information about the practices of different Chocó subgroups (Emberá, Catio, Chami, Wounaan) or Chocó regions representing river systems (e.g. Atrato, Baudo, San Juan). Among the numerous themes examined, there is reference to clothing, hairstyles, body decoration and adornments. The scope of this large – in geographical terms – unit of analysis includes the Emberá of rivers Sambú and Balsa in Panama, even though Pineda and Gutiérrez de Pineda focus more heavily on the Chocó in Colombia. Despite this wealth of comparative information, and admirable geographical range, *Criaturas de Caragabí* is rather descriptive in nature and does not engage directly with wider theoretical debates. It does provide, nevertheless, a firm point of comparison with older classic accounts of the Chocó in Colombia, such as those of Wassén (1935, 1955), Reichel-Dolmatoff (1960, 1962), Vasco Uribe (1985, 1987) and Ulloa (1992).

Of the literature on the Emberá in Colombia, one monograph in particular has been more relevant than others to my interest in Emberá dress. This is Astrid Ulloa's (1992) study of body painting and designs, which is presented with systematic accuracy and artistic sensitivity. This work is by no means as theoretical as Ulloa's later monograph, *The Ecological Native* (2005), which engages with the non-indigenous proclivity to perceive Amerindians in naturalised terms. Her 1992 study focuses more narrowly on body painting, and its contribution is twofold: firstly, it encourages us to see Emberá body painting as an everyday Emberá practice, not solely a shamanic ritual, and secondly, it makes available an impressive collection of body-painting designs. The variety presented by Ulloa is remarkable, and as I will outline in Chapter 6, has inspired some Emberá at Chagres to diversify their body-painting applications. In this last respect, Ulloa's collection of designs has the potential to make an applied contribution to contemporary Emberá representation through tourism.

Undoubtedly, the authors mentioned above have each shaped the production of this book in a different way: Howe and Taussig, by turning my interest in the Emberá towards their exoticised reception of Others; Isacsson, by considering Emberá meaning in symbolic terms; Herlihy, by framing my spatial awareness of social change; Kane, by refusing to compromise with conventional ethnographic presentation; and Torres de Araúz, by constructing an ethnographic orthodoxy that invites complication. These are only some of the ethnographic voices that haunt my text and frame, as written records of the Emberá past, my ethnographic nostalgia. They are complemented by many other accounts to which I refer to as points of comparison – Norderkiold (1928), Reichel-Dolmatoff (1960, 1962), Faron (1961, 1962), Lowen (1963a, 1963b), Kennedy (1972), Tayler (1996), Pineda and Gutiérrez de Pineda (1999), Mortensen (1999), Wali (1989), Ulloa (1992). Together with some authors who had been writing about the same time as me about the Emberá (Colin 2010, 2013), the Wounaan (Velásquez Runk 2009, 2012), the Guna (Fortis 2012a, Margiotti 2013, Martínez-Mauri 2011a, 2011b) and the Ngäbe (Karkotis 2012), they comprise, to my mind, an imagined community of knowledgeable 'specialists' who dialectically address a dilemma: to exoticise [Panama's indigenous people] or not to exoticise?

An ideal community to confront the exotic

On my first trip to Panama I travelled with a friend, Yannis Tzortzis, a renowned photographer. I was looking for a community in which to start new anthropological fieldwork. He was looking for spontaneous, out-of-the-ordinary photographic views. So, we visited many Emberá communities, debating along the way the authentic and the exotic. As I have briefly described in a previous essay (Theodossopoulos 2013c), my friend the photographer saw authenticity as an inherent, non-verbal quality in people and things: a spontaneous tiny spark that lay beyond linguistic and cultural barriers, immediate and communicable through the senses. He raised his camera and took photos of people – exceptional photographs I must admit – without always asking permission or following the protocols of contact. He maintained his own code of ethics – the ethics of spontaneity – which were in sharp contrast with my conventional anthropological research guidelines and fuelled my apprehension and irritation.

There was a special sparkle emanating from meeting a new Emberá community for the first time. And Tzortzis, the photographer, used his camera to capture the hesitant first point of each new arrival, often the canoe embarkation point of one or another community in Darién. By the time I had introduced myself to each community's leader and explained who we were, Tzortzis had already made numerous friends, whom he immortalised with his heavy, roll-film camera. I found his excessive photographing embarrassing, but everyone else appeared to be charmed by his friendly and immediate personal style. In fact, his ability to establish a sense of rapport with the Emberá put to shame my slow and step-by-step approach. 'Anthropologists salvage the authenticity of Others with their writing', he said, 'I do so with my camera.'

That anthropology was no longer a mere salvaging project was my main thrust of argument. That art could transcend any barriers set up by cultural difference was his. On one thing we agreed: that all the Emberá communities we met in Eastern Panama had received us with welcoming hospitality. Those closer to Panama City that received visitors regularly, and those in Darién that did not. And the Emberá in many of these communities were willing to organise a special cultural celebration for us, to entertain us with 'traditional' dance and music, to show us their culture. It was easier for us to accept such invitations in the 'touristy' – as Tzortzis called them – communities that performed for several visitors, than in the inaccessible communities where whole villages were willing to get mobilised to organise an event especially for us, their only two visitors.

By 2005, and this particular trip, the idea of developing tourism had spread throughout Emberá society in Panama. Even the most inaccessible communities – located a several-hours canoe ride away from the main transportation arteries – were aware that occasional Western travellers may come, interested in Emberá culture. And most communities had a good general idea of how to entertain Western visitors (see Theodossopoulos 2007). This included performances of Emberá dance and music, sometimes a short speech about the community or the methods of constructing Emberá artefacts, wood sculpture and basketry (see Theodossopoulos 2010a, 2011). And there was some expectation that visitors would buy some of these artefacts, which are normally directed (through various middlemen) to major markets in Panama City or sold to other Emberá communities that entertain large numbers of tourists (see Velásquez Runk 2001; Colin 2013).

So we travelled and met several Emberá communities, my friend and I, and had heated discussions along the way. Which was the most authentic community? Which was the best community for future fieldwork, or the one with the most spontaneous photographic opportunities? We were pulling together different referents and criteria of authenticity – essentialist, ethnocentric, artistic, anthropological – entangling ourselves in the convoluted tentacles of a misleading search: there was not one authenticity to be sought, but many (see Theodossopoulos 2013a, 2013b), dependent upon shifting, relational concepts – 'tradition', 'modernity', 'indigeneity'. It transpired that the community that provoked the most heated debate between us, was the very first one we had visited: 'the most touristy one', said Yannis Tzortzis. 'No, the most globalised one', said I.

It was the community of Parara Puru in Chagres National Park, renowned among the Emberá for its success in developing tourism; one of the six Emberá communities in the general Panama Canal area that received and entertained foreign visitors regularly. This recent success with tourism – emerging from a hesitant experimentation in the mid-1990s – was what most other communities in Darién were trying to emulate: a direct relationship with foreign tourist audiences. In this respect, Parara Puru and the other six communities in the Canal area comprised a contact zone for cultural exchange (Clifford 1997), from which emerged a wide array of research opportunities. To realise the importance of these, I had, as a first step, to free myself from a nostalgic expectation – rooted in the anthropology of the early- and mid-twentieth century: the idea of conducting fieldwork in a community removed, as far as possible, from the influence of Western civilisation (see Angé and Berliner 2015; Berliner 2015).

Having worked previously in rural and urban European contexts I had developed a critical perspective towards the classic anthropology of the exotic-looking, 'tribal' or indigenous people and the inconsistencies inherent in such categorization (see Beteille 1998; Kuper 2003; Barnard 2006). The field of European anthropology in the 1990s – the period in which I developed my anthropological identity – was permeated by a strong critical perspective towards geographically defined areas of study in anthropology. The collapse of the notion of the 'Mediterranean', the field of my early work, came from the destabilisation of the exoticising perspective (see Goddard, Llobera and Shore 1994; Just 2000), the search for anthropological subjects in some faraway land. For that reason, a part of me wanted to challenge the vision of isolated society and focus instead on global interconnectedness. But there was another part of me resisting the anthropologist I had become, the nostalgic voice of the anthropologist I was trained to be: a dedicated fieldworker devoted to the recording of detail, the *imponderabilia* of social life (Malinowski 1922). Were the little details (that can pass so easily unnoticed) more important than the great events (that are made explicitly obvious)?

Inadvertently, although for different reasons, Parara Puru appealed to both anthropological voices within me. The daily rhythm of the community shifted effortlessly between cultural representation and private social life, encompassing the two with ease and unpretentious simplicity. There was a time of the day when I shared my relationship with the community with many other Westerners, and a time of the day when I was a privileged guest, the only other outsider, 'a white Emberá' (*Emberá torro*) – a person that I deluded myself into believing that I could become. The desire for 'exclusive contact with Otherness', itself a dimension of the nostalgic view, was back then, as it is now, a constant temptation. During the course of my fieldwork I saw the same desire in many visitors, tourists and off-the-beaten-track travellers, who wished, as I did in those early days, that all other Westerners would vanish, leaving no trace, no reminder of the rest of the world.

I can now rationalise my nostalgia retrospectively, and explain why I chose Parara Puru as my fieldwork site. As a site of interface between global tourist audiences and Emberá culture, 'Parara' – as its residents call their community informally – made visible the relationship between indigenous representation and the idealising admiration of international audiences. This provided me with opportunities to engage critically with the exoticisation of myself and other outsiders, but also with emerging narratives about an indigenous Self. And at the same time, Parara, as a site of cultural performances, provided glimpses of 'tradition' – conceived as representativeness – comparable to past practices and the ethnographic record, which in turn triggered my ethnographic nostalgia and an antiquated commitment to seeking out connections with previous written descriptions of Emberá culture.

Was Parara Puru representative of old and relatively unchanged Emberá traditions, as these were described by Reina Torres de Araúz (1966) and Reverte Coma (2002) in the 1960s? Or representative of change and Emberá political emancipation as described by Kane (1994) and Herlihy (1986) in the 1980s? As I came to realise much later, the residents of Parara responded, at a different pace and to different degrees, to both these standards (or ideals) of Emberá authenticity conceived as representativeness. During the time they devoted to entertaining tourists, dressed in traditional attire, they embodied an aspect of their identity that partially conformed to an ideal vision of Emberá culture in the time of their grandparents – as ethnographically recorded in the 1960s. After the tourists departed, they dressed in modern or mixed indigenous/non-indigenous clothes and negotiated a social life representative of many other contemporary Emberá communities in Eastern Panama, which addressed dilemmas related to the reorganisation of Emberá social and political life as this was recorded ethnographically in the 1980s.

Nonetheless, at the time I chose Parara Puru as the field site of my research these thoughts had not fully crystallised within me. From where I stand now, I can only see that Parara provided me with valuable lessons, including a direct confrontation with nostalgia, my uncontained admiration for the Emberá dressed in the old dress code, 'their own clothes' as they often referred to them. And when, after some time, I caught myself admiring the Emberá in Western clothes too, I learned another valuable lesson: that the dichotomy between tradition and modernity was much less rigid than I previously thought.

Looking back retrospectively I now feel that it was not merely that I chose Parara Puru; its residents also chose me, in the very same slow and steady manner that they cultivate warm relationships with other Western admirers of their culture – missionaries, NGO practitioners, Peace Corps volunteers, teachers and academic scientists, photographers and filmmakers – with whom I learned to share the Emberá despite my romantic and selfish desire for an exclusive relationship. But once these others left, I was the lone non-Emberá in the village, engaging in everyday life as it unfolded. Over the course of my fieldwork, in the absence of tourists and passing visitors, I had opportunities to discuss and reflect upon the Emberá way of life – introducing themes that I read from previous ethnographers and had structured my ethnographic nostalgia. By describing facets of what other ethnographers had written about the Emberá, I had an opportunity to explain to the Emberá what anthropologists do, and that ethnography can provide a repository of knowledge (see Theodossopoulos 2015). A great number among the Emberá I met, both in Chagres and in Darién, have been very keen to discover information about the history of their culture, but also about other cultures, a growing interest to which I refer in Chapter 6 as representational self-awareness.

Through the many themes that I introduced I sought the opinions of my interlocutors, in one-to-one conversation, or by addressing groups of individuals: men and women, younger and older members of the same family, and clusters of friends. The resulting conversations almost always evolved in unpredictable directions, encompassing a variety of unrelated themes. On the whole, unsolicited conversations far surpassed those I had introduced. They provided a reality check – a challenge to ethnographic nostalgia – and an invitation for empirically led research. The topics of my first publications on the Emberá,[10] and those that I explore in this book, emerged from a wide array of potential themes that had been previously discussed in Parara Puru during my fieldwork. Obviously, the involvement of the community in tourism, and the desire of its residents to improve their cultural representation, fuelled my interest in their aspiration to reach out to the world and make some aspects of their culture more widely available – topics that I have explored theoretically in previous work (see Theodossopoulos 2010b; cf. Comaroff and Comaroff 2009). From this broader concern with the politics of representation, my interest in Emberá clothes emerged; an interest encouraged by the fluid and continuous shifts in the dress code of the Emberá at Chagres and Parara Puru in particular. The latter I was able to observe in daily life: at home, during manual work, in tourism, or in preparation to exit the community.

The resonance of my conversations in Parara Puru – and especially those about clothes – inspired further travel to Darién, where, over the course of several trips, I was able to visit most of regions settled by the Emberá in Eastern Panama.[11,12] The purpose of my journeys to Darién was to obtain a broader view of contemporary Emberá society in Panama, in an effort to conceptualise the connections and networks that united the Emberá world. In many cases I travelled with Emberá men, and in one occasion with a friend from Parara Puru, commenting and comparing along the way, from the perspective of the Emberá who live in Chagres.[13] During these trips, which lasted between four to ten days each, I talked with several Emberá, especially community leaders, and acquired a broader – although horizontal and not profoundly deep – sense of their concerns. However valuable this experience, I do not claim that I have undertaken systematic fieldwork in Darién – definitely *not* in the longitudinal sense in which I conducted research at Chagres. In all respects, my fieldwork anchor was Chagres, where I returned after each trip in Darién to share with the residents of Parara every little detail of my impressions of the greater Emberá world. They had been equally generous in sharing their comparative views and impressions, for most of them travel frequently to Darién to visit relatives.

I should emphasise here that during fieldwork I enthusiastically embraced the standard anthropological practice of living in the site of my research, where I followed the rhythm of daily activity.[14] Working in a community that entertains tourists invites misunderstanding: the fieldworker can be taken as a tourist, or the community itself as a tourist spectacle. As I emphasise throughout this book, Parara Puru is very much the everyday home of its residents. It was also my primary home and point of reference during fieldwork. To extenuate the nostalgic echoes of my role as a participant-observer, I attempted to strengthen my participation, pursuing an engaged approach to anthropological research (see Sillitoe 2015). As I returned to Panama each year – from 2007 to 2012[15] – for one, two or three months each time, I became better attuned to the needs of the community and learned how to put aside my academic concerns and make my academic knowledge available to the community – all that I learned from reading books about them. Every time I returned I brought one or another book about the Emberá with me, which I laid on the floor by my sleeping bag, inviting the Emberá to search its pages with curiosity. On my laptop screen I shared photographs from previous visits and journeys in Darién, or ethnographic sketches and images from previous Emberá ethnographies, which invited countless conversations about the past and present, and authenticity as representativeness.

In 2011, my friends in Parara – as by that time I came to dislike the awkward term 'respondents' – told me that I had come much closer to what they secretly expected me to become: somebody who could contribute a little something to community life – helping the kids to prepare their homework, printing photographs and body-painting designs from older ethnographic accounts, preparing photo exhibitions or laminating textual descriptions of cultural practices, or even

1.3   Emberá children browsing the pictures of Donald Tayler's ethnography

copying high-resolution maps to help the local leaders plan their land-claim cam-
paign (Theodossopoulos 2015). And I was glad that I was given opportunities to
repay the knowledge I was given, with fragments of the knowledge I systematically
collected about Emberá culture. In fact, I felt that in time my dilemmas about
authenticity and representativeness became more relevant to them. Or maybe it
was them who had been leading and influencing my interests in authenticity and
cultural representation all along.

About the sketches

The art of drawing is a neglected practice in anthropology (see Ingold 2011;
Taussig 2011; Wettstein 2011). Before the wider availability of photographic
cameras, ethnographic depictions heavily relied on drawings of objects and
people. Drawing provided additional time to establish a relationship with what
was represented, a relationship that contributed to a deeper understanding of
form and detail (see Wettstein 2011). We may choose to mourn nostalgically the
demise of ethnographic drawing, and its replacement by photography, but we
should also remember that sketches of indigenous people from earlier eras foregrounded indigeneity as exotica and stereotyped the 'wild' tribal Other – very
much as early photographic images did (see Taussig 1987; Nugent 2007). As with
a photograph, a drawing of an ethnographic object or subject can be interpreted
(or presented) as a prototype or standard of authenticity, an undifferentiated
singularity that contradicts the complexity of social life; see, for example, my
sketch of the typical Emberá attire (as this is statically conceived) at the beginning of Chapter 2.

1.4   Nostalgic sketch of an Emberá facial *jagua* design

At the same time, drawings can also de-essentialise by generating a sense of incompleteness. As argued by Taussig, ethnographic drawings work against realism by 'being suggestive of a world beyond', capturing what may be only partially invisible or auratic (2011: 13). Since its replacement with photography, the art of anthropological drawing has found refuge in fieldwork notebooks, often hidden from public view, in unpublished form. In this often playful, informal use, unpublished anthropological sketches have a secret life, obtaining a destabilising role that departs from the motionless precision of stylised 'posed' photography. Instead of reaching finality and closure, anthropological drawing thus encourages an open-ended imagining of social life (Ingold 2012). Far from freezing the world into a supposed-to-be-authentic, prototypical form, sketches drawn by anthropologists sometimes point towards a reality that 'does not have to be explicitly recorded' (Taussig 2011: 13).

Despite these obvious advantages, there are not that many ethnographies that extensively use sketches and drawings. My list of favourites includes Alfred Gell's sketches of body decoration in *Metamorphosis of the Cassowaries* (1975); they are full of grace and movement, and emerge from the pages as if they have a life of their own. Emma Tarlo's *Clothing Matters* (1996) relies mostly on photographs, but also includes sketches of design motifs and a good number of cartoons from previous eras. Mukulika Banerjee and Daniel Miller's *The Sari* (2003) uses photography in a dynamic manner that includes cartoon-like interventions such as thought balloons and lines that pinpoint particular explanations or denote a sequence of movement. This creative use of lines brings to mind Tim Ingold's book, *Lines* (2007), which is animated, as appropriate, with drawings and illustrations of lines that substantiate – as if his lines have a voice – anthropological arguments. Steve

Nugent's *Big Mouth* (1990) is illustrated with sketches of everyday people unsupported by captions, which point towards the type of non-prescribed exposition contemplated by Michael Taussig, whose book, *I Swear I Saw This* (2011), highlights the dynamic potential of fieldwork drawings, and includes, unsurprisingly, several sketches of his own.

Recent works have attempted to reconstitute anthropological drawing as 'an inscriptive practice in its own right' (Ingold 2011: 2), and encourage us to consider the re-emergence of 'graphic anthropology' (Ingold 2011) or 'design anthropology' (Gunn and Donovan 2012), or the value of ethnographic sketches (Taussig 2011). Following this enticing call, I have transformed a number of photographs I took during my fieldwork to sketches, taking one experimental step towards a perspective that borrows stylistic elements from the comic book and the graphic novel. I have used a variety of digital filters to desaturate and blur my original photographs, before altering the resulting images by hand (drawing on paper and digitally). In other cases, I draw my own depictions of people or objects completely by hand. Through this creative transformation, I have tried to destabilise the authority of the photographic depiction, and de-exoticise the self-exoticising posture of my Emberá friends and interlocutors, most of whom are tourist professionals accustomed to reenacting a prescribed image of indigeneity (tuned to meet the exoticising expectations of their visitors).

In creating new versions of my photographic images, I attempt to reanimate my fieldwork experience – since drawing can be seen as restoring life to anthropology (Ingold 2011) – and promote a view of incompleteness that departs from the usual motionless depictions of the Emberá posing in traditional attire. Instead of providing 'objective' visual records of 'how the Emberá dress' – as if all Emberá dress in the same manner – I try to suggest to the reader that the images presented are first and foremost imperfect sketches: they represent an incomplete view of Emberá practices, shaded by my incurable ethnographic nostalgia, and my (not fully successful) struggle to escape from it; both of which I am trying to expose, as constructive lessons about the imperfection and dynamism of the anthropological description.

In this final respect, the abstracted sketches of my photographs – and on occasion the sketches inspired from the photographs of Westerners who had previously visited the Emberá[16] – are filtered by my subjective reading of Emberá social life, and my memory of fieldwork, which at the moment of writing is infused with nostalgic recollections. So, undeniably my sketches exoticise – probably as much as photographs do – but they do so as artistic and incomplete depictions, not absolute records of an unchanging reality. It is this very imperfection in my sketches that I try to challenge and use as a medium for reflection, deconstruction and learning. My descriptions, drawn as either pictures or written as text, do not claim to represent a singular depiction of normative authenticity – e.g. 'this is the authentic Emberá costume' or 'this is the way all Emberá dress' – but only an example. They do not attempt to 'impose closure', but rather, I hope, 'allow for everyday life to carry on' (Gunn and Donovan 2012: 1).

Box 2

Some useful terms

- *Emberá* – In the Northern Emberá dialect spoken in Panama, Emberá means 'a person' (Mortensen 1999: 1) or 'the people' (Torres de Araúz 1966: 7) or more liberally 'the humans'. As Ewart (2013) observes, Amerindian ethnic groups frequently name themselves as 'people' or 'human beings' (see also Walker 2013: 8). This exact meaning is often underestimated by ethnographers – and non-indigenous neighbours – who use autodenominations as generic names to differentiate one group from another (Ewart 2013: 16). In Panama the term *Emberá* is widely used – by the Emberá and their neighbours – to signify a language and an ethnic group (ideally endogamous) (Velásquez Runk et al. 2011). Ethno-linguists recognise several sub-groups of Emberá speakers in Colombia, with up to six dialects (Mortensen 1999) or nine dialect areas (Loewen 1963a). They have all been referred to collectively as 'the Chocó' (the people from Chocó, Colombia), a generic term that also includes the Wounaan, a separate ethnic group with a related but distinct language (Velásquez Runk 2001, 2009).
- *Wounaan* – From the Emberá point of view the only other people that share the attributes of Emberá-ness (and are nominally acceptable as marriage partners) are the Wounaan, a linguistically and historically related ethnic group (see Kennedy 1972; Tayler 1996; Velásquez Runk 2009). They have been also referred to as Chocó.
- *Chocó* – In Panama, the term *Chocó* (or *Chocoes*, in plural) has been used as a negative ethnic stereotype to accentuate the Colombian origins of the Emberá and the Wounaan (see Theodossopoulos 2010a). Until the 1960s, ethnographers used the term *Chocó* extensively, as a useful category for analysis and comparison (Nordenskiold 1928; Wassén 1935; Reichel-Dolmatoff 1960; Torres de Araúz 1966, 1980; Kennedy 1972; Tayler 1996; Pineda and Gutiérrez de Pineda 1999; Reverte Coma 2002). As an analytical category, the term is still useful nowadays, especially when one attempts to address the shared histories and common cultural practices of the Emberá and the Wounaan (see, for example, C. Williams 2004). Nevertheless, the tendency to examine both ethnic groups in the same ethnographic studies often produces confusion, especially since some communities have both Emberá and Wounaan residents (see Velásquez Runk et al. 2011: 31). My infrequent use of the term *Chocó* attempts to accentuate the shared history of the Emberá and the Wounaan; otherwise, I avoid using the term altogether.
- *Jurá* – The Guna are referred to in Emberá as *jurá*. They were once the traditional enemies of the Emberá (see Vargas 1993; C. Williams 2004; Isacsson 1993; Martínez Maori 2011). The term *jurá* also translates in Emberá as 'enemies' (see Isacsson 1993: 87–8, 225, 226, 246). Since the mid-twentieth

century the Guna have become allies of the Emberá in struggles to secure indigenous rights. The Emberá have borrowed many ideas from the Guna in their efforts to organise themselves politically and manage their semi-independent territories (Herlihy 1986; Kane 1994; Howe 2009).

- *Kampuniá* – The Emberá refer to people who are not Amerindians as *kampuniá* (see Kane 1994; Theodossopoulos 2013a). The *kampuniá* are further subdivided into Spanish-speaking black people (*kampuniá paimá*) and Spanish-speaking white or *mestizo* people (*kampuniá torro*), who the Emberá of Eastern Panama also call *colonos* (because they came from Western Panama to colonise their land). More recently, one hears a new adaptation of the *kampuniá* term: *kampuniá gringo*, to describe white North Americans and Europeans.

- *Indigenous* – The Emberá understanding of who is indigenous accords with wider Latin American 'structures of alterity' (Wade 1997: 36–7), which associate indigenousness with 'Indian-ness' and an ancestral connection with the Americas. When they migrate – from Colombia to Panama or from the rainforest to the city – they remain indigenous for as long as they remember their language and they desire to associate with an indigenous identity. Children raised in Panama City who do not speak Emberá are absorbed to the flexible category of *mestizo*, and may potentially become *Latinos* (Spanish-speaking, non-indigenous people). All Amerindian groups of Panama – including the Guna, the Ngäbe and the Wounaan – are recognised by the Emberá as indigenous. In this respect, the term indigenous is also a racial signifier referring to all people of Amerindian descent: from the Emberá point of view, black or white Panamanians (or foreigners) can never be indigenous.

- *Indians* – The Emberá are aware that non-indigenous Panamanians often use the term *Indians* (*indios*) in a pejorative manner to indicate social inferiority and a less 'civilised' status. This is why many Emberá prefer the term *indigenous* (*indígenas*) as a more politically correct alternative, as it acknowledges a historical connection with the Americas. Unlike *Indian*, which was used in a discriminatory way in the past to exclude or stigmatise inferiority, the term *indigenous* is associated with the more recent politics of indigenous representation, and the official nomenclature of the nation state. In this respect, the term *indigenous*, unlike the term *Indian*, conveys a certain degree of respect and official acceptance.

- **Emberá,** *instead of* **indios** *or* **Chocoes** – In recent years, the word *Emberá* has been increasingly used in Panama, even by non-indigenous Panamanians. Two separate processes have contributed to this change. Firstly, the formalisation of Emberá political structures, which included the appointment of Emberá representatives at community and regional levels, where the Emberá, like all other Panamanian groups, are referred to by their self-chosen name (see Herlihy 1986, 2003; Kane 1994; Colin 2010). Secondly, the development of indigenous tourism in the last fifteen years, which was supported by national advertisement campaigns that presented Emberá culture as an asset to Panamanian diversity (see Theodossopoulos 2011, 2014; Velásquez Runk 2012).

Notes

1 Here, I borrow the term 'first wave' from O'Hanlon (2007: 4); yet it should be noted that this broad characterisation does not represent a homogenous type of anthropology, or a sub-field. It rather represents a particular era, when anthropological attention on clothes and body decorations lead to analyses of other, more established anthropological topics of enquiry.

2 A good example of using clothes as a means to a theoretical end is Roland Barthes's semiological analysis, *The Fashion System* (1985). Notwithstanding his perceptive and penetrating critique of bourgeois culture, Barthes is not interested in the materiality of clothes, but rather on the meaning-making of fashion.

3 For example, Faris (1972); T. Turner (1969, 1980, 1992a); Strathern and Strathern (1971); Strathern (1987); Knauft (1989).

4 Epitomised by classic accounts such as Terence Turner's 'The Social Skin' (1980).

5 A definition of dress by Eicher and Roach-Higgins beautifully combines the elements of both types of dress codes I outlined above (that is, those relying to a greater or lesser extent on woven clothes). Eicher and Roach-Higgins define dress 'as an assemblage of body modifications and/or supplements displayed by a person in communicating with other human beings' (1992: 15).

6 See Kane (1992) for a structuralist-inclined analysis.

7 For example, several of my undergraduate students over the years who approached Kane's book with the intention of extracting basic ethnographic information to use in their assignments.

8 Reverte Coma lived in Panama from 1950 to 1968, after which he returned to Spain.

9 Note that the publication year of *Tormenta* is somewhat misleading of the Emberá experiences captured by this book: Reverte Coma's portrait illuminates aspects of the Emberá world witnessed between 1955 and 1965.

10 Such as, for example, the similarities in how accessible and inaccessible Emberá communities approach tourism (Theodossopoulos 2007); the Emberá perception of the tourists as 'resources' in tourism (Theodossopoulos 2010); the negotiations of tourist expectations in the Emberá tourist encounter (Theodossopoulos 2011); the reintroduction of the indigenous attire (Theodossopoulos 2012, 2013a); the Emberá dancing tradition (Theodossopoulos 2013c); the elusive concept of authenticity (Theodossopoulos 2013a); the representational self-awareness of the Emberá in tourism (Theodossopoulos n.d.); and the exoticisation of indigeneity in the tourism imaginary (Theodossopoulos 2014); and, finally, my role as a researcher and my dilemmas regarding anthropological engagement (Theodossopoulos 2015).

11 At river Sambú, I have travelled from Puerto Indio to Pavarandó, and at river Venado, all the way to Borovichi. At river Chico, I have travelled to the communities of Comun, Naranjal and Corozal. At river Chucunaque, I have travelled from Lajas Blancas to El Salto, while I have also taken two times the long journey along river Ucurganti, with the community of Tortuga as my final destination. At river Tuquesa I have visited the community of Nuevo Vigía. I have also travelled to La Palma and Garachiné, and to Yaviza twice, where I visited Emberá who are settled in these non-indigenous towns. While visiting the Emberá communities on the above-mentioned rivers, I have always obtained permission from the *nokó* of each community. Before starting these journeys, I presented myself to the Cacique General at Puerto Indio, while in 2008 I obtained written permission to travel in Darién by the Head of the National Police in Panama City. At Chagres, I obtained permission by the *nokó* of Parara Puru, who subsequently became a close friend, and the Cacique Regional for the Chagres area.

12 I use the term 'Eastern Panama' to denote, according to the archaeological tradition, the lands that extend to the east of the Panama Canal; these include the Panamá province (where the Emberá communities at Chagres are located), San Blas, and Darién.

13 The memoirs of this trip I plan to present in a future publication.

14 I interacted during fieldwork with all families of the community, and sometimes with their frequent Emberá guests, usually relatives from other communities in Chagres or Darién. I followed the tourist presentations, chatting about representational issues during the frequent intervals, but I also spent time with the local residents during non-representational time: relaxing closer to the river, or eating with them at their family homes. The leaders of the community always arranged that I take my meals – breakfast, lunch and dinner – with different families, prioritising those that needed, due to unforeseen circumstances, the modest financial assistance I offered in exchange for my food. I have always eaten what everybody else has eaten, and through commensality, I solidified my links with the local families, sharing aspects of their – but also my own – life, the episodes of which the Emberá and I have followed in the last ten years. During fieldwork I communicated with the Emberá in Spanish and, occasionally, in Spanish embellished with a few Emberá sentences or words. I kept my fieldnotes in a mixed idiom of Greek, Spanish and Emberá.

15 The seventeen-month fieldwork experience that informs this book was spread over seven years from 2005 to 2012, during which I visited Panama, usually in between academic terms or during periods that I was relieved from teaching, for one to four months at a time. I spent the greater part of this time in Parara Puru. Every seven or nine days I would leave the community to spend three or four days in the city, where I washed my clothes, collected published and unpublished sources about the Emberá written in Spanish, or visited my wife, who, at various periods during my fieldwork, undertook her own research in other parts of Panama.

16 In the cases that I have drawn themes from old photographs from the early twentieth century, my reproduction is highly selective. The end is affected by my ethnographic nostalgia and, by all means, is my art, not a copy of the original picture. Some sketches inspired by older books have been drawn by the artist Tasia Kolokotsa.

2

Static sketches in transformation

Describing the Emberá attire – a costume representative of a previous era – can be metaphorically compared to a series of photographic snapshots that capture only a small dimension of Emberá life: in the case of the Emberá costume, we see as much as fits in the frame of a picture, for example one that contains the representative male and female attire as an ideal type. As with other ethnographic portraits of 'tradition', the descriptions of the Emberá clothing are haunted by a proclivity to freeze a set of vibrant practices into a formalistic and narrow typology. In the case of what the Emberá call 'traditional' clothes – the clothes of the times of their grandparents – the mere act of description can foster essentialism and a static view of Emberá culture represented by singular – more or less authoritative, but rigid – version of authenticity: 'here is the traditional Emberá attire', 'this is what it consists of'.

Aware of the problems with this motionless form of representation, I offer in this chapter a series of descriptive snapshots that freeze small fragments of the Emberá reality in time: they provide a static depiction of a transforming practice, 'the Emberá costume or attire', described and simplified in an outline that can be understood and appreciated by the generic, undifferentiated 'non-Emberá', the *kampuniá*[E], or the *kampuniá* reader. Interestingly, Emberá leaders and friends in the field have encouraged me to produce exactly that: a structured account of the old Emberá costume, referenced in a scholarly way and put in written form, sketching out an indigenous authenticity of a sort;

2.1 The male and female Emberá attire as an ideal type

one that relates, as I argue in the following chapters, to a variety of 'indigenous essentialism' (Howe 2009: 240–1). Such a limited and constrained version of authenticity is partly encouraged by the Emberá themselves as it legitimises indigeneity through academic authority and persuasion: it puts their culture on the record, yet in a motionless form frozen in time. Here, the anthropological denial of coevalness (Fabian 1983) provides indigenous politics of representation with a sense of authority: fixed, defined, immutable indigeneity.

These are the considerations that underlie my ambivalence about describing the standard traditional Emberá attire in a generic form. Therefore, I would like to forewarn the reader that the three sections of this chapter are devoted to an imperfect task, limited by what it seeks to provide: a simple description, not the unravelling of a process. As I proceed from the description of male and female attire to the description of body painting with *jagua*, the reader will agree with me that Emberá practices do not fit prescribed typologies. My typological description merely provides a starting point, which enables me to tell the story of Emberá clothing in the next chapter, but also, indirectly, to frame my account of the Emberá clothing in terms of previous ethnographic descriptions. Comparisons with the past provide the foundation for ethnographic nostalgia, evident here in my search for underlying patterns of continuity in Emberá culture. However limiting is this task, it will open the way for realising that the Emberá attire – as this is now reintroduced in presentations for tourists – is not merely a static 'tradition', but has been recently transformed to another, alternative dress code. As we shall see in the following chapters, the Emberá attire as this is normatively conceived, is as subject to change and variation as any other cultural practice.

'Traditional' clothes for men

The loincloth (*andeá*[E], *guayuco*[S]) is one of the most iconic constituents of the male 'traditional' Chocó (Emberá or Wounaan) attire. It is a plain piece of cotton fabric, without designs, in a single bright colour (usually red, yellow, green or blue) tied around the waste with a string (see Torres de Araúz 1966: 55; Pineda and Gutiérrez de Pineda 1999: 105; Reverte Coma 2002: 209). It is used nowadays only for cultural presentations and celebrations. The Emberá and Wounaan are the only indigenous groups in Panama that consider the loincloth as part of their 'traditional' costume. In the past, they made their loincloths from bark-cloth (*kuéporo*[E], *damagua*[E], *cocuá*[S]) from the bark of the *cocuá* or *damagua* tree (*Poulsenia armata*[L]) (Pineda and Gutiérrez de Pineda 1999: 74–5).[1] Ethnographers and travellers have noticed Emberá loincloths made from bark-cloth in the early twentieth century (Isacsson 1993: 63), but by this time cotton loincloths were already predominant (see Verrilll 1921, 1931; Nordenskiold 1928; Marsh 1934).

Within the contemporary Emberá world, the use of the *andeá* is associated with adherence to the old ways, 'the times of the grandfathers' and life in dispersed settlement, before the foundation of concentrated communities. For

 amburá

andeá

2.2 The *amburá* and the *andeá*

non-indigenous Panamanians, the loincloth or *guayuco* is considered to be emblematic of life in the jungle, a stereotype of primitiveness or ignorance of 'civilised' life: the Indian in a loincloth is caricatured as an 'uncivilised' man living in the forest, 'uneducated', stripped of modern clothes, unaware of how to behave in the city. The contemporary Emberá are very much aware of these stereotypical connotations. Nevertheless, their considerable reluctance to wear the *guayuco* is sometimes mediated by an emerging sense of pride in upholding an Emberá identity. In the communities that host regular presentations for tourists, wearing the loincloth is particularly associated with an emerging representational confidence.

The *amburá*[E] is a wide layer of glass beads (*chaquira*[S]) that male Emberá wear on top of their loincloth. In older ethnographies it is described as a broad 'girdle' (Wassén 1935: 70; Stout 1963: 270) or a wide belt of beads (Pineda and Gutiérrez de Pineda 1999: 120) with geometric patterns created by glass beads of different shades.[2] Reverte Coma (2002: 213), reflecting upon the *amburás* that he saw in the 1960s, says that their beautiful designs make them 'authentic works of art and patience'. These items of clothing were used in social and ritual celebrations in the past (Torres de Araúz 1966: 56; Reverte Coma 2002: 213), and have been reintroduced for tourist presentations. In some communities, such as Parara Puru, every adult male has one, while in some other communities the men refuse to wear the *amburá*, even if it is solely for the entertainment of tourists. They say that they feel 'more comfortable wearing only the *andeá*', but when prompted they reveal that they dislike the *amburá* for its skirt-like and womanly appearance. Contemporary *amburás* tend to be approximately three to four centimetres wider than the ones used in the past. As I discuss in Chapter 7, this increase in width of the *amburás* is an adaptation aimed at increasing the cover provided by the male attire.

When dressed in traditional attire Emberá men wear long beaded strings, an item of dress referred as *kotiábari*[E]. They loop over the shoulder and reach to the opposite hip, and two or three such beaded strings – or multiple threads of glass beads (Torres de Araúz 1966: 56) – are worn over each shoulder, crossing at the centre of a man's chest. The beads (*chaquiras*[S])[3] come in a variety of colours, mostly white, blue, red, green and yellow, and nowadays they can be bought, like those used for the *amburás*, from shops in the Chinese neighbourhood in Panama City. Most contemporary Emberá in Eastern Panama, who dress in traditional attire to participate in cultural presentation, use them. In the past they were especially

2.3 The *amburá* is worn on the top of the *andeá*, but the edge of the latter falls in front of the former

preferred by young men looking to attract the attention of young women (Pineda and Gutiérrez de Pineda 1999: 119).

In addition to the *kotiábari* necklaces, which hang shoulder to hip, most men, but also boys and adolescents, also wear small necklaces. These are formed of beads interspersed with small cold-hammered silver pendants or, more rarely, animal teeth. These items are all in frequent use in Parara Puru and other communities in Chagres that entertain tourists. In the past, seeds and animal teeth were more common, and if we consider the importance attributed by the Emberá of the seventeenth century on possessing the teeth of their enemies (Isacsson 1993; Nordenskiold 1928: 99), we may extrapolate that triumphant warriors sported necklaces made from Spanish or Guna teeth. To avoid entertaining such an exoticising assumption, I prefer to imagine that the precursors of glass beads were seeds, while silver pendants came, as is often the case nowadays, from cold-hammered coins.

Another constituent of the traditional Chocó attire, as it is conceived today, are the arm cuffs or bracelets (*pulseras*[S], *maniyia*[E]). They are open to accommodate the thickness of the wrist (Reverte Coma 2002: 221), and are often embellished with punch work. In the past they were made from cold-hammered silver, and nowadays from stainless steel. According to Isacsson (1993), the Chocó once had lip and nose ornaments as well. The former are reported in early colonial documents, although reference to them becomes progressively infrequent towards the late seventeenth century (Isacsson 1993: 35, 38–9). In contrast, nose ornaments appear to have survived into later centuries, probably until the late nineteenth century, as Isacsson reports after scholastic archival research. By 1927 when Nordenskiold visited Docampadó and Docordó rivers – in the Colombian Chocó homeland – elderly men had removed their nose ornaments, but their perforated septum was still visible (Isacsson 1993: 39; Wassén 1935: 70–1). The Emberá that I have met in the twenty-first century make no mention of such adornments. In contrast to the Emberá, nose rings have been an important adornment for the Guna women. The attempts of the Panamanian government to constrain their use in the second decade of the twentieth century excited the Guna struggle for self-determination (see Howe 1998: 125–6, 179, 2009: 32, 56, 67).

In many old photographs, we can see Chocó men posing with headdresses made of coins and long earrings.[4] The Emberá in Chagres no longer wear headdresses, and little mention is made of them these days. On the contrary, most Emberá men and women – from Chagres or Darién – who have seen my digitised collection of old ethnographic photographs speak with enthusiasm and nostalgia about the multi-layered earrings worn by men in times gone by. I was told that such long and elaborate silver earrings were used by the Emberá men in Eastern Panama until the 1960s, and in Darién some men still have them. Ethnographers of previous generations report that Chocó-earrings were long and composed of interlinked – often crescent-shaped – silver pendants usually created from cold-hammered coins (see, for example, Reverte Coma 2002: 214, 233; Pineda and Gutiérrez de Pineda 1999: 116). Despite the care they take dressing up in formal 'traditional' costume to welcome tourists, the Emberá in Chagres do not wear earrings, although some women still possess and wear silver earrings that resemble smaller versions of the male Chocó earrings. My view is that male earrings, as with other adornments that are viewed in non-indigenous society as feminine, became less popular in Emberá society when a new genera-tion of Emberá started attending mainstream primary schools and being indoc-trinated by occidental gender aesthetics in the 1970s, 1980s and 1990s.

'Traditional' clothes for women

2.4 Girls wearing *parumas* and *ubarís*

I would like to start this section with an inter-esting observation made by ethnographers who worked with the Emberá in the past. Torres de Araúz (1966, 1980) and Reverte Coma (2002), reflecting on their ethnographic observations in the 1960s, reported that among the Emberá, the women's code of dress was more modest and less flamboyant than that of Emberá men. Although women wear a variety of adornments too, 'it is the men who take pride in decorating their bodies with ornaments of different sorts' (Isacsson 1993: 35), particularly younger men (Pineda and Gutiérrez de Pineda 1999: 116). Coquetry is not an exclusive trait of women, comments Torres de Araúz: male adolescents dedicate a great deal of time every morning to taking care their personal appearance (Torres de Araúz 1966: 58, 1980: 224), often painting themselves carefully (Reverte Coma 2002: 236), especially when they wish to attract the oppo-site sex (Pineda and Gutiérrez de Pineda 1999: 115). Similar to Nordenskiold's observa-tions from the second decade of the twentieth century (1928: 48, 82), Pineda and Gutiérrez de Pineda (1999) add that children, women and elderly men and women decorate themselves to a lesser degree in comparison with younger men.

Torres de Araúz clarifies in direct and authoritative style that the female dress contrasts, in its simplicity and austerity, with the rich masculine attire (Torres de Araúz 1966: 58), because the ornaments of women are much reduced and much simpler than those of men (Torres de Araúz 1975: 272; 1980: 171). Reverte Coma (2002) corroborates these observations and maintains that in this indigenous group we very often see an exaggerated narcissism in men, while the women are diminished in their affectation in dress (Ibid.: 213), care less about their appearance (Ibid.: 231), and do not have the silver ornaments that adorn men (Ibid.: 235). It is clear from these descriptions, that until the last quarter of the twentieth century, women traditionally wore far fewer adornments than men. In fact in some cases, the only adornments for young girls were flowers – in particular hibiscus flowers – attached to their long hair (*budá*[E]), and/or a simple necklace. Nowadays, Emberá women of all ages take good care of their hair, combing it carefully and frequently, and when dressed in traditional attire, they weave crowns – from *nahuala*[S] or *bijao*[S] fibers[5] – onto which they attach flowers.

In the past, men also used to put flowers on their hair (see Nordenskiold 1928: figs. 29 and 39), a practice that they avoid nowadays, because – as with the use of *achiote* in facial body painting – it is considered effeminate. When I tried to discuss the former inclination of males to wear more adornments than women, my Emberá interlocutors in Parara Puru became uncomfortable. The heavy decoration of men in the old times, I was given to understand, inspired the mockery of non-indigenous neighbours, who were much less polite about this than Torres de Araúz and Reverte Coma, and equally as opinionated. Nowadays, however, some women – especially in communities that entertain tourists – wear a good variety of adornments, while, as I will explain below, certain female items of clothing have become more elaborate, are extended in size to cover a greater part of the woman's body, or, as in the case of the *parumas* have obtained their own distinctive fashion.

The *paruma*[S] (*wuá*[E]) is a quintessential Chocó garment that communicates the ethnic identity of its bearer, and is emblematic of an indigenous identity more generally. In non-indigenous Panamanian towns, Emberá and Wounaan women can be easily recognised by their colourful *parumas*, in a similar way that Guna and Ngäbe women can be identified by their own distinctive dresses. Here, women's dress is emblematic of indigenous identities, as it is elsewhere in Panama (Young 1971: 10–15; Tice 1995: 28, 47, 81; Howe 1998: 17, 125, 178; see also Chapter 7). A majority of the Emberá men and women living within the two districts of the semi-autonomous reservation in Darién insist that their wives and daughters should wear the *paruma*, an item of clothing that is also popular in Emberá communities outside the reservations and throughout Eastern Panama.

The *paruma* is essentially a rectangular piece of cloth, which is wrapped tightly around one's hips like a skirt – or a 'sarong' (Reverte Coma 2002: 233) – with the loose-end carefully tucked in at the waist (see Pineda and Gutiérrez de Pineda 1999: 105–6). The skirt then falls to about knee-length. It is worth noting that the term *paruma* is used by the Emberá and the Wounaan to describe a rectangular piece of cloth, usually three yards in length.[6] In contrast, non-indigenous Panamanians refer to the *parumas* (in plural) to describe its use as an indigenous (and specifically Chocó) skirt. Nowadays the *parumas* are available in a variety of different colours and patterns, making them easy to match with a top. As a result, it is easy to combine this traditional item of dress with modern clothes. On the one hand, the continued use of the *paruma* represents a desire to identify with an indigenous identity. On the other hand, the practice of matching the *paruma* with t-shirts, vest tops, tank tops and cropped tops provides an aesthetic combination acceptable to non-indigenous society, as it ensures that the upper female body remains covered.[7]

The overwhelming majority of Emberá women I have met in Chagres and in Darién need little persuasion to wear the *paruma*. Apart from being recognised as a very light and comfortable garment amenable to the tasks of everyday life, the *paruma* has also emerged as a type of dress with its own distinctive fashion. Nowadays the *paruma*-cloth is manufactured in Asia according to Emberá size specification and design preferences, normally nature motifs: flowers or birds in vivid colours. It is available in retail shops in Panama City alongside textiles – also fabricated in Asia – for the Guna. I discuss this issue in further detail in Chapter 8, although I should stress here that each indigenous group purchases only the fabrics made specifically for them. Even though the new *paruma*-cloth available at the market is made specifically for the Emberá and the Wounaan, the contemporary naturalistic *paruma* designs bear no similarity with the 'traditional' designs used in body painting, as was probably the case in previous centuries when *parumas* were made from bark-cloth (Torres de Araúz 1966: 59).[8] Before the introduction of the new style of *paruma*-cloth from Asia, the Emberá of Eastern Panama bought fabrics from shops in the non-indigenous towns of Darién or during the occasional trip to the capital (Torres de Araúz 1966: 58).

As mentioned above, the standard length of a *paruma* is three yards – and has been so at least since the last quarter of the twentieth century (see Torres de Araúz 1966: 58; Pineda and Gutiérrez de Pineda 1999: 105). The *paruma*-cloth, when sold in bolts of three yards, is wide enough to be cut lengthwise to produce two *parumas* (of the same length). The most recent designs are always more expensive, and Emberá women eagerly await the arrival of the new season's *paruma*. Every new *paruma* pattern is printed in a variety of colour combinations, adding to the overall variety of *parumas* available. In this respect, and as with some *mola* themes among the Guna (Salvador 1976), particular *paruma* styles become fads (see also Chapter 8).

Another item of clothing with a long history, which has lately been adapted to accommodate the non-indigenous aesthetic of covering the upper body, is the *ubarí*[E] (*pulsera de plata*[S]), a heavy beaded necklace that covers the chest with lines of coins interposed between the layers. The coins could be dollar quarters, but also old or contemporary coins from different countries. Reverte Coma describes seeing nineteenth and early twentieth century coins from Ecuador, Colombia, Chile and Peru on the necklace of a shaman's wife in Darién (Reverte Coma 2002: 232), and I have witnessed Emberá women collecting foreign coins from tourists for the same purpose. In the last twenty years, the beaded component of the *ubarí* has evolved so that it looks more like a top than a necklace. This adaptation

2.5 Contemporary *ubarís* are larger and cover a woman's chest

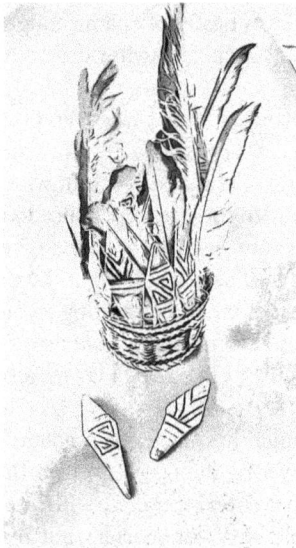

2.6 Emberá crown

provides some cover for the otherwise topless female bodies of Emberá women dressed in traditional attire, and is another example of conforming non-indigenous aesthetics and principles of modesty into Emberá clothing practices.

The standard female Emberá attire also includes small necklaces that are worn around the neck – that is, much higher than the *ubarí* (which falls lower at the point of a woman's chest). These necklaces are composed of small pendants made of silver or from cold-hammered coins and are virtually identical in style to those worn by men. Nowadays women also wear all sorts of inexpensive earrings. In the past female Emberá earrings were similar in style and manufacture to the old multilayered earrings sported by men. They were also made of silver, but were smaller and shorter than their male counterparts (Torres de Araúz 1980: 172; Pineda and Gutiérrez de Pineda 1999: 116).[9] While most male earrings have either been sold to outsiders, or melted or cold-hammered to produce other ornaments, a good number of old female silver earrings have been kept. As I explained in the previous section, this observation allows us to appreciate the influence of non-indigenous ideas of masculinity on Emberá traditional attire.

Some dancing troupes in Darién use crowns of balsa wood, cut into the shape of feathers, and painted with *jagua*. These crowns were common in the past, but were worn mostly by men (see Nordenskiold 1928: 51, figs. 27, 32; Torres de Araúz 1980: 171), particularly shamans, on special occasions (Torres de Araúz 1980: 169; Isacsson 1993: 35). Figure 2.6 shows one I drew in 2010, previously used by Emberá women living close to Yaviza. I have seen videos of Emberá women performing traditional dances wearing such crowns in community celebrations in Darién and in Colombia.

Emberá body painting

One would be seriously mistaken to understand Emberá body painting merely as a feature of 'traditional' Emberá attire. Certainly, body painting is an ingredient of 'traditional' Emberá-Wounaan attire, as this is used to reenact a dress code of the past. But it is also a creative and dynamic representation of the Emberá present, one that was not eradicated with the introduction of mass-produced clothes. As I will further explain in Chapter 7, body painting can be used in combination with modern clothes, adding, as with the *paruma*-skirts, an element of indigeneity to styles of Emberá and Wounaan dress that rely on Western clothes. Although not all contemporary Emberá in Eastern Panama systematically practise body painting – and admittedly not to the degree that they did a few decades ago – many apply it for the sheer pleasure of ornamentation and because they value the medicinal properties of the painting medium, the juice of the *jagua*^{S} fruit (*kipará*^{E} or *chiparrá*^{E}, *Genipa americana*^{L}).

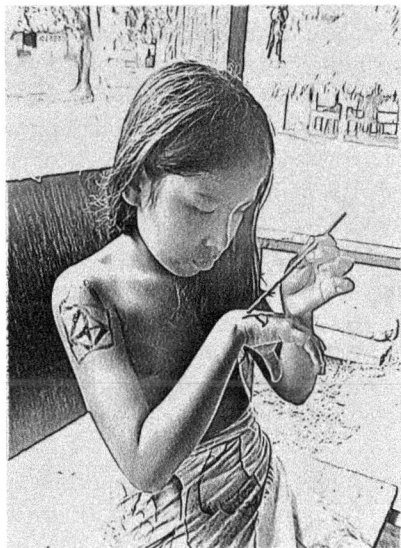

2.7   Experimenting with *jagua* paint

Jagua provides a dark blue, almost black colour, which fades away eight to twelve days later – depending on one's exposure to water. The Emberá, who shower or bathe in the river very frequently, say that *jagua* designs usually last for eight days, while foreign tourists or travellers sometimes manage to maintain the designs for a few days longer. The temporary nature of *jagua* design encourages variation and artistic experimentation. As the Emberá helped me to understand, it is not the end of the world if you make a mistake when painting with *jagua*, as the paint will fade away after a few days. Children in particular often indulge in creative applications of *jagua* body painting. Sometimes they make mistakes with their paint strokes or spill *jagua* on their skin while painting their friends or siblings. As an Emberá friend once disclosed to me, if you do not like a pattern or you wish to rectify a mistake, there is a simple solution available: to paint a bigger portion of your body, or even your whole body completely black, covering old or unwanted designs.

The *jagua* juice is extracted when the *jagua* fruit is still green. At first it is transparent, but it gradually acquires its characteristic dark blue colour through oxidisation. When it is applied on the skin it is grey in appearance, but soon becomes dark blue, almost black. *Jagua* trees grow in the wild, but if necessary the Emberá transplant one or two closer to home. The ones in Parara Puru are still too young to produce fruit, but other communities in Chagres are lucky enough to have fully grown *jagua* trees, and their residents paint their bodies much more frequently. To prepare the paint, the fruit is peeled and its fleshy part is scratched. Then the pulp is squeezed to extract the juice (for example, through a piece of cloth) and the juice is poured into a metal container and placed over fire. With the increase in temperature, the transparent juice turns black as the heat accelerates the process of oxidisation (Reverte Coma 2002: 223). Sometimes ash, preferably from balsa wood, is added to the mixture, to stabilise the paint (see Torres de Araúz 1966: 57; 1980: 169; Ulloa 1992: 179–180; Isacsson 1993: 32). Some Emberá prefer not to 'cook' the *jagua*, as the juice eventually acquires the desired dark colour simply through exposure to the air.

A thin stick of bamboo (*bakurú*[E]) is usually used to paint the *jagua* on the body. In the past, and also more rarely today, the Emberá used painting sticks with two or three points to paint symmetrical parallel lines (see Torres de Araúz 1980: 169; Isacsson 1993: 33; Pineda and Gutiérrez de Pineda 1999: 113; Reverte Coma 2002: 225; Ulloa 1992: 181), which can be compared with painting styluses used by other Amerindian groups (cf. Ewart 2013: 99). Previous ethnographers of the Emberá mentioned the frequent use of wooden painting stamps (*pintaderas*[S]) with prefabricated designs (see Nordenskiold 1928: 51–2; Torres de Araúz 1966: 57, 1980: 169; Reverte Coma 2002: 224–6). The older Emberá of Chagres nostalgically recognised these *pintaderas* in my collection of digitised photographs from older ethnographies, but they no longer have any. When they wish to paint a large part of their body completely black they use their hand to apply the *jagua* juice. In most cases the hands of those who have extracted the juice, or have worked extensively with it, painting themselves or others, absorb a great quantity of *jagua* juice and appear intensely black.

Body painting with *jagua* in Darién was recorded in early colonial documents (Reverte Coma 2002: 222). It is an example of a more widespread practice common among many other lowland South American groups, such as the Kaipó (see T. Turner 1980, 1992; Vidal and Verswijver 1992), the Piro (Gow 1999) or the Panará (Ewart 2013), while the Guna, neighbours of the Emberá, use it as well (Salvador 1997; Margiotti 2013). In the past, apart from the black/blue colour of the *jagua*, the Emberá also used red, which they extracted from the seeds of the *achiote*[S] tree (*kanyí*[E], *Bixa orellana*[L]) (Torres de Araúz 1966: 56; Reverte Coma 2002: 221; see also Wassén 1935: 72; Isacsson 1993: 33; Tayler 1996: 52).[10] The use of red in contemporary body painting in Eastern Panama is rare, with the exception of women using *achiote* as a medium of makeup to colour their lips and cheeks (Torres de Araúz 1975: 274). But nowadays in this case, inexpensive makeup products – in particular lipstick – are preferred (see Torres de Araúz 1966: 58; Isacsson 1993: 33; Pineda and Gutiérrez de Pineda 1999: 114; Reverte Coma 2002: 221).

It is interesting to note, however, that in the past facial designs with *achiote* – usually in combination with *jagua*-black – were favoured by men, rather than women. As the contemporary Emberá explain, face painting with *achiote*-red was sported especially by young men who wanted to attract the attention of a girl – or more generally, adolescents wishing 'to impress those around them' (Isacsson 1993: 32, 265). This practice was frequent, according to the contemporary Emberá, up until the 1960s (see Reverte Coma 2002: 236), and it appears that back then young single men painted themselves more often, and with more care, than women (see Pineda and Gutiérrez de Pineda 1999: 113). A wide variety of facial designs that combine both red and black – '*achiote* with *jagua*' – can be seen in Ulloa's (1992) impressive ethnographic collection of Emberá body-painting patterns.[11] In general, *achiote*-red is applied on the face – and, according to Isacsson, indicates an intention to attract either an enemy or a person of the opposite sex (Isacsson 1993: 257–8, 264–5)[12] – while *jagua*-black is applied from the upper lip downwards. Most contemporary young and middle-aged Emberá men in Eastern Panama consider the application of red designs on their face effeminising, well aware of the gendered connotations of red lipstick in non-indigenous society.

With the exception of the contrast between the colours red and black, and unlike other Amerindian groups (cf. T. Turner 1980), the Emberá have less to say about the colour of body painting, and more about the design.[13] In traditional curative ceremonies, the shaman (*jaibaná*[E]) will choose carefully what pattern to apply, after consulting an aiding spirit in his sleep. It is believed that the body of the patient has been invaded by the spirit of an animal, plant or object, which is responsible for the disease, and which the shaman has to expel (see Torres de Araúz 1966; Pineda and Gutiérrez de Pineda 1999; Reverte Coma 2002; and among the Guna, Fortis 2012a: 41). For this purpose the shaman calls other spirits that will either scare the 'illness-inflicting' spirit away or entice it (e.g. through sexual attraction) to depart from the patient's body. Usually, during the first night of the curative process, the shaman attempts to ascertain the nature of the problem – that is, which spirit is causing the illness. The following day, he paints – as he feels is necessary – the torso, arms and legs of the patient with a geometrical design representing an appropriate animal, plant or object. The shaman might also paint his assistant – a woman who helps him during the ceremony – with a different design.

Each shaman has two or three favourite body-painting designs that he applies most frequently. For example, the last practising shaman in Chagres relied on the designs of *saú*[E] (calabash, *totumo*[S]) and *damá*[E] (snake) (see figure 2.8). The designs themselves are pronounced *damá-pa* and *saú-pa*, the drawings of the snake and the calabash.[14] I have recorded variations of the same and different designs from other shamans (see figure 2.9 for another version of the calabash [*saú*] and a pattern called 'the sun' [*beséa*] drawn by two shamans from Darién), while Ulloa (1992) presents us with a variety of these and many additional designs, mostly, but not exclusively, from the river Atrato in Colombia. What is important to note here is that the procedure followed by a shaman for each cure is by no means identical: complex considerations relating to the interrelationship between different spirits may influence the shaman's decision, and his choices

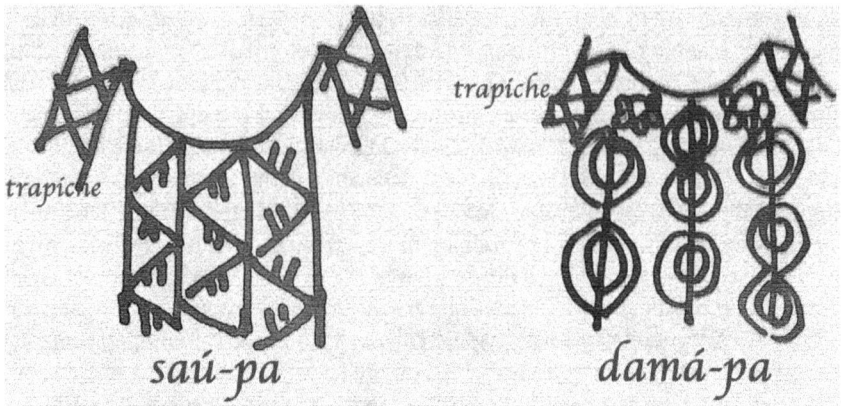

2.8 *Damá-pa* and *saú-pa*, the drawings of the snake and the calabash

with respect to body painting and design. In addition it should be noted that the shamanic practices of the Emberá of Panama, although still popular, are meeting with considerable opposition from Emberá who are committed to Evangelical Christianity. There are still a few practising and well-known *jaibanás* who attract some patients, but all those I have met complain that younger Emberá are not particularly interested in succeeding them. In Parara Puru and most other communities in the Canal area there is no *jaibaná*, but they occasionally receive visits from Emberá shamans[15] who come for two or three days to perform a particular cure (see Chapter 8).

In the past, body decoration with *jagua* was a standard element of preparation for participation in a wide variety of social occasions, including all sorts of gatherings or ceremonies that involved the consumption of alcohol, or marking an event or accomplishment (completion of a new canoe or house, cooperation in agricultural labour or a transition in a young person's life) (see Ulloa 1992: 238). In this respect, and considering its widespread use in the past, it is difficult to separate ceremonial from social occasions, as the preparation of the traditional *chicha*-beer – consumed in most social gatherings – involved the participation of spirits and was managed by shamans, who played an integral role in Emberá everyday life. Undoubtedly, many particular ritual practices that involved *jagua*-painting until as recently as the last quarter of the twentieth century are no longer common in Eastern Panama. These include, for example, the naming ceremony, during which the one-year-old child is painted black, as well as the seclusion period that marks a girl's puberty, during which the girl is rinsed by her mother with *jagua* sap (see Nordenskiold 1928: 74; Torres de Araúz 1966: 57, 1980: 223; Ulloa 1992: 235; Isacsson 1993: 17–18).

Nowadays, there is a weaker association between the activities supervised or instigated by the *jaibanás* and the use of *jagua* body paint. Nevertheless, the

(a)   (b)

2.9a The painting of the sun   2.9b The painting of the 'calabash of the
(*beséa-pa*)   mountain' (*saú méa devéma-pa*)

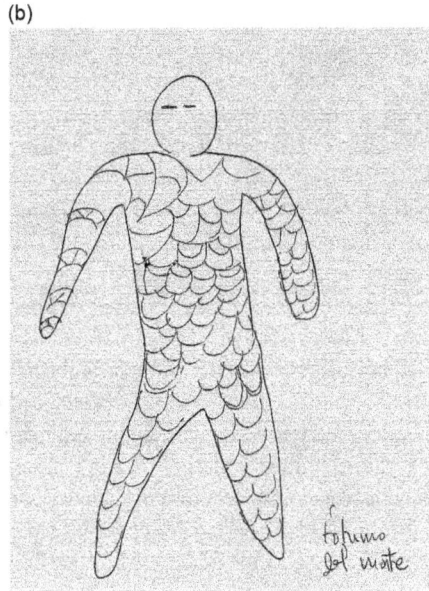

Emberá of Eastern Panama use it frequently to prepare for community events and celebrations – for example, commemorating the foundation of a community – that may involve drinking canned beer, dance and music, or athletic competitions (usually basketball matches). On these occasions, dance troupes (of women or schoolgirls) who perform in front of an audience, but also adolescents who want to flirt or impress, and older women who are used to this practice, dedicate time and attention to decorating their bodies with *jagua* designs.

Besides shamanic practices, social gatherings and celebrations it is important to note that there are a myriad of other occasions on which body paint is applied throughout an individual's life. The Emberá use *jagua* in their normal day-to-day working life, and often cover their bodies with it in a less ceremonial manner. Astrid Ulloa in her monograph *Kipará: Dibujo y Pintura, dos formas Emberá de representar el mundo* (1992) takes special care to emphasise that *jagua* body painting occurs in different contexts and occasions that stretch from ceremonial to everyday events. Similarly, choice of design may reflect contextual considerations that range from participation in curing ceremonies to an intention to flirt or to project an identity related to a new institutional role – for example, 'governor' or 'health promoter' (Ibid.: 140–141, 250). Unmarried women pay more attention to the patterns chosen and applied, while married women often resort to the easier practice of painting their whole body completely black and/or adding a smaller design on their lower cheek and jaw.

Most Emberá I know accentuate the medicinal or ornamental uses of *jagua* over its ritual significance. The former include *jagua* working as a sunscreen and insect repellent – attributes that are praised by the Emberá and their eth-nographers (see Wassén 1935: 74; Torres de Araúz 1966: 56, 1975: 272; Isacsson 1993: 32; Pineda and Gutiérrez de Pineda 1999: 115; Reverte Coma 2002: 221, 228). Reverte Coma, who was trained as a medical doctor, comments on the anti-pruritic and antifungal qualities of *jagua* (2002: 228). In addition, many Emberá men and women, and especially the elderly, use *jagua* to darken their hair (see Torres de Araúz 1966: 58, 1975: 274; Reverte Coma 2002: 238),[16] a practice that deludes those tourists who are suspicious of inauthentic indigenous performances into believing that there are no elderly people in communities that host tourism. Newborn babies are also painted with *jagua* (see Wassén 1935: 74; Torres de Araúz 1980: 171; Isacsson 1993: 32; Pineda and Gutiérrez de Pineda 1999: 142, 155) to ensure, as my respondents maintain, beautiful, smooth skin into their adulthood. Overall, sick individuals and children, as I was told on many different occasions, benefit from the medicinal properties of *jagua*.

More generally, *jagua* body paint – nowadays as in the past – is applied for the sheer pleasure of ornamentation. The designs used are often geometric simplifica-tions of old shamanic patterns, or playful natural motifs (such as leafs, birds and flowers). In Parara Puru, individuals have their own favourite simplifications of older shamanic designs, for example 'the monkey tail' (*rabo del mono*), and the *trapiche* (the sugar cane grinder). These, as Ulloa (1992: 109) explains, sometimes represent the whole object. This is true in the case of the butterfly (*bagábaga*) or the snail (*kogoró*). On other occasions, they represent only a characteristic element of the object, for example, the footprints of the jaguar (*imamá*) or the spots of a snake (*damá*). In Chagres such older designs are often reduced to their particular components, or applied only on the arms. Some Emberá say that one or another design is 'one of ours' – or 'from Parara' – by which they mean that the residents of their community use it more frequently than others do. This tendency to associate particular designs with particular people or communities resonates with the old-times use of body paint as a signifier of local or ethnic identity. In all cases, *jagua* body painting, like other types of dress, receives the attention not only of curious visitors and tourists, but also of the Emberá themselves, who notice and comment on each other's designs.

Referring to its ornamental use, most Emberá will agree that *jagua* paint is, more or less, like clothing (*como un vestido*) – or, from an anthropological per-spective, a type of 'social skin' (T. Turner 1980). While travelling in Darién, I saw Emberá painted with *jagua* in communities outside the semi-autonomous res-ervations, including the Emberá and Wounaan neighbourhoods that have only recently emerged in the suburbs of the old Darienita towns (for example in Yaviza, La Palma and Garachiné). In the main streets of these towns, the visitor can observe middle-aged (*paruma*-wearing) Emberá women whose palms are stained black from grating *jagua*, or young adolescent girls dressed in modern clothes for an afternoon outing (with girlfriends or a boyfriend), whose arms or face are deco-rated with beautiful *jagua* designs. Similarly, the Emberá of Chagres, most of whom decorate themselves to receive tourists, may choose to make their body-painting

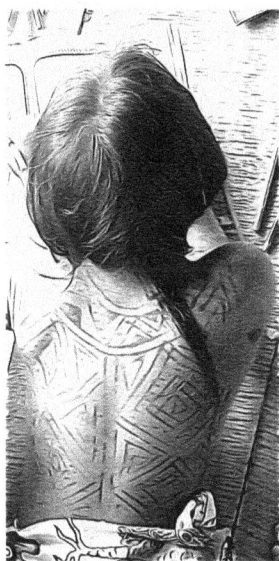

2.10 Combination of designs drawn by a mother on her daughter's back

patterns more or less visible when they go out of their community, either by applying *jagua* to those parts of their body that are covered by a t-shirt or those that are not (for example, arms or face). In all cases body painting conveys an indigenous identity, and non-indigenous Panamanians see body painting as an exclusively Chocó (Emberá-Wounaan) practice.

Body painting is applied in the context of preparations to host tourists in communities that have developed tourism, but also in those that entertain only occasional visitors. The Emberá often ask the visitors if they desire a *jagua*-tattoo and paint on the arm or leg of those who agree a 'traditional' geometric pattern. This is usually one of three or four favourite ones that the indigenous artist applies frequently on the bodies of other Emberá. Some tourists ask to be painted with a non-traditional design, usually a naturalistic representation, such as a flower or a bird. In most cases, the Emberá are able to accommodate these requests as they frequently experiment with non-traditional designs themselves. The tourists pay two or five dollars to the indigenous body painter, who could be an adult woman or a young man – *jagua* painting is not, strictly speaking, a gendered activity among the Emberá, although it is more often carried out by women.[17] Several tourists have shared with me their excitement at this experience, which, as I will examine in Chapter 8, represents a playful opportunity to temporarily embody an artful dimension of Emberá culture and explore difference through imitation (Taussig 1993).

Generating further ethnographic nostalgia

'To debunk classic ethnography', argues Knauft, 'perpetuates rather than attenuates a sense of moral distance and superiority of the new author over his or her predecessors' (1999: 213). Interestingly, it was my younger authorial voice that best identified with Knauft's insightful observation. Instead of evading description – the rather lazy approach – I chose to record and describe the dress code that the Emberá present as their 'traditional' attire. And in fact, it was an Emberá representational preference that led me to organise my account in this order: male attire, female attire, *jagua* body painting.[18] Throughout the process, I took the views of the Emberá respectfully on board, while at the same time I compared what the Emberá told me with the accounts of my predecessors, former ethnographers of Emberá culture. These provided me with a comparative stepping stone to frame the normativeness of Emberá clothing practices in the present, setting a measure to compare more complicated clothing combinations that diverge from a static conception of the 'traditional'. In these respects, ethnographic description of cultural practices has a role to play in the generation of new standards of authenticity, being itself a form of authentication. It is thus irrevocably linked to the politics of cultural representation, from which it derives inspiration and to which it contributes through a mutually defining dialogue (see Howe 2009). This is a topic that I will discuss in further detail in later chapters. For now, I want to highlight one more time the contribution of the ethnographic practice in generating nostalgia.

To the degree that ethnographic description situates the cultural practices of a people in time, it sets up the parameters for the emergence of a certain nostalgic feeling, one that seeks continuities with the standards of representativeness that emerge from the ethnographic record. The ethnographer is tempted to frame authenticity with respect to an ethnographic past, since his or her book is itself only an addition to this existing body of work. If previous ethnographies provided me with the comparative vantage point for my developing ethnographic nostalgia, each ethnographic chapter in this book sets the parameters for the nostalgia that haunts and inspires the rest of the book. It is a nostalgia that grows, mutates and disguises itself under new forms and pretexts, resisting my attempts to uproot it. But it is also a nostalgia that leads to further ethnographic engagement, encouraging a more complicated picture to emerge. Complexity engenders a more nuanced description, which may not completely expunge nostalgia, but can make it redundant, at least temporarily.

Such is the power of ethnographic description. Not only does it provide the authenticating standards that may shape – in the present or future – a people's cultural representation, it may also structure an author's position with respect to social change. The static sketches of Emberá clothes I provided in this chapter will frame, as a pivotal step of comparison, the analysis that follows, and inevitably set up new challenges in my constant struggle to contain nostalgia. How many elements of traditional Emberá attire that I described in this chapter can be identified in the present? How many times will I nostalgically rejoice when I see them unravelling in Emberá practices? And would I ever have made such discoveries – about either the clothes of the Emberá or ethnographic nostalgia – without having embarked from a static ethnographic description in the first place? To find out the answers to these questions, you will have to keep reading this book . . .

Notes

1 Isacsson (1993: 63, 71, 73) provides a slightly implausible etymological interpretation of *damagua* bark-cloth, which provides a metaphorical link between human clothing and snakeskin. If such a connection exists, it is not one maintained by the majority of contemporary Emberá who are not shamans or specialists in esoteric matters.
2 It is difficult to speculate about the history of this item of dress. Pineda and Gutiérrez de Pineda (1999: 107) refer to a description by Uribe Ángel published in 1885, which clearly portrays what we understand today as a Chocó *amburá* (see Ángel 1885: 522).

3 Contemporary Emberá understand that the word *chaquira* is Spanish. However, Isacsson (1993: 143) attempts to provide an alternative etymology of the term – once more, a bit implausible – which links it to Emberá language and symbolism.

4 See Krieger 1926, pl. 12; Nordenskiold 1928: 81, 99; Wassén 1935: 71, 1963: 67; Torres de Araúz 1966: 11, 99, 1975: 273; Pineda and Gutiérrez de Pineda 1999:: 117, 120; Reverte Coma 2002: 73, 123, 215; Howe 1998: 221.

5 *Nahuala* (*Carludovica palmata*[L]) is also known as the Panama hat plant; *bijao* is a species of *Calathea*[L] plant. The fibres of both are used in basketry (see Velásquez Runk 2001; Callaghan 2002).

6 Many Emberá in Chagres, but also in Darién, use the Spanish word *paruma*, instead of the indigenous word *wuá*, even when they speak in Emberá. I believe that this is a consequence of the wider popularity and visibility of the *paruma*-cloth in Panama. The *paruma* is an item of dress that is recognisable and discussed beyond indigenous contexts. My preference for the word *paruma* reflects this wider use.

7 Tice describes a similar shifting of dress codes among Guna girls, who unlike the Emberá, make more definite choices about which style of dress, Western or traditional, to adopt in adult life (1995: 82).]

8 Reina Torres de Araúz (1966: 59) entertains this possibility reflecting on a photo of bark-cloth with *jagua* designs in the ethnographic collection that emerged from the Marsh Darién expedition in 1923 (see Krieger 1926: 105, pl. 19). She explains that the bark-cloth fabrics she has seen in Darién, as those I have seen, were not painted. Nevertheless, we must consider that *jagua* decorations easily fade away with time.

9 For photographs of women with traditional Emberá earrings, see Torres de Araúz 1966: 148, 1980: 170, 173. I have seen similar ones at Chagres, but I did not have permission to photograph them.

10 In the seventeenth century, the Emberá, as well as the Guna, painted their faces with *achiote*-red in preparation for war (Isacsson 1993: 256). If we believe Isacsson's (1993: 253–8, 264–7, 271) structuralist interpretation, which I am not in a position to corroborate with contemporary ethnographic data, *achiote*-red was applied in times of war to attract the enemy (to offer yourself to the enemy as a sexual appetizer), while *jagua*-black was applied after the battle (that is, after killing or consuming the enemy, indicating that the killer is pregnant with his foe). Note that Isacsson does not refer to anthropophagy, and his analysis is purely symbolic.

11 See Ulloa 1992: 171, 174–8, 191, 195, 200–1, 216, 251–7, 262–3, 276–80, 284, 290–6.

12 In fact, according to Isacsson, there is a connection in Emberá symbolism between meeting the enemy in war and sexual intercourse – because the enemy, from the point of view of his adversary, is compared to a woman (Isacsson 1993: 264, 256–65).

13 For a similar emphasis on design among the Guna, see Fortis (2010, 2012a, 2012b). Fortis is exploring the role of design in relationship to Guna ideas about aesthetics and personhood, and with special reference to Guna art and woodcarving. The precision of his analysis invites comparison with the Emberá, which I cannot provide in this book, as I do not possess sufficient data. A more systematic comparison of Guna and Emberá symbolism is a promising field for future anthropological investigation.

14 Isacsson (1993: 60) records the snake design as *damámbu*, and roughly translates it as 'where the snake is'.

15 The visiting shamans come from Darién or the indigenous neighbourhoods in the suburbs of Panama City.

16 Reverte Coma, reflecting on his experiences among the Emberá in the 1960s, mentions that sometimes we may see an elderly man or woman with white roots on their hair. Yet,

he adds, when they go to the next fiesta, they appear 'with their hair well dyed and oiled' (2002: 238).

17 Even in the context of shamanic ceremonies the painting pattern chosen by the *jai-baná* can be executed by his female assistant, who could be the his wife or daughter. There are also a few women *jaibanás*, who are usually widows or daughters of male shamans.

18 This corresponds to the order of presentation in the explanation the Emberá give to tourists. In Parara Puru, and most other communities at Chagres, each group of tourists listens to a speech by a community leader (see Chapter 5), which includes a brief description of male and female attire and the medium of body painting.

3

A story about Emberá clothes

The same sequence of events can be narrated from different perspectives, follow-ing different experiential pathways, coloured by particular histories and context-ual parameters. Some anthropologists, and I am one of them, hesitate to give a single authoritative version of a people's history. The formalism of much Western history, based on 'the assumption that the past is disconnected from the present', can hide from our view the degree to which 'the past, present and future are mutu-ally implicated' (Hirsch and Stewart 2005: 261, 265). As Hirsch and Stewart (2005) aptly explain, within Western historicism there is a proclivity to exoticise the past by locating it in an objectivised and radically different world. This possibility is more imminent when we are referring to the history of an indigenous people who are already exoticised as living in a different world – and time (Fabian 1983), dressed with minimal clothing, entering into our view as if they arrived through the mist of some primordial time.

In providing an account, in a linear fashion, of the transformations that have taken place in the social life of the Emberá, this chapter runs the risk of promot-ing a simplified view: one disconnected from the present, placed in an irrevocably altered world, entrapped by its own subheadings: as if Emberá history can be con-fined to discrete phases of change. Aware of these limitations, and for the benefit of the reader who knows very little about the Emberá, I decided nevertheless to tell the story of Emberá clothes. To this end, I hope that the ethnography in later chapters will challenge the singularity of this narrative, by making visible the com-plexity and unpredictability of Emberá social life. The story I provide here is, after all, a story of change, so it is by definition incomplete. Yet, my particular interest in Emberá clothes provides me with an excuse to tell it, making obvious that its scope and ambition is limited: this does not constitute a comprehensive social history of the Emberá in Eastern Panama. It should instead be received as yet another story, a partial rendition of 'what was before' and 'how it is now', which illustrates some social experiences and leaves many others unsaid.

In all these respects, the following narrative is customised to fit the topic of the book: my focus on Emberá clothes is one among many possible threads that con-nect three particular episodes of the Emberá past: (a) social life in dispersed settle-ment, which is seen by the Emberá of today as 'traditional' life (those times when

3.1   A sketch of the Emberá of the old times inspired by a photograph by
Nordenskiold (1928)

they were mostly dressed in 'traditional' clothes), (b) the foundation of nucleated
communities, and the reorganisation of Emberá society as a result of a closer relationship with the state and non-indigenous neighbours (a relationship that led the
Emberá to rely more heavily on mass-manufactured clothing) and (c) an emerging
stage of increased national and international visibility, that encourages the revalorisation of Emberá dress and other cultural practices. In later chapters I will try
to go beyond the linearity of this sequence of transformations – and the misplaced
assumption that they move simply from tradition to modernity. The interface
of what is locally considered 'tradition' and 'modern' is more complex than this
account reveals.

Episode one: in the mists of time and up to the 1960s

There was a time, not that long ago, when the Emberá wore very little clothing in
their day-to-day lives: the women wore only a *paruma*-skirt, and the men only a
loincloth. They painted their bodies with simple or elaborate black designs using
the juice of the *jagua* fruit, or occasionally completely black. Small necklaces of
animal teeth, glass beads, seeds or silver pendants complemented their less formal dress, as well as flowers that both men and women adorned their hair with.

This light, simple and comfortable dress code was followed during work and routine activities in daily life. Westerners who met and photographed the Emberá of Darién in the 1920s – for example, traveller/author Hyatt Verrill (1921, 1931), explorer Richard Marsh (1934) and ethnologist Erland Nordenskiold (1928) – saw the use of minimal clothing as evidence of a lack of contamination by Western society. Ethnographers Torres de Araúz (1961, 1966, 1980) and Reverte Coma (2002) recorded the persistence of this simple daily dress code in Eastern Panama until the 1960s.[1]

During that time not so long ago, lasting approximately until the 1960s, there was a second, more elaborate Emberá dress code for participating in celebrations, ceremonies and social gatherings. To attend such occasions they prepared themselves with closer attention to detail and used a wider array of adornments. Generally, the men were adorned with items of greater value, such as long multi-layered silver earrings, silver bracelets or headdresses with coins. A girdle of beads, the *amburá*, was placed on top of their loincloths and layers of long beaded strings across their chests. Women on the other hand used ornaments of smaller size and value than those of men, such as earrings and necklaces. They preferred to wear, when possible or affordable, a new – or newer – *paruma*-skirt for festive occasions. Some married women possessed heavy, long necklaces with coins and beads, the *ubarís*, which stretched gracefully down their chests. In addition to black *jagua* body paint, Emberá women and men painted their faces with *achiote*-red and wove flowers into their hair. This general code of dress represented what Torres de Araúz called (1980: 168–9), with a minor touch of irony, 'gala dress' (*vestimenta de gala*).

The period when the Emberá followed the formal and informal dress codes

3.2 An Emberá couple dressed according to the old formal dress code. The sketch is based on a photograph from the Marsh Darién expedition of 1924–1925 (see Krieger 1926, pl. 12) and was drawn by Tasia Kolokotsa

described above falls within the living memory of the elderly. The same period of time can be fairly described as 'when the Emberá lived dispersed', each family house located at some distance from the next, usually at the next river bend, or approximately 200 meters away (see Herlihy 1986: 270). All houses were built on stilts close to a river, but dispersed settlement provided easier access to land. Fruit trees were usually planted close to home, with plantains, rice or maize in cleared plots farther away, but always close to the river and the domestic compound. Dispersed settlement also made the extraction of natural resources easier, and this is one of the reasons – according to the older Emberá of today – that they preferred to live at distance from each other, so that there was enough game, fish and timber for all. Families, as they grew, spread along particular rivers, and when land or marriageable partners were no longer available, some family members would move to a new river (see Farron 1962; Herlihy 1986; Kane 1994). Back then, as is the case nowadays, the Emberá and Wounaan social worlds were organised around river networks and these provided the necessary communication channels (Velásquez Runk 2009).

Through this adaptive strategy of dispersal to inaccessible rainforest locations (C. Williams 2004; see also Isacsson 1993; Kane 1994), the Emberá spread from their ancestral homelands in the department of Chocó in Colombia to the prov-ince of Darién in Panama (Torres de Araúz 1966; Pineda and Gutiérrez de Pineda 1999). This was an ongoing movement that started in the late-eighteenth century (Herlihy 1985b, 1986: 78–9, 2003: 318),[2] and has continued, at a slow and gradual pace, up to the present. Although the Emberá established themselves firmly in some parts of Darién in the nineteenth century – for example, at river Sambú – the growing Panamanian Emberá population was augmented in the twentieth century by a steady stream of Emberá born in Colombia, many of whom intermarried with those born in Darién.[3] Many Colombian Emberá entered Panama as young men, exploring new possibilities, and after settling in they encouraged their siblings or their whole families to join them in Darién (see Reichel-Dolmatoff 1960: 150).

As a result of the continuous search for new hunting or fishing grounds, land suitable for plantain cultivation, and marriage partners, the demographic expan-sion of the Emberá in Darién stretched from the rivers Sambú, Balsa and Tuira to the Chico, and gradually the Chucunaque and its many tributaries (see Herlihy 1986: 79–86).[4] This slow and gradual migration was facilitated by the retreat of the Guna, the former archenemies of the Emberá,[5] towards San Blas, Bayano, and the upper reaches of river Chucunaque (Herlihy 1986; Howe 1998). In many cases, the Emberá settled on rivers previously occupied by their old enemies, though not always as a result of war or competition, and this process lasted until the middle part of the twentieth century.[6]

Darién, under-populated and not easily accessible due to the dense rainforest and lack of road infrastructure, offered considerable geographical independence, an attribute that the Emberá in particular appreciated (Faron 1962; Kane 1994). Living in relatively unapproachable locations up the river, usually a few hours by canoe from non-indigenous towns, the great-grandfathers and grandfathers of the contemporary Emberá maintained their language and their characteristic style of dress. By the turn of the twentieth century, the use of commercial cotton cloth, employed increasingly by the Emberá 'from the eighteenth century onwards' (Isacsson 1993: 63), had already replaced bark-cloth (kuéporo[E], damagua[E], cocuá[S]), although bark-cloth mattresses were in frequent use until the middle part of the twentieth century (see Nordenskiold 1928: 65; Wassén 1935: 75), and a small number survive even to this day.

With the intensification of banana and plantain cultivation in the twentieth cen-tury (Faron 1962; Torres de Araúz 1966; Loewen 1985, 1975; Herlihy 1986; Colin 2010), the Emberá were able to afford – more easily than before – 'Western' com-modities, such as cotton clothes; in fact, as Herlihy (1986: 146) argues, their desire for Western commodities was what encouraged them to invest in cash-earning cultivation in the first place. With their canoes full (first) of bananas and (later) plantains,[7] they visited the towns of the Darienitas – the black, Spanish-speaking inhabitants of Darién – where they sold their produce and bought market goods, including fabrics to make *paruma*-skirts and loincloths. In the towns, wealthier Emberá men commissioned Darienita silversmiths to cast them silver jewellery (primarily earrings), while the Emberá themselves cold-hammered silver coins to produce pendants (Torres de Araúz 1966: 56; Reverte Coma 2002: 214, 233; Isacsson 1993: 35).

Up until the 1960s, Emberá use of non-indigenous clothing[8] was reserved mostly for visits to non-indigenous towns. Men would put long-sleeved shirts on top of their loincloths during the canoe journey to the Darienita towns downriver, while women covered their shoulders and chest with cotton cloth.[9] Dressed with such 'additional' clothes, both men and women entered the towns with their upper bodies covered, only to happily relinquish themselves of this burden on their return journey upriver (Reverte Coma 2002: 209). It is worth mentioning here that all people in Panama – indigenous or not, women or men – are required by law to cover their upper body in public spaces. As Torres de Araúz (1975: 272) reports drawing from her observations in the 1960s, when Emberá women went to the non-indigenous towns they were obliged to dress in clothes of 'European type'. In the Darienita towns – La Palma, Pinogana, Chepigana, Yaviza or El Real – and by order of the authorities, the 'Indian' women had to wear a shawl draped over their shoulders, reaching down to their breasts to remove them from the view of curious non-Indians, who were not 'accustomed to seeing their women in this way' and sometimes inspected them 'too intensely', noted Reverte Coma (2002: 235).

While the general Emberá population still lived in dispersed settlement, small groups of Emberá migrated even farther westwards, out of the geographical limits of Darién, into the province of Panamá. By the mid-to-late 1950s, they had established themselves at various locations along river Bayano (Wali 1989: 36–7) and Chagres (Caballero and B. Araúz 1962: 48–53; Herlihy 1986: 90). Once more, migration followed the flexible pattern of dispersed resettlement described above. Many Emberá settlers at Chagres, the westernmost settlement of the Emberá, had stayed for a short period of time in Bayano. The apical settler of the Chagres community, Tomé (or Antonio Zarco), arrived at river Chagres in the years after the Second World War (Koster 2005) and invited close relatives to join him initially at river Chagres, and much later in Camboa. Additional Emberá families arrived from the rivers Sambú, Chico and Balsa in the late 1950s, and many of them settled in dispersed settlement at the river San Juan de Pequeni, a tributary of the Chagres (Caballero and B. Araúz 1962).

From the 1960s onwards, the use of Western items of clothing by the Emberá – t-shirts, shirts, shorts and long trousers – gradually increased, albeit at a different pace in different communities in Eastern Panama. In most cases, proximity to non-indigenous communities influenced the speed and degree of these changes. Torres de Araúz observed that, by the 1960s, the Emberá of the Bayano area were generally dressed in clothes of European type (1966: 144). Caballero and

B. Araúz made similar observations about the Emberá of Chagres, adding that changes in dress were more evident among men, although Western elements were also observable in the clothing of women (1962: 54, 59). Nevertheless, it seems that the Emberá of rivers Chagres and Pequeni encountered slightly less pressure to adopt Western clothes than those in other locations that were similarly close to non-indigenous populations. For example, Guzman (1966) reports that the Emberá in Bayano who lived close to the town of Chepo[10] had already completely abandoned the old Emberá style of dress by the 1960s (encouraged by rigorous evangelisation), yet those who lived upstream and closer to what is now the Bayano water reserve negotiated mixed Emberá and Western dress combinations as they moved into or out of the gaze of Others. Even their Guna neighbours were unhappy to see them with their bodies uncovered (Guzman 1966: 225–6).

If local authorities in Eastern Panama strived to cover the uncovered Emberá body, the pre-1980 descriptions of sympathetic Westerners – travellers-*cum*-explorers (Verrill, Marsh) and ethnographers (Nordenskiold, Torres de Araúz, Reverte Coma) – saw in the appearance of the Emberá a deep-rooted connection with a vanishing tribal way of life. Dressed in only a few clothes made of fabric – a loincloth or a *paruma*-skirt – the Emberá of the 1920s and the 1960s seemed to have emerged from the mists of time. Explorers rushed to portray them as confirmation of a lost primordial world, while ethnographers located them in typological descriptions: 'the Emberá are like that', as if the Emberá have always been the same. In this respect, the mystical image of the Emberá with the loincloth or the *paruma*, hides from view the possibility that Emberá life had always embraced change. As we are about to see, the Emberá would soon modernise their wardrobe and reorganise their political representation, only to rediscover their 'traditional' clothes once more.

Episode two: resettling in concentrated communities

The next episode in my story of Emberá clothes marks a turning point in Emberá dress practices, which coincides with a more profound change in the social history of the Emberá in Eastern Panama: the foundation of concentrated communities. Once more, I invite the reader to see this change through the lens of the shifting dress codes that transformed the Emberá appearance. While in the middle part of the twentieth century the Emberá generally covered the upper body only to enter non-indigenous spaces – for example, the Darienita towns down the river, in the last quarter of the twentieth century, their use of modern clothes spread from such temporary occasions to everyday life, and became a permanent feature. Two important factors contributed to this change: the desire of many Emberá for their children to attend school (see Loewen 1985; Herlihy 1986: 161–2), and the commitment of some Emberá to evangelical Christianity. In both cases, the Emberá were exposed to occidental aesthetics and the values of modesty promoted by non-indigenous schoolteachers, pastors and missionaries.

These two factors – national primary education and evangelical worship – are, in turn, connected to a much greater process of transformation in Emberá social life: the foundation of concentrated communities with organised political leadership and primary schools. In the narratives of most Emberá I know the provision of primary schools was as important an incentive to live in concentrated communities as being able to elect their own leaders (thus benefiting from political representation). In addition, to qualify for government-sponsored education a number of dispersed families had to be concentrated in a particular area. The government rewarded those who resettled by establishing primary schools, even in the most inaccessible river sectors (see Herlihy 1986: 163–83, 274). It also provided schoolteachers to teach Emberá children in Spanish, who often had to negotiate long river journeys to reach the new communities. For their part, Emberá children, like all children in the country, had to be dressed to attend school. For several (now middle-aged) Emberá this was the first time they had to wear shirts and shoes.

In most but not all cases, evangelical Christianity had a similarly inhibiting effect on the use of the old dress codes, in particular with respect to covering the upper body. *Paruma*-skirts were often tolerated – due to their modesty – but women who were receptive to the Christian message started covering their upper bodies systematically, and a few also felt that it was appropriate to wear non-indigenous skirts. Groups of evangelised Emberá also felt the need to resettle in concentrated communities so that they could attend church more frequently. As a result, a few of the first Chocó nucleated villages in Darién were founded by groups of Emberá and Wounaan who were directly supported by particular churches (Loewen 1975, 1985; Herlihy 1986). Here it is helpful to note that evangelical missionaries radically diverged from their Catholic counterparts with respect to the importance attributed to regular church attendance. If Emberá allegiance to the Catholic church was often nominal,[11] North American evangelical churches expected a much more serious commitment, expressed through regular worship. They also provided tangible – and much needed – material aid and medical care. Overall, evangelical missionisation was facilitated by village formation (Velásquez Runk 2009: 460), and as a consequence an increasing number of Emberá have come closer to Christianity; they avoid participation in shamanic practices and attend church regularly, especially the women (see Chapter 8).

The resettlement of the Emberá in concentrated communities did not happen overnight. 'At first, villages were composed of a few huts surrounding a thatched-roofed schoolhouse' (Herlihy 1986: 162). Then more families joined these settlements, some of them reluctantly, often when their children reached school age. Herlihy (1986) describes in detail how the first few communities were founded in the 1950s, and how they multiplied in the 1960s and 1970s. By the 1980s, the majority of the Emberá adopted concentrated settlement. This gradual process of Emberá resettlement in villages changed the relationship of the Emberá with their cultivated land – which was now located farther away from home – and accelerated deforestation, especially closer to the new communities (Herlihy 1986). Loewen (1985: 252–4) reported that life in villages brought about an increase in marital breakups and premarital sex, while Kane (1994: 170–2) noticed how women's land claims became destabilised. Women undoubtedly started spending more time at home while their children attended school (Colin

2010: 190, 2013: 495). Yet, from the 1990s, many women used their time at home productively to construct basketry, which provided them with earnings comparable to, or even higher than, those of men (Velásquez-Runk 2001: 79; Colin 2010: 135, 187, 193, 2013: 496).

Most contemporary Emberá agree that the most significant consequence of Emberá resettlement in nucleated communities was the enhancement of Emberá political representation; in fact, it would be more accurate to present the political reorganisation of the Emberá as an incentive for – rather than a consequence of – founding villages. Torres de Araúz, the leading anthropologist of Panama at the time, summarily noted that up until the 1960s the Emberá had no political organisation of their own. In Darién, she argued, 'it is impossible to find tribal chiefs or caciques, and the same occurs in Colombia' (Torres de Araúz 1966: 78; cf. Reichel-Dolmatoff 1960: 109–10). There is no doubt that in the past charismatic shamans possessed a certain amount of authority, but this was merely – as Clastres (1977) would have argued – a representational role. In a subsequent publication Torres de Araúz indirectly echoes Clastres's thesis on the anti-authoritarian orientation of tribal societies when she underlines that it is wrong to identify the Emberá shaman as the chief, a figure who in fact does not exist (1975: 250). Yet, only five years later, in her book *Panama indigena*, she admits that the Chocó of Panama have, and have had for the previous ten years, a new political pattern, an issue that she overlays without much commentary in her previous description of Chocó cultural practices (Araúz 1980: 192–5).

The Emberá of today remember the transition from dispersed household autonomy to structured political organisation in a generally favourable light. They often make critical remarks about the narrow family-oriented logic that governed their previous dispersed organisation. This they often condemn as selfish and short-sighted, a position echoed by an expression I've heard many times during fieldwork: 'before' or 'in the past' 'every man was the chief of his own family!' Even now, the Emberá argue, many leaders tend to promote the interests of their family, 'as if they still live in the past'. In conversations about indigenous politics, they often juxtapose the quaint image – or memory – of the old grandfather with the loincloth, illiterate and set in the old ways, with the ideal type of the contemporary Emberá leader, who is fluent in Spanish and able articulate arguments about indigenous claims with fluency. A good contemporary leader is not necessarily conceived of as ignorant or unappreciative of tradition; in fact, knowledge of the Emberá ways is necessary for making and sustaining a line of reasoning as a political representative.

In two subsequent pages of her monograph, Kane (1994) presents the clothing preferences of two men in the 1980s. Their choice of dress can serve as a metaphor for what was then an emerging transformation in Emberá political consciousness. On the one hand we see Kane's key respondent Dzoshua: he is elderly, 'the only man in his village who wears a loincloth'; he came from Colombia when he was only a child, surviving in his early life hardship and loss; he honestly admits that he doesn't understand the politics of indigenous congresses (common in the 1970s and 1980s) and that 'he looks like a toad' in such a formal context (Ibid.: 24).

On the other hand, we see Benjamin, an Emberá man 'who wears an elegantly pressed shirt and slacks with black leather polished shoes'; he owns a store in a non-indigenous town and has held a leadership role before; on his way to participate in an indigenous congress, he shares with the ethnographer traditional tales and Emberá exotica, well aware of how to impress an educated foreigner (Ibid.: 25).

In the last quarter of the twentieth century, the Indian with the *guayuco* who lives dispersed in the forest is gradually transformed into a Panamanian citizen with an identity card and a community marked on the map. Moving away from a fundamentally egalitarian structure (Herlihy 1986: 269), the Emberá resettled in villages and elected their political representatives. The process started in 1968, and gradually developed, over a number of indigenous congresses through the 1970s and early 1980s (Herlihy 1986; Colin 2010), leading to the foundation of a semi-autonomous reservation, the Comarca Emberá-Wounaan in 1983. The political structure of the new *comarca* borrowed many elements from the preexisting Guna reservation at San Blas (Torres de Araúz 1980: 194; Herlihy 1986: 168, 170, 274; Kane 1994: 10).[12] The *comarca* has demarcated boundaries, which protect its lands from the incursion of non-indigenous settlers, and its own charter of regulations, consolidated in 1999 (Colin 2010: 172). Each community elects a leader, the *nokó*, while the *nokóes* in turn elect a leader for their district, the Cacique Regional, and an overall head, the Cacique General.

The Emberá gradually became more confident in running their own affairs and a new generation of younger leaders with Western education soon replaced the first generation of caciques, some of whom were shamans. The new leaders, experienced in 'urban, non-Indian ways' (Kane 1994: 10), set new standards for appearance and contact.[13] This is easy to visualise in terms of dress preferences and choices. For the modern Emberá man, the loincloth is not an option anymore, unless of course one wishes to entertain tourists or make a political statement in protest of, for example, a road block. In contrast, for the Emberá women who live within the *comarca*, the *paruma*-skirt – identified as a specifically Emberá-Wounaan dress – is the most widely used clothing item. Matched with a simple t-shirt, or an inexpensive vest top, tank top, or cropped top, the *paruma* provides the basis for versatile indigenous-modern combinations. As I will describe in the following chapters, community leaders and parents discourage young women from wearing shorts, and they promote the use of the *paruma*, which has recently obtained new popularity prompted by a seasonal fashion.

Nowadays the new *paruma*-cloth, manufactured in Asia, is bought in Panama City, often on the very first day of its release (see Chapter 8). It is often sold by Emberá men and women, acting as middlemen, at slightly higher prices all over Eastern Panama. Mass-manufactured clothing and a wide variety of other material commodities travel along the Pan-American Highway, which unites the Emberá communities in Darién[14] with those scattered in Panamá Province. The highway was extended in the early 1980s to the border of Darién, and, by 1984, it reached Metetí (Wali 1993: 117). The expansion of the highway accelerated social change in Eastern Panama, encouraging modernisation (Velásquez Runk

2015), the circulation of consumer products, but also easily accessible markets for Emberá plantains and lumber (Herlihy 1986: 153–4; Wali 1989: 49–51, 107; Colin 2010: 161). Although bus fares are still quite costly for most Emberá, many travel extensively – between Darién and Panama City, or to the communities located in the Canal area[15] – to visit relatives or sell artefacts.

It is important to stress at this point that not all the Emberá and Wounaan in Eastern Panama live within the semi-autonomous *comarca*. At the time of its foundation, the Comarca Emberá-Wounaan excluded approximately half of the Emberá population in Darién (Colin 2010: 106; Velásquez Runk 2012: 30) and all Emberá in Panamá Province. The many Emberá whose communities fall outside the geographic limits of the *comarca* – such as, for example, the communities at Chagres – have their own community leaders and district representatives, but no entitlement over their land. In other words, they have political representation, but no land rights. This means that they could – hypothetically – be evicted or relocated, as in the case of the communities in Bayano in the 1970s, when the government decided to build a large hydroelectric dam (Wali 1989, 1993). Since 1996, the Emberá and Wounaan who live outside the *comarca* have formed an organisation – later subdivided into separate congresses – to pursue collective rights for their lands (Velásquez Runk 2012: 30), an initiative to which most Emberá refer as *Tierras Colectivas*. The leaders of the communities involved in this meet (usually on an annual basis) and continue their struggle to secure legal recognition of their immediate territories: a process that is still unravelling, albeit at a rather slow pace.

In a recent thesis, Colin has argued that 'the indigenous regions outside the *comarcas* are lost from view' (2010: 106). I would like to add to this astute observation a similar one: it may be true that most Emberá communities outside the semi-autonomous reservation have some form of political representation, but this formalisation (and endorsement) of indigenous politics detracts attention from the reluctance of the government to provide land titles. The Emberá have a representational avenue to express their claims, while the government may choose to continue ignoring them. Herzfeld (1992) has described this attitude as the social production of indifference. In Panama, it is epitomised by the rhetoric of multiculturalism adopted by recent governments that favour neoliberal policies of economic development (see Wickstrom 2003, Horton 2006, Velásquez Runk 2012). 'Neoliberal governance', argues Velásquez Runk, 'has led to diminishing indigenous rights to environment and lands', despite the superficial impression that it supports such rights (2012: 23). Overall, neoliberal reforms have generated greater economic insecurity and inequality for most Panamanians, indigenous or not (Rudolf 1999: 25).

As Velásquez Runk suggests, it may be legitimate to expect that state-sponsored multiculturalism can lead to the marginalisation of indigenous groups and the promotion of the interests of the elites (see Hale 2002, 2005). Horton (2006) has recognised a proclivity among the governing Panamanian elites to co-opt multiculturalism. Yet at the same time, she has also identified that in the few cases where multiculturalism is supported from the bottom-up – for example, in the mobilisation of indigenous autonomy and land rights – multicultural rhetoric can also be

3.3 Nokó Claudio Chami, the elected leader of Parara Puru, has led his community with confidence for the last twelve years

empowering (Ibid. 2006). If it is hard to see such an empowerment in the recent initiatives of *Tierras Colectivas* – frustrated as they are by government inaction – undeniably the foundation of the Comarca Emberá-Wounaan in 1983 established a precedent that all Emberá and Wounaan communities with unrecognised land rights aspire to match. The official endorsement of the *comarca* signalled considerable recognition for those two indigenous groups: they are no longer the Indians from Chocó, Colombia – 'naked' and scattered forest dwellers – but an integral part of the Republic, indigenous groups with their proper and chosen names.

Episode 3: the return of indigenous attire

The adoption of Western clothes by the Emberá in the last quarter of the twentieth century can be seen as an iconic representation of their changing relationship with their nation-state. As we have seen so far, the Emberá – dressed in more clothes than before and resettled in concentrated villages – entered the national community: they elected leaders and acquired identity cards, and their children went to primary school. Their new communities became the 'regional foci of the Emberá's first political organisation linked to the state' (Kane 1994: 1). In the new nucleated Emberá villages men abandoned the loincloth for shorts, long or cropped trousers, while women, who up until then preferred to go about their daily activities topless, began wearing cotton tops most of the time, which they combined with their *paruma*-skirts.

By the turn of the twenty-first century, it may seem that occidental aesthetics and rules of conduct had become dominant tropes in the modernising political economy of Emberá representation. The stage was set for modernising politicians to reflect upon 'progress' (understood in terms of Western civilisational values) and for idealist Western travellers to grieve for the demise of indigenous culture and its inevitable retreat in the face of an onslaught of Western civilisation. The latter perspective, indicative of what Rosaldo (1989) calls imperialist nostalgia, and communicated through 'the lament for things lost' (Howe 2009: 249), relies on the conceptualisation of 'an unspoiled and irrecoverable past' (Herzfeld 2005: 109). This, in our story, is epitomised by the image of the Emberá dressed in traditional clothes: the loincloth and the uncovered upper bodies of Emberá men and women stand for a vision of indigeneity lost in the mists of time. It is this timeless image that will eventually become a costume, the Emberá attire, a representation of tradition – an exaggerated code of dress that heightens the communication of an identity that is not directly visible (see Shukla 2015: 4–5).[16]

In a fine twist of irony, a nostalgic inclination to recapture what modernity has hidden from view – Emberá distinctiveness as explicit Otherness – contributed to the reinstatement and revalorisation of the Emberá attire as a costume, a tool in the service of indigenous representation. As the image of the 'uncivilised' Emberá – the unclothed rainforest dweller – faded away, another complementary icon gradually re-emerged, that of the socially accepted indigenous Panamanian, dressed in traditional garb to represent at once the nation's present and the nation's past. The nation's present projects a vision of cultural diversity, and invites the world to visit, experience and consume indigeneity as cultural difference. The nation's past is encapsulated by a firm connection between Panama's indigenous people and the American continent, a link that stretches back to pre-colonial times to establish a primordial relationship between what was before, what came after and what the nation is now.

As soon as the Emberá became citizens – residents of communities that can be pinned down on the map – their cultural legacy became an asset of the multicultural national community, and their costume an iconic representation of what Panama was and what it might become: a tourism provider, among many other things. Driven by financial motivations, cultural tourism became the force that encouraged the Emberá themselves to re-evaluate and revalorise their own traditions. More broadly, the development of cultural tourism as a national project was associated with the promotion of Panamanian cultural diversity, which Emberá culture was a part of. The latter obtained national and international visibility, as now showcased in tourism (see Theodossopoulos 2010a, 2011, 2013a; Guerrón-Montero 2006a; Velásquez Runk 2012), which came to complement the government's endorsement of Emberá resettlement and political organisation in the last quarter of the twentieth century.

For most of its history, the Republic of Panama foregrounded its official representation on its Spanish and Latino roots (see Guerrón-Montero 2006a: 65–7). Elements of indigenous history – for example, the heroic figures of past indigenous leaders – were selectively appropriated as symbols of anti-colonial resistance, for example in Panamanian literature (Howe 2009: 165–9; see also Karkotis 2012). An appreciation for indigenous identities, depoliticised and repackaged as 'culture' or 'tradition' (Howe 2009) – and comparable to Latino folklore, became evident in Panamanian national narratives from the 1940s, and linked national identity with the music and dress of the majority *mestizo* population of 'the interior' provinces (southwestern Panama) (see Tice 1995: 66; Horton 2006: 836). In the last twenty years, tourism provided a new angle to talk about cultural diversity, this time not merely as a component of *mestizaje*, but also as ethnic distinctiveness valued on its own terms. The appreciation for cultural difference promoted by tourism, has become part of the new multiculturalism endorsed by the state; it embraces all Panamanian indigenous groups in an encompassing, but rather superficial, neoliberal guise (see Horton 2006;

Velásquez Runk 2012). The dress of indigenous people – not only the costume of the *mestizos* – has now emerged as just such a superficial (politically 'benign') cultural marker of difference (Horton 2006: 840).

It was first the Panamanian government, via the Panamanian Institute of Tourism (IPAT), who encouraged cultural or indigenous tourism and created a plan for its development in the 1990s (see Guerrón-Montero 2006a: 66, 69).[17] Images of the Emberá and of their better-known neighbours, the Guna – who had been tourism icons for much longer (see Salvador 1976; Swain 1989; Tice 1995; Howe 2009; Pereiro et al. 2010) – were included in national advertising campaigns for tourism. Like the Guna, the Emberá shared visually compelling cultural traditions, such as their dances and artefacts, yet their traditional costume conformed much more closely to stereotypical Western expectations of Amerindian rainforest dwellers. Quite conveniently, the appearance of the Emberá dressed in traditional attire has not been supported by textual elaboration: it falls unequivocally within conventional Western registers of indigeneity, as Amazonian Indians do (see Conklin and Graham 1995; Conklin 1997).

Since the 1990s, government officials, NGO practitioners and a new generation of Emberá leaders have attempted to promote the idea of developing tourism at the community level. After all, one of the advantages of community life – as opposed to the individualistic egalitarianism of dispersed settlement – was that it enabled collective undertakings and the organisation of labour required for their fulfilment. Cultural presentations for tourists demand preparation, trained teams of dancers and musicians, sufficient quantities of food for the visitors, appropriate community spaces that conform to Emberá architectural principles. Thus, by pooling their knowledge and resources, most Emberá communities in Eastern Panama were in position to organise and deliver cultural presentations for tourists.

There was however one major problem. Even though many Emberá communities shared the determination to develop tourism, most were located away from the flow of tourists. For the most part, Panamanian tourism is concentrated in the capital or in areas around the Canal, where the majority of hotels and museums are located and cruise ships make short visits. As a result of these factors, the communities at the westernmost edge of the Emberá distribution have benefitted the most from tourism, in particular those that are now located in the broader Canal area, usually less than two-hours driving distance from Panama City or the landing points of cruise ships. As I have already outlined, the Emberá reached this part of Panama in the 1950s and initially established themselves in dispersed settlement in the wider area that now falls within the limits of the Chagres National Park, and later in two additional locations, Gamboa and Gatun.

It was meant to be the descendants of these groups of Emberá – whom Caballero and Aráuz (1962) described as experiencing deculturating change – who fulfilled the promise of developing tourism.[18] By the 1990s, young Emberá men from Chagres had never in their lives worn a loincloth, and though women still used *paruma*-skirts in daily life – interchangeably with non-indigenous skirts and trousers – most were accustomed to covering their torsos. As several Emberá of this generation described to me, the idea of putting on 'traditional' clothes – or taking off modern clothes – to entertain tourists posed a challenge, because it invited mockery from non-indigenous neighbours. Most Chagres-born Emberá did not live in homogenous Emberá communities, and this was a serious obstacle to developing tourism. There was only one politically organised Emberá community on the Chagres, Emberá Drua, formed by families that emigrated from Darién in the 1970s. Arriving later than others, this group had experienced the growth of nucleated villages in Darién and knew how to represent themselves politically. They had a head start in developing tourism in the 1990s.

The remaining Emberá in the area, who called themselves 'natives of Chagres' (*nativos de Chagres*) – that is, 'Chagres-born', the descendants of the earlier generation that arrived in the 1950s – felt that they were equally entitled to benefit from tourism. Since 1985, the establishment of a national park that incorporated their scattered settlements had curtailed normal subsistence activities, such as systematic cultivation, logging and hunting. After a decade of surviving in the face of these serious restrictions, the idea of delivering presentations for tourists appeared to be the ideal solution. Following the advice of travel agents, members of NGOs, and the Panamanian Institute of Tourism, the Emberá developed a fairly standardised pattern of cultural presentations for tourists visiting on short trips. It included traditional dance, music, food, a speech about Emberá culture, and the sale of artefacts. This particular type of tourism had a low environmental impact, which meant that the Emberá could remain in the park, but secure a small and fairly sustainable income.

These considerations encouraged several Emberá families from the area to regroup and form new ethnically homogenous communities at riverside locations, convenient for the easy transport of tourists.[19] In the new communities they felt more confident dressing 'as their grandparents' and inviting their guests to experience facets of Emberá culture in an environment conducive to a respectful reception of indigeneity. The agencies advertised and transported the tourists to the Emberá communities, collected the money from the tourists and paid a small percentage of the income to the hosting Emberá community – usually a per-capita fee for each tourist entering the community. For their part, the Emberá provided the cultural presentations and substantiated indigeneity dressed up in traditional attire, welcoming the tourists to their – now ethnically homogenous – communities.

The desire to develop indigenous tourism has created a set of asymmetries in Emberá society. These relate to the accessibility of the flow of tourists, who are perceived by the Emberá as an asset (see Theodossopoulos 2010). Obviously, the tourism agencies exercise greater control over the number of tourists that go to each particular community.[20] They often put the different Emberá communities in competition with each other, expecting them to lower their per-capita fee when tourist groups are particularly large. Due primarily to geographical restrictions, not all Emberá communities are seen as desirable tourist destinations. Those in the wider Canal area receive a regular number of tourists throughout the year and the majority of their residents work for tourism on a full-time basis. A few other communities close to the Pan-American Highway receive occasional visitors, sometimes students of Panamanian educational institutions on a day trip or small groups of tourists who may stay for a couple of days, always accompanied by a tourist guide.[21] However the majority of Emberá communities in Eastern Panama, and especially those in the *comarca*, receive no tourists at all, due to their inaccessible locations and the overall reputation of Darién as an inhospitable area unsafe for visitors (Velásquez Runk 2009: 460, 2015; Colin 2010: 149; see also Frenkel 1996).

In the last twenty years, the leaders of most Emberá communities that do not receive tourists have spent a considerable amount of time assessing the benefits of cultural tourism. Some rely on attracting irregular, off-the-beaten-track tourists or on developing ecotourism, and have organised the construction of 'traditional' communal houses in which to receive irregular visitors. Aware of the financial rewards of tourism at Chagres, many community leaders in Darién stress – for example, during community meetings – the value of keeping cultural knowledge alive. They encourage young girls to learn the traditional dances that are indispensable components of tourist presentations (see Theodossopoulos 2013), and they praise women who wear the *paruma* and young people who use the Emberá language.

At the same time, a great number of Emberá women in the most inaccessible communities earn a modest, but for them significant, income from weaving masks and baskets (Callaghan 2002; Velásquez-Runk 2001; Colin 2010; 2013). These artefacts are sold at tourist markets in Panama City, or to Emberá communities that do receive tourists, such as those in the Canal area. The commodification of Emberá basketry, as Colin explains in a recent article, reflects 'the expansion of Panama's tourism industry', but also 'the expansion of capitalist processes within indigenous areas' (2013: 487). At the local level, income gained by women through basketry challenges gender roles and ideals (Colin 2010, 2013) and has partly empowered Emberá women, whose position in Emberá economic and political life was marginalised in the period following their resettlement in concentrated communities (Kane 1994). Looking at the broader picture, the growth of Emberá 'tourist arts'[22] – to use an expression introduced by Graburn (1976) – has generated economic flows that benefit the wider Emberá society in Eastern Panama and add visibility to Emberá culture. The neighbours of the Emberá, the Guna, who are known for their distinctive textiles, the *mola*, experienced similar transformations at least two decades earlier (see Salvador 1976; Swain 1989; Tice 1995; Margiotti 2013; Martínez Mauri 2012).

Despite the asymmetries it has generated,[23] indigenous tourism has transformed the visibility of Emberá culture, promoting, instead of hiding, cultural difference. The superficial attention it pays to the 'cultural' side of ethnic diversity (Howe 2009) has so far been transformative for particular communities. In this respect, the multiculturalism promoted by tourism represents one of few instances in Panama where state-endorsed multiculturalism is empowering for indigenous representation (see Horton 2006). If tourism campaigns have added a sense of official endorsement to Emberá culture and costume – recognisable at the national level – the tourist encounter itself has generated a dynamic that has made the Emberá visible internationally. As the tourists disseminate their experiences, photographs and videos through various forms of social media, countless images of the Emberá – dressed in full attire – can be 'googled' with a simple click. There are now multiple URLs for Emberá culture (see Comaroff and Comaroff 2009). Although very few Emberá have access to the internet, the admiration of the international public is communicated to them by the tourists themselves, most of whom do not hide their enthusiastic reception of Emberá culture during their visits to particular communities. As we shall see in Chapter 5, the interest of the tourists is expressed in the questions they ask, their participation in the dancing, and their overall gratitude, which is not only conveyed verbally, but often via small monetary donations.

From the point of view of the Emberá, the positive attention of the outside world is a new phenomenon. The adult residents of the communities that entertain tourists were raised with the expectation – originating from the wider Panamanian society – that they should learn Spanish, dress in modern clothes and adopt Western practices. In the context of previous discrimination and stereotyping in Panama, Emberá culture was caricatured as 'primitive' or 'uncivilised'. Since the introduction of tourism, the Emberá have started to realise that their culture is now respected by foreigners who come from countries that are more powerful and wealthier than Panama. This realisation has encouraged the Emberá to identify more closely with their indigenous identity, and to project it to outsiders more confidently. Instead of hiding away or retreating from the non-Emberá world, an adaptation strategy that served them well in the past (Williams 2004; Kane 1994), they are now reaching out to the international community, taking advantage of the new opportunities offered by an increasingly globalised world to represent themselves (Theodossopoulos 2010b).

The promotion of indigenous culture as an 'ethno-commodity' has provided opportunities for the Emberá to see and hear 'themselves enacting their identity'

3.4   Emberá dress as a costume

(Comaroff and Comaroff 2009: 26). As part of this process, and as the Comaroffs highlight, indigenous actors objectify their subjectivity and homogenise their self-presentation in abstract terms. In most Emberá communities in Panama, regardless of the degree to which they benefit from tourism, indigenous leaders, performers and individuals who specialise in producing cultural artefacts have introduced to their discussions the notions of tradition and authenticity, conceived as representative of the way of life of the grandfathers. In a manner that greatly resembles the work of anthropologists of previous eras, Emberá men and women attempt to identify the characteristic attributes of authentic practices: what are the constituents of traditional Emberá dress, dance and art? The transformation of the dress code of the grandparents to a costume – widely recognisable and emblematic of Emberá culture – is related to this self-exploratory attempt of the Emberá to negotiate representations of their own culture. 'The act of dressing up in costume', to perform or accentuate their identity, can be seen as 'a means of achieving a self-conscious definition of the self' (Shukla 2015: 4). We will see many examples of how this process unravels in everyday life in the chapters that follow.

Notes

1 Anthropologists writing about the Chocó (Emberá and Wounaan) in Colombia provide similar descriptions of Chocó daily clothes based on ethnographic observations that range from the 1930s to the 1980s (cf. Wassén 1935; Reichel-Dolmatoff 1960; Pineda and Gutiérrez de Pineda 1999; Ulloa 1992).
2 See also Guzman 1966: 133; Howe 1998: 214; Wali 1989: 26; Williams 2004: 224.
3 Nordenskiold (1928), who visited river Sambú in 1927, corroborates the established presence of the Emberá in the middle and upper sections of the river, as well as the continuous migration of Emberá from Colombia to Panama.
4 The last stages of this process of geographic expansion in Darién took place in the twentieth century and, in some areas, such the Eastern tributaries of Chucunaque, lasted until the 1970s.
5 Back in colonial times, and even before the Emberá migrated to what is now the Republic of Panama, the Emberá fought wars with the Spaniards and other Amerindian groups and, in particular, the Guna (Vargas 1993; Williams 2004; Isacsson 1993; Martínez Maori 2011). Fragments of stories about battles and brave deeds against the Guna are still narrated today in Emberá communities in Eastern Panama.
6 When the Guna abandoned, for example, upper river Chico and the middle sections and tributaries of river Chucunaque (see Verrill 1921, 1931; Marsh 1934; Howe 1998).
7 The commercialisation of banana cultivation in the 1930s provided the Emberá of Darién with their first opportunity for sustained cash income (Herlihy 1986: 149–50; Colin 2010: 179). The resulting affluence was terminated with a banana disease, the 'sickness of Panama'. From the late 1950s, plantains took over as the main cash crop of the Emberá.
8 Here, I consider cotton cloth used for *parumas* and loincloths as an element of indigenous dress; from the Emberá point of view *parumas* and loincloths are distinctively indigenous items of dress.
9 As many women do nowadays, when they use a second *paruma*-cloth as a shawl (see Chapters 7 and 8).

10 For example, those settled at river Mamoni (Guzman 1966: 226).

11 In colonial times, the Emberá resisted Christian proselytising, aided by their dispersed settlement and migration to inaccessible locations (Williams 2004). When Christian missionaries did gain influence, they discouraged 'the "barbarian" habit of decorating the human face with lip and nose ornaments' (Isacsson 1993: 38). Later, in the early twentieth century the Emberá dealt with the pressure of the Catholic church by avoiding direct confrontation. When priests and missionaries departed, the majority of the Emberá continued to rely on the guidance of their shamans.

12 For an acknowledgement of the influential role of the Guna model in the emancipatory politics of other Panamanian indigenous groups, see also Herrera 1972; Martínez Mauri 2003; Horton 2006: 831; Howe 2009.

13 The emancipating role of the new generation of Emberá leaders with Western education can be compared with the contribution of Guna native scholars (Howe 2009) and NGO activists (Martínez Mauri 2008) in shaping Guna political representation. The major difference between the two ethnic groups is that the Guna educated elites made their mark evident since the mid-twentieth century, preceding the Emberá by at least two generations.

14 The Emberá of the rivers Sambú, Balsa and Mogue start their journey to the Panamá province by canoe and boat, then board on little coasters, and finally join the highway at the town of Metetí, where they can take the bus to Panama City or travel eastwards or westwards towards other Emberá communities.

15 Owing to their involvement in tourism, the communities in the Canal area provide a market for large quantities of Emberá-Wounaan artefacts produced all over Eastern Panama. Indigenous middlemen, or the producers themselves, travel from Darién or Bayano to Chagres to sell their basketry or woodcarvings to the Emberá of Chagres, who, in turn, sell those items directly to tourists.

16 In a recent book, which I read while revising this manuscript, Pravila Shukla (2015) redefines costume beyond its connotations as indicating what is out-of-the-ordinary (see Roach-Higgins and Eicher 1995: 7, 10) or what is related to performance (Eicher 2010: 152). Costume, like dress, argues Shukla, 'is the clothing of who we are' but 'it signals a different self, one other than that expressed through daily dress' (Shukla 2015: 3).

17 Tice further clarifies that 'tourism has been promoted by the Panamanian government since 1939, but not in a systematic fashion until 1962.' (1995: 66)

18 With the exception of the community of Mongue in Darién which started entertaining small groups of tourists in the 1980s (Herlihy 1986: 247). This community is located within reach of cruise boats approaching from the gulf of San Miguel, which solves the problem of access and transportation.

19 In Chagres National Park these are Parara Puru and Tusipono at river Chagres, and Emberá Puru at river Pequeni, an affluent of Chagres. The communities of La Bonga at river Pequeni and Emberá Drua at river Chagres have a slightly longer history.

20 The tourism agencies make the greatest profit from this particular arrangement. They argue that their costs are greater, as they have to pay for the cost of transportation, advertisement, their business premises, bills and the salaries of non-indigenous tourist guides who act as interpreters. 'The Emberá do not pay taxes or electricity and telephone bills', say some of the travel agents rather apologetically.

21 The police check passports and identity cards on at least two points on the Panamerican Highway, and discourage foreign tourists from travelling to Darién without a tourist guide. Tourists are prohibited from entering certain parts of the *comarca* that are closer to the Colombian border.

22 Emberá tourist arts do not only involve basketry, but also wood and *tagua* sculpture, a
job undertaken by men.

23 For example, not all Panamanian groups have benefited equally from tourism. An
experience that reproduces earlier inequalities and encourages us to reconsider
Bourgois's (1998) observation that different indigenous groups in Panama have mobilised their ethnicities with different measures of success in mediating their relationships
with the state and the outside world.

4

Ghosts of Emberá past

In so many exoticising narratives, the negative stereotyping of indigeneity coexists with its idealisation, albeit ambivalently. In this chapter I will examine these two prevalent tropes of exoticisation – both the idealisation and the derision of difference – in the accounts of two early-twentieth-century authors, Verrill (1921) and Marsh (1934), who provided us with detailed descriptions of the appearance of the Emberá in the 1920s. Their un-deconstructed commentaries – romanticised but infantilising and occasionally racist – present us with a diachronic perspective of the exoticising ambivalence of a particular Western perception, that of the 'naked' indigenous body. Nudity here is interpreted as an index of naturalness and used to sustain an illusion of distance from Western modernity, which, in turn, legitimises exploration as authentic discovery. Since colonial times, difference in Latin America has been 'discursively constructed through a rhetoric of clothing', where nakedness was used and reused as a trope of barbarism or mark of a lack of civilisation (Meléndez 2005: 17, 20–4).

Evident in the accounts of Marsh and Verrill is an ambivalent stance towards Western civilisation: Western civilisational achievements are admired, but concomitantly perceived as destructive for indigenous innocence. This ambivalent orientation, which fluctuates from admiration of indigenous spontaneity to imperialist nostalgia (Rosaldo 1989) and sentimental pessimism (Sahlins 2000), offers a valuable insight into the contradictions of the exoticising gaze (see Berliner 2015). The Emberá emerge from Verrill and Marsh's narratives as attractive, strong and uncontaminated by civilisational vices, but also as childlike, naïve, passive victims of non-indigenous agents. Here a particular Western perception of Emberá nudity consubstantiates a vision of unclothed freedom (as in nature) with a contrasting view of unclothed primitiveness. The resulting combination of exoticised contradictions has framed the image that outsiders have of the Emberá and, as I will demonstrate in Chapter 5, is not considerably different from the expectations of contemporary tourists.

In this respect, Verrill and Marsh can be seen as predecessors of contemporary tourists and off-the-beaten-track travellers. In their adventurous journeys to the rainforests of Eastern Panama, the two authors did not come across any undiscovered people or lands; no matter how much they hoped they would. Nevertheless, the narratives of their explorations provided Western imagination with new ways to think of the Emberá as an exotic people. Their ambivalence about modernity and the indigenous inhabitants of the Panamanian rainforest, combined with their longing for exclusivist contact with Otherness, has certain diachronic qualities: qualities that can help us appreciate Emberá politics of representation in the present. And yet, in one final respect, the accounts of Marsh and Verrill, however heavily exoticised, contain a good deal of descriptive information that may be used as a comparative vantage point to see contemporary Emberá practices, such as, for example, the way the Emberá host notable non-indigenous outsiders.

Verrill's fascination with Emberá nudity

Hyatt Verrill (1871–1954) was a North American explorer and inventor and an author of 115 books, addressing an impressive array of topics. Zoology, archaeology, and travel writing represent only a fraction of his interests. One of these books, *Panama, Past and Present*, first published in 1921, is a portrait of the Republic of Panama based on the author's travel and observations in the period after the First World War. Verrill's inquisitive curiosity and inclination to travel off the beaten track provide us with an outsider's view of the Republic in its early formative years. His vivid descriptions, valuable for the eyewitness detail they include, reflect the position of a cosmopolitan Western traveller writing for a North American audience. At times, Verrill is politically incorrect, reproducing racial stereotypes and an ethnocentric view of Otherness. Nevertheless, in certain passages he complicates received knowledge by drawing on his own direct observations. During such moments he appears to be reflexive, nostalgic and indecisive about which type of exoticisation to prioritise: the idealisation or the derision of difference.

Verrill locates his descriptions of the Emberá in the context of his journey to Darién, which followed the course of the main communication route at the time. He journeyed by steamboat from Panama City to the gulf of San Miguel, stopping at the Darienita towns of Garachiné, La Palma, Chepigana and El Real. His portrait of these towns is particularly gloomy. He depicts local living conditions as unhealthy and poverty ridden, a perception rationalised as the result of the 'laziness' and the 'apathetic' attitude of the 'colored' inhabitants.

4.1 A sketch of Verrill

His commentary on these people,

whom we recognise today as the Afrodarienitas, is condescending. He describes them – perpetuating a particularly Western perception of tropical idleness (see Frenkel 1996) – as 'killing their time', gambling their limited money in cockfights.

Verrill's unenthusiastic portrayal of the Afrodarienitas sharply contrasts with the idealising attention he devotes to the Amerindian inhabitants of Darién, who captured his imagination unreservedly. After meeting some Emberá at El Real – to whom he refers as the *Chokois* – Verrill decided to travel along river Tuira in a dugout canoe to see 'the primitive Indians at home' (Verrill 1921: 181). This trip provides us with an early-twentieth-century sketch of the Emberá settlement along that river, a description of their houses and the items found in them. More important, for the purposes of this book are of course his descriptions of their dress code. This information is found in the penultimate chapter of *Panama, Past and Present* (Verrill 1921), 'Darién the Unknown', and it was later cut and pasted in a subsequent reproduction and extension of the book, under the new title *Panama of Today* (1931).

'Both men and women are practically nude', Verrill maintains, 'the men wearing merely a cloth breech and the women a loin cloth' (Verrill 1921: 186). In the description that follows, the terms 'naked' and 'nude' are used interchangeably in every other paragraph to describe the Emberá. It is interesting to note that references to nudity are delivered in parallel with a description of Emberá costume and an emphasis on their extensive use of body painting. From an Emberá point of view, the stress that Verrill places on nudity contradicts his obvious understanding of the Emberá use of adornments and body painting. For the Emberá, adornments and body painting represent a form of dress that conceals the naked body. Yet, for Verrill, writing for early-twentieth-century consumers of the exotic, the emphasis on indigenous nudity, however inaccurately this is communicated, served a more particular purpose in bearing witness to the claim that the explorer has (intrepidly) ventured outside Western civilisation.

Thus, here, Emberá nudity legitimises the framing of travel as exploration: it is used as a literary device that aims to validate the adventurous spirit of the writer-explorer and his exotic testimony – his 'discovery' – of a world far removed from the Western civilisational experience. The following passage is indicative of Verrill's narrative style:

> The first sight one has of the aborigines is a big dugout, drifting down the river towards the settlements, filled with fruit and rice and with naked Chokois standing at bow and stern guiding the craft with their long poles, their scarlet breech-cloths gleaming against the brown skins while, seated amid the cargo, are half-nude women and naked brown-skinned children who gaze curiously at the white strangers as they pass. Meeting them here upon the river in the wilderness, the traveller feels that he is remote from civilization, that he is indeed out of the beaten track; that at any moment he may meet with adventure; that just around the next bend of the stream some strange, unexpected sight may be in store. (Verrill 1921: 188–9)

The unexpected sight around the next bend of the river for Hyatt Verrill was 'the Chokoi village'. His use of the word 'village' comes to us as a surprise, considering that the Emberá lived in dispersed settlement at the time (as later generations of Emberá and ethnographers have established indisputably). I extrapolate from his overall description that Verrill refers to an extended family compound along river Tuira, where several other Emberá families, forewarned of his imminent visit, had arrived to greet the foreign visitor and participate in a *chicha*-festival;[1] a dozen canoes were drawn up at the bank, he notes. It is necessary here to resort to Verrill's own words to convey his fascination with the dress code and overall appearance of the Emberá, which he sees as emblematic of 'the primitive savage', a figment of Western imagination to which he subscribes with minor reservations:

> Short, thickset; with slender limbs and wonderfully developed shoulders and chests; with masses of thick, black hair falling to their shoulders; with brown skins decorated with blue, scarlet and white paint; with enormous earrings of beaten silver and scarlet or blue breech-cloths the Chokois completely fulfil one's ideal of the primitive savage. But they are savage only in name and with broad smiles, and speaking in broken Spanish, they shake hands, shoulder our luggage and lead the way up the bank to their homes. (Verrill 1921: 189)

Verrill's reserved and moderately patronising idealisation of the exotic appearance of the Emberá communicates the desire of a well-intentioned Western visitor to experience cultural difference, yet without fully embracing it; a desire expressed in a profoundly nostalgic predisposition. In a final passage we can see this nostalgia – 'imperialist', in Rosaldo's (1989) terms, and un-deconstructed – emerging from the author's self-reflection:

> As they dance and prance about to the dull boom of tom-tom and the shrill notes of reed flutes it is hard to believe that we are scarce one hundred miles from the Canal, that, within two days travel, is Panama with its crowded traffic, its trolley cars and electric lights, its department stores and motor cars; that only the distance from New York to Philadelphia separates these primitive, painted, naked Indians from the roaring trains, the busy shops, the great hotels and the teeming, civilized, modern life of Balboa and Christobal. (Verrill 1921: 192)

At this point it is convenient to leave Verrill wondering in his lingering, nostalgic and ambivalent way – is 'naked' innocence preferable to marvellous but noisy modernity? – to appraise another contrast in his exoticising description. This is one between two types of 'Indians' that he encountered in Darién. Here, comparisons of the 'naked' *Chokois* with the Guna, who 'wear clothes', as Verrill plainly describes, provide us with an opportunity to appreciate the role of clothing and dress in determining Western ideas about primitiveness and civilisation. For example, Verrill argues that the Guna 'in many ways are more civilized than their Chokoi neighbours' (1921: 184) and uses their respective codes of dress to substantiate his claim. But while the Guna are described as more civilised overall, they are further subdivided to 'tame' and 'wild' Gunas, a division that reflects the reputation of a certain segment of the Guna population at the time: the wild Gunas dwelling 'in the unknown, unexplored district extending from the upper Bayano to the Membrillo River' (Ibid.: 184; see also Howe

1998). As I will illustrate shortly, Marsh (1934) made similar observations a few years later.

The image of exotic-*cum*-dangerous Panama described by Verrill in *Panama, Past and Present* (1921) is appreciably toned down in a later edition of his account. In the four new chapters added to the book for its subsequent republication as *Panama of Today* (1931) we detect similar idealising tendencies, now moderated by a greater degree of observational accuracy. One of the new chapters, 'Indians of Panama', comprises a commendable attempt to compile his knowledge of Panamanian indigenous groups in an orderly account that bears similarities with ethnographic description, especially when the author relies on personal observation and disregards rumours. In the text published in 1931, Verrill critically re-examines exaggerated beliefs, especially with regard to the myth of dangerous Indians who pose a threat to the lives of visitors. Close comparison of his 1921 and 1931 accounts reveals that new travel experiences and a closer acquaintance with Panama have encouraged a turn away from explicit primitivisation to a more careful repackaging of the image of indigenous groups as a potential attraction for Western visitors.

Good examples of Verrill's (1931) later attention to detail are his sketches of Guna and 'Guaymi' (Ngäbe) items of clothing. Following his 1921 publication, the North American author visited Panama once more – an experience that added new elements to his existing knowledge of the Guna, the Ngäbe and other groups.[23] However, it appears that he did not travel to Darién again. As a consequence, his understanding and opinion of the Emberá (and their attire) remained mostly unedited.[4] Considering the increased accuracy in Verrill's writing style and his gradual move away from unexamined primitivisation, it is unfortunate that he did not travel again to lands inhabited by the Emberá, since this would undoubtedly have resulted in more precise descriptions. Before examining the testimony of another North American writer, whose exoticising tendencies are less constrained, I will evaluate briefly some of the descriptive information made available in Verrill's account.

Box 3

Material for comparison

- Verrill's eyewitness testimony corroborates later ethnographic descriptions of Emberá attire. In the second decade of the twentieth century, the Emberá are depicted as wearing most of the recognisable Emberá items of dress that comprise the standard Emberá attire today: coloured fabric loincloths (for men), a cloth equivalent of the *paruma* (for women), beaded strings across the chest, broad belts of woven beads, crowns of painted wood and bamboo, silver ornaments – 'of their own manufacture' (Verrill 1921: 186) – such as enormous silver earrings, bracelets and necklaces, simple shell necklaces, and hibiscus flowers adorning women's heads, as well as body painting. Verrill also refers to women wearing bits of 'rubber bark about their hips' and 'bunches of the soft inner bark of the rubber tree' (Verrill 1921: 190), which comprises valuable testimony to the use of bark-cloth for making *parumas* and sleeping mats as recently as the early twentieth century.[i]

- A close reading of Verrill's account elucidates additional dimensions of Emberá social life and material culture that resonate with ethnographic descriptions from the 1960s (cf. Torres de Araúz 1966; Reverte Coma 2002). For example, he describes 'Indians' 'dressed in loin cloths' and 'often painted' who visited the Afrodarienita towns to trade (Verrill 1921: 181), an observation that (a) confirms a pattern in the Afrodarienita-Emberá trading relationship identified by later ethnographic accounts, but also (b) implies that use of Western clothes by the Emberá for the purpose of visiting the town was possibly less widespread in the early twentieth century (than in the 1960s). He also describes some items found in the Emberá house, such as 'bright colored cloth' (coexisting with bark-cloth mattresses), 'earthen pots' (testimony to the once widespread Emberá ceramic tradition[ii]) and wooden figurines 'fastened to posts' and 'gaudily painted' (such as those used in shamanic ceremonies nowadays) (Ibid.: 190–1).[iii]

- A close comparison of the two editions of Verrill's book reveals a few small but notable changes, indicative of his shift towards a perspective of greater accuracy. In the 1931 version of the book there are: (a) a sub-clause explaining that the Emberá men wear at times a ragged shirt, presumably combined with their loincloth, which attests to the Emberá hybrid modern-traditional style of dress that I discuss elsewhere (see Chapter 2), which has also been observed by other ethnographers (cf. Torres de Araúz 1961, 1966), (b) an improved description of what we know today as the Emberá *paruma*: 'a strip of calico' worn 'about the waist and falling to the knees' (Verrill 1931: 216–17), (c) a passing comment that 'the Chokois are seen at their best' 'when a dance or a feast is in progress', which substantiates the contextual and celebratory use of the full Emberá attire (Verrill 1931: 218) and, finally, (d) an acknowledgement that the Chokois 'nearly all speak Spanish,[iv] they have adopted most of civilized man's vices, and they are far from over cleanly in habits or persons' (Verrill 1931: 217).

[i] For references to the use of bark-cloth by the Emberá see Chapter 2; see also, among many other corroborating sources, Nordenskiold 1928; Marsh 1934; Wassén 1935; Torres de Araúz 1966; Isacsson 1993; Pineda and Gutiérrez de Pineda 1999.

[ii] The Emberá have their own distinctive style of pottery (see Krieger 1926; Wassén 1935; Reichel-Dolmatoff 1960, 1962; Torres de Araúz 1966, 1980;

Vasco Uribe 1987; Tayler 1996; Pineda and Gutiérrez de Pineda 1999; Reverte Coma 2002), a tradition they kept alive until recently, but one that it is now dying out, along with the last Emberá potters who still remember its secrets (see Mendizábal and Theodossopoulos 2012).

iii The fact that the wooden figurines were fastened onto the columns of the house suggests that Verrill probably arrived during a shamanic ceremony, which also justifies the number of canoes and people on that particular site.

iv In his 1921 account Verrill refers to the Emberá as 'speaking in broken Spanish' (Verrill 1921: 189).

Marsh seeing the Emberá as 'naked' and 'child-like'

4.2   A sketch of Marsh

Richard Oglesby Marsh is another North American writer – but also explorer, adventurer, businessman and agitator of indigenous insurrection[5] – who travelled in Darién in the 1920s. He left detailed accounts of his experiences and his own racist-*cum*-idealising views regarding Otherness. His search for a mythical tribe of 'white Indians' and his conviction – despite all evidence to the contrary – that such people exist, spurred Marsh on to travel among the people that are nowadays known as the Emberá and also the Guna, and to pay careful attention to their appearance. His provocative views have inspired extensive commentary from two prominent anthropologists, Michael Taussig (1993) and James Howe (1998), who have also used Marsh – and, in particular, his unconstrained ethnocentrism – as a platform from which to launch a critique of the Otherising process instigated by Western visions of exploration.

Marsh conceived, fundraised and organised the 'Marsh Darién expedition' of 1924–1925, supported financially by prominent US industrialists and the Smithsonian (Howe 1998). The expedition was composed of its heart and soul, Marsh himself, a few officers from the US military, several supportive staff (mostly Panamanian citizens of Afro-Antillean origin) and a small team of scientists who collected data on natural history and human physiology and indigenous material culture (to be stored later in the ethnology division of the United States National Museum in Washington, see Krieger 1926). Shortly after the expedition, Marsh's impulsive character and his sympathy for the Guna (which culminated in his involvement in the 1925 Guna revolution) earned him many critics and enemies, some of whom opposed Marsh's political views (favouring Guna separatism), while others were affronted by his racist assumptions and his belief in a non-existent race of 'white Indians' (Howe 1998). Marsh himself defended his idiosyncratic vision in a self-flattering book, *White Indians of Darien* (1934). This 'is the story of an amazing episode in the life and dream histories of the New World', Taussig comments, and is 'more valuable for being clichéd and sensationalist – tropical, colonial, hysteria' (1993: 152). Therefore, Marsh's account presents a good opportunity to study the treacherous path of exoticisation.

As with Verrill, one of Marsh's principal literary devices for exciting the interest of his readership is the alluring risk of danger in the confrontation with Indian Otherness. Danger and Otherness are located within the 'unexplored' and potentially threatening province of Darién – a 'blind spot' of Latin America, 'about the worst type of jungle' (Marsh 1934: 11, 12) – which few Westerners had penetrated, and those who had had either faced peril or never returned. In Darién, Marsh maintains, one can discover tribes who do not allow strangers to stay overnight, 'savage Indians perpetually on the warpath' (Ibid.: 5), an unexplored wilderness awaiting 'discovery' by the white, 'civilized' 'man', only 'fifty miles away' from the Panama Canal (Ibid.: 11, 15–16): so close, and so far away! Taussig wonders how curious it is that Marsh locates alterity only a grasp away from the world's shipping artery: 'the closer you get, the greater the mystery becomes' (1993: 173–4).

Marsh, more explicitly than Verrill, manipulates the echo of danger to credit himself with having succeeded where everyone else had failed. According to Marsh, everyone else had failed to capture Otherness, to find white Indians, to recognise a new world of exciting tribes in the misleading – and presumably wrongly charted – geography of Darién. Marsh's self-justificatory tactic underestimates the motives, resilience or geographical awareness of other 'white' men – sailors, explorers, rubber cutters or gold prospectors (Marsh 1934: 17). Verrill, who travelled along a similar route before him, is not mentioned. How would Marsh have felt if he had met Verrill on an accidental encounter at rivers Tuira or Chucunaque? Would such an accidental encounter have spoiled the exclusiveness of discovery for both? We will never know.

Another striking similarity between Marsh and Verrill is Marsh's comparative idealisation of 'Indian-ness', juxtaposed with the denigration of blackness (see also Howe 1998: 9; Taussig 1993). Here the two faces of exoticisation – naïve romanticism and denigrating contempt – are applied to indigenous and black Panamanians respectively. The Afrodarienitas are depicted as 'bush niggers', 'negroes' (Marsh 1934: 5, 16), 'degenerate blacks', 'less civilized than when they came from Africa' (Ibid.: 16, 25) and Yaviza, one of their towns, 'a negro settlement of a few score filthy bamboo huts' (Ibid.: 16, 25), 'black babies everywhere, flies, mangy dogs, garbage, rubbish and mud' (Ibid.: 25). The last phrase – quoted by both Taussig (1993) and Howe (1998) – illustrates Marsh's vivid, but overtly racist depiction of Afrodarienita poverty, which resonates so keenly with that of Verrill. In the early twentieth century, Darién was indeed a province forgotten by its government, yet, as with Verrill, poverty in Marsh's narrative is more explicitly projected onto the Afrodarienitas, not the Indians who were viewed as living in a dignified state of nature. Such a perception of naturalness hid Indian poverty from view.

There is another interesting instance of exoticising ambivalence, which concerns the juxtaposition of the Emberá with the Guna. Marsh, as well as Verrill, portrays the Guna as having more 'dignity' (a sense of civilised, clothed decorum) and the Emberá as being closer to nature (bare bodies, childish naivety). In his book, Marsh introduces this view as a first impression in a description of a group of Guna visitors: 'the new visitors were a silent, dignified group, very different from the joyous, child-like Chocois' (1934: 89). The leader of this first group of Guna maintained 'a ceremonious, almost austere, dignity which contrasted sharply with the irresponsible spontaneity of the Chocois' (Ibid.: 90). He was kind and gentlemanly towards his wife, Marsh further describes, unlike the Emberá men who do not reveal such affections publicly (Ibid.: 101–3).

While the Guna had their own reasons to be mistrustful of the Emberá – a 'traditional' enemy of old – Marsh takes the opportunity to superimpose his denigrating view of the Emberá on that of the Guna:

> 'The disdain which the Cunas felt for the Chocois was very evident. They apparently considered themselves far superior, a superiority borne out of their manner if not by their physique. The Chocois were taller, and decidedly more muscular. But mentally, there was no question as to the superiority of the Cunas.' (Ibid.: 90)

For Marsh, the visible embodiment of such superiority, apart from Guna manners (their silent, austere outlook), is their dress code: the Guna men appeared in 'straw hats, cotton shirts and short dark-blue trousers', while the 'the costumes of the women showed most clearly the great difference' between the two groups; the Guna women wore 'long skirts of brightly appliquéd cotton quilting', instead of 'the short loin cloths' of the 'Chocois' women (Ibid.: 100).

Marsh also detects a certain sad quality hiding behind Guna dignity, which he contrasts with the 'carefree' attitude of the Emberá. While reflecting on the troubled Guna of Tacarcuna, he writes in a reflexive mode that 'there is a definitely grim, sinister, and serious side to the Tule [Guna] nature which is never found among the simple peace-loving childlike Chocoi' (Marsh 1934: 105). Later in the book, he admits that his attitude towards the 'Indians' gradually changed in the course of his time in Darién: 'I was delighted from the start with the Chocois, but I considered them merely charming children', he confesses, alluding to his perception of Guna superiority and the superiority of both Amerindian groups over black Panamanians (Ibid.: 190). Howe (1998), in his comparison of Marsh's book with Marsh's diary, complicates our view of Marsh's sentiments, which were more ambivalent than the book alone reveals them to be. Such an ambivalence – or, in Marsh's own words, 'sentimental idealism of the Indian' (Marsh in Howe 1998: 234) – provides us with a striking example of imperialist nostalgia (Rosaldo 1989).

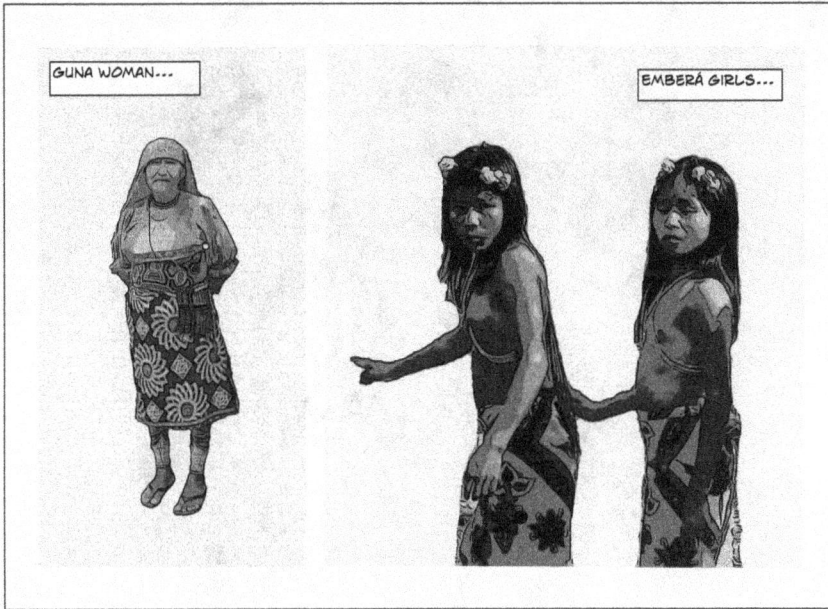

4.3 Marsh described Guna demeanour as serious and dignified, and the Emberá dress code as indicative of childlike innocence

Marsh seeing the Emberá as white

Let us now have a quick look at how Marsh describes the Emberá. His first encounter was in 1923, during a short trip to Darién on a 'little coastal boat', 'diesel engine, negro crew' (Marsh 1934: 18). The purpose of the trip was to evaluate the suitability of Darién for rubber planting. Marsh – accompanied by two lawyers, whom he characterises for their dislike of adventure – entered Darién through the usual route at the time, the Gulf of San Miguel, the very same course undertaken by Verrill a few years earlier.

There, at the outskirts of Yaviza, Marsh had a profound experience – an unexpected exotic encounter – with three 'white' Indian girls. These females, as a photograph taken by Marsh clearly shows,[6] were two Emberá girls and a woman (potentially their mother) all dressed in typical Emberá attire, residing in what is undeniably (from Marsh's own description) a typical Emberá house (see also Howe 1998: 206). They appeared to have slightly lighter-coloured skin than the average Emberá. This is a frequent occurrence among contemporary Emberá,[7] though those with lighter skin are never confused or equated with white people. Yet on this occasion Marsh chose to detect or, to put it more accurately, to superimpose, a description of Aryan whiteness on the Emberá body: 'ethereal, otherworldly, golden-haired nubility' (Taussig 1993: 162).

4.4   Marsh's mirage – the three white-Indian girls. Sketch inspired
by Marsh's original photograph

Marsh's perception of whiteness was, as Howe explains, 'an illusion, a combination of preconception, romantic folklore, racist theorizing, and wishful thinking' (1998: 206). In this instance, as nowadays, the image of the not fully covered female Emberá body conforms to conventional male Western fantasies about exotic beauty and sexuality. Marsh's misperception of whiteness in this accidental encounter reflects the glowing intensity of his astonishment: seeing in naked flesh the embodiment of a vision so highly exoticised; too exotic to be true! This was for Marsh, remarks Taussig, an 'epiphany': 'white-fleshed nakedness and pubescent women making a mockery of, yet heightening, all that seems emotionally at stake where racism, labor discipline, and sexual desire come together for a flashing moment in a clear, elusive image' (1993: 161).

The intensity of the exotic encounter as experienced by Marsh leads to hyperbole: the distortion of a clear Emberá identity. As I mentioned above, some Emberá have lighter skin than others, and a few Emberá children and young adolescents have light-brown rather than black hair, but they are neither mistaken by others – indigenous or non-indigenous – for Latinos or *gringos*, nor do they long to be mistaken as such.[8,9] Additionally, Marsh, by the time he wrote his book, recognised very well the ethnic category of the particular group, whom he called

'Cholas', 'Chocos' or 'Chocoi'. During his expedition, he spent months in close interaction with them, an experience that informed the writing of his book and several detailed descriptions of the Emberá physical appearance and attire. Yet, a year before, he had chosen to see the 'three white girls', as well as an Indian chief dressed in full Emberá attire (see Howe 1998: 207–8),[10] as 'white Indians', members of a lost, not-yet-'discovered' tribe.

As we have seen so far, during his early encounters with the inhabitants of Darién, Marsh projected his fantasies of Indian 'whiteness' onto the Emberá. Eventually, his quest for 'white Indians' led him to identify strongly with the Guna and to support their political cause (Howe 1998). Retrospectively we may realise that the North American explorer merely sought an alibi: a Holy Grail for his very own crusade, 'the Marsh Darién expedition', which he accomplished a year after meeting 'the three Emberá girls'. Progressively during his expedition, Marsh's attention (and exoticising idealisation) shifted towards the Guna, and Marsh recognised (and described in detail) the Emberá as an existing – as opposed to a mythical, undiscovered – indigenous group.

Marsh describing the Emberá body and attire

> I have never seen the equal of those Darien Chocoi Indians. And yet they are not big men – in fact, in stature they are rather small, seldom over 5 feet, 4 inches in height, with symmetrical well-shaped bodies, full deep chests, powerful shoulders and finely muscled legs. (Marsh 1934: 67)

Marsh pays tribute to the physical strength of the male Emberá body early in his account of the Darién expedition. The opportunity emerged when 'one particularly powerful Indian' managed to carry a 370-pound trunk up the steep river slope. This was Marsh's treasure-trinket trunk (see also Howe 1998) containing gifts for the 'Indians'. In New York the trunk was handled by four professional baggage men, says Marsh, and in Panama by an even higher number. Yet, a single Emberá man, remarks Marsh with astonishment, was able to do the job of many with remarkable ease and efficiency. And Marsh continues:

> It is not the size of their muscles so much as the quality, which gives them their great physical power. I later saw them pole their dugout canoes up swift mountain streams, from daybreak to midnight with never a sign of weariness, while our most powerful negroes became so exhausted after one hour of the same work that they literally fell overboard from sheer exhaustion.[11] (Marsh 1934: 67–8)

Here, Marsh attempts to accentuate a comparison between the generalised African American and the undifferentiated Indian, using the one, as Taussig (1993: 142) comments, to purge the other. This type of implicitly racist comparison was a familiar trope among North American expats in Panama in the early- and mid-twentieth century. Howe identifies this 'sentimental preference for the Indian' among the Zonians – the US citizens of the Canal zone – who acted on several occasions as an international support group for Indian rights, and helped the Guna in their struggle for autonomy (2009: 99–100). Marsh's crypto-racist comparisons, which idealise the Indians and denigrate African Americans, resonate with this particular historical context.

Taussig (1993) has used Marsh's admiration of the male Emberá body as an illustration of a particular type of sensationalism that underwrites visible power asymmetries. 'You feel something acutely at the level of the body, the male Indian body as celebrated in Marsh's *White Indians of Darién*', comments Taussig in a particularly pointed style:

> You feel him ogling this sturdy musculature, the eye grasping what the hand can't, lovingly scrutinized by Marsh's writerly eye, like a sculptor running his hands over the rippling flesh, like the magician deploying the magic of Contact, and there is something of the evaluative eye of the employer of muscle-power in this paean of praise to the uncorrupted Primitive body too. (Taussig 1993: 152)

During my own fieldwork, I have witnessed Marsh's colonial sensationalism – which I see as representing a characteristic Western exoticising trope – re-emerging in the commentary of contemporary tourists and travellers. The Emberá of today use outboard motor engines on their canoes and rely on them heavily for long trips upstream. Nevertheless, they still apply their old poling techniques to navigate through the shallows or difficult river passages – or for shorter canoe rides closer to home. They do so with a sense of ease, which elicits the admiration of contemporary Westerners who visit Emberá communities – in Emberá canoes – on tourist excursions (see Chapter 5). The tourists' fascination with the Emberá male body, strength and canoe-poling skill – which I admit has also put my ethnographic nostalgia to the test – echoes Marsh's idealisation ninety years earlier. To the extent that such an exoticising view reveals a post-colonial asymmetry in the tourist encounter, it fully deserves Taussig's rather unforgiving critique.

We have seen so far that the Emberá appearance and ways of dressing inspired Marsh's sensationalist and infantilising references. Yet, surprisingly, when he attempts to give an account of the Emberá attire, Marsh puts aside his idealising and patronising proclivity and instead presents us with a detailed, 'neutral' description:

> The Chocoi men wear a 'gee-string' or loin cloth, sometimes of cheap traders' cotton and sometimes of a native-made bark cloth, while the chiefs and leading men generally have hand-beaten silver wrist bands, occasionally large silver earrings, and as many beads of gay colors as they can drape across their chests and around their thighs.
>
> The women wear larger loin cloths of the same material wrapped around the waist extending nearly to the knees, and as many necklaces of beads, shells, and silver ornaments as they possess.
>
> Both men and women of the Chocoi wear the hair long, falling down over the shoulders, though some of the younger women trim the hair to 'bangs' in front. Avellino and some of the leading men on festive occasions wore a girdle or circlet of braided yellow flowers on their heads. (Marsh 1934: 72–3)

What we see in this testimony from 1924 is, more or less, the code of dress approved by the Emberá nowadays, with the exceptions that bark-cloth has now disappeared

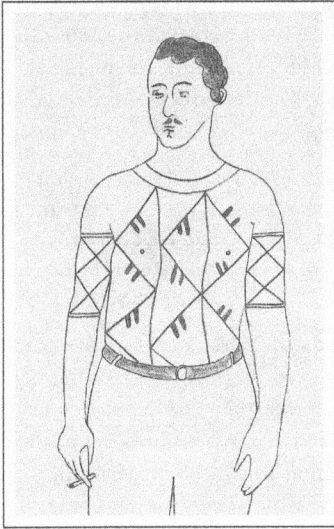

4.5 Marsh painted in Emberá body-painted designs. My sketch is inspired by photographs from the Marsh expedition, although the design (*saú-pa*, the calabash) is one I was taught by the Emberá in Parara Puru

and that contemporary Emberá men – aware of Latino representations of femininity – avoid wearing flowers on their heads. Marsh also discusses the Emberá preference for silver ornaments, as opposed to the Guna who prefer gold, a comparison also underlined by Verrill. He further explains that young boys, as it is often the case nowadays, are 'generally frankly naked', but young girls, Marsh clarifies, 'invariably' wear their 'loin cloths' (Marsh 1934: 96), which is also standard practice today.

During the early stages of the expedition Avellino, an Emberá shaman, befriended Marsh, and became his guide and gatekeeper in the explorer's encounters with other Emberá. Avellino invited Marsh to visit his house on the river Chico and, later, to participate in an Emberá harvest festival. This was a typical Emberá celebration, centred around the preparation of alcoholic beer (*chicha*), a great opportunity for Emberá from dispersed households to meet and solidify their bond. In the contemporary Emberá world of concentrated communities, similar celebrations involve the consumption of great quantities of canned beer, basketball matches, traditional 'animal' dances (performed by women), but also performances of the rumba and cumbia to Emberá music (during which men dance with women) (see also Theodossopoulos 2013c), as well as non-indigenous music styles, such as the Panamanian *típico*. On such occasions, many contemporary Emberá indulge in body painting with *jagua* (see Chapter 2), as the Emberá of river Chico did during the festival attended by Marsh back in 1924. Marsh's detailed description provides valuable testament to this practice – and its application on strangers – in the early part of the twentieth century:

> … We were told, it was necessary for all of us to be formally adopted into the tribe. This ceremony consisted of decorating the entire body from the face to the knees with painted designs in a vegetable pigment which darkened quickly to a deep blue. The design was generally painted on with a small brush, but in my case I was to be honoured by having the chief's eldest wife decorate me by means of a carved wooden block[12] which was first covered with pigment and then pressed against the bare skin. (Marsh 1934: 93)

The Emberá women used the medium of body paint to 'prepare' the Western men for the celebration and welcome them, according to Emberá tradition, as members of the group. Contemporary Emberá see body painting as an opportunity to help visiting tourists experience – and more literally, to embody – a dimension of what it means 'to be Emberá'. In Chapter 8, I will explore the reversal of the exoticising gaze that painting strangers entails. In the case of Marsh's scientific team, the act of dressing up as a 'native' encouraged a shift in Marsh's attention, from the body of the 'Indian' to the body of the Western observer:

> The scientists who had stayed with Avellino were already stripped to make-shift gee-strings and painted in various designs. Brin, the *botanist*, was covered with circles and triangles. Baer, the Smithsonian *anthropologist*, had curved designs like feathers. Breder, the *ichthyologist* from the American Museum of Natural History, was decorated with snakes and frogs in dark blue. (Ibid.: 93, my emphasis)

So for a short period of time we see the scientists of Marsh's crew – the botanist, the anthropologist, the ichthyologist – stripped of their clothes and the fields of scientific knowledge they represented. They expose their naked bodies to the touch of the Emberá painting-stick, they become excitable and lose concentration: laughing, they enticed the indigenous women to giggle, undermining the 'gravity that the Indians attached to the ceremony' (Ibid.: 94). Avellino's intervention re-established good order politely.

Later on the same day, a group of Emberá girls decorated themselves in preparation for the shamanic dance, which we recognise from Marsh's description and expedition photographs as a typical Emberá animal dance.[13] Marsh observed the details with ethnographic accuracy: 'Their bodies were elaborately painted, their long black hair was decorated with bright flowers, beads, carved wooden figures, shells, bright red seeds, and silver' (Ibid.: 95). He also noted that 'the four leading girls wore crowns made of short upright wooden spear-heads, painted and decorated' (Ibid.: 95), like the ones used nowadays by some contemporary Emberá dancing troupes (see Chapter 2). Marsh noticed that some girls wore 'rather shabby cotton loin cloths',[14] which provided him with an opportunity to offer – as, he clarifies, an American parent buys a dress for an American daughter – strips of his 'gold cloth' to be used as new *parumas*.[15] Throughout his account of the harvest festival, Richard Marsh, the paternalistic and idealising author-explorer, emerges for a short interval as a participant-observer, corroborating the historical embeddedness of contemporary Emberá practices. I discuss some of his observations in detail below, for the benefit of those with a particular interest in the anthropology of Panama.

Box 4

Material for comparison

Despite his many shortcomings – for example, racism, arrogance and boastfulness – Marsh took care to provide us with valuable descriptions of the Emberá as he encountered them in 1924. As with Verrill (1921), it is Marsh's exoticising enthusiasm and curiosity that inspires his vivid descriptions of Emberá practices. Three of his chapters in particular – 'The Chocoi Indians',

'Avellino's house' and 'Harvest festival' – deserve the attention of contemporary ethnographers of Panama.

Geographical observations

During an early airplane survey, a single 'reconnaissance' flight that Marsh took before launching his expedition, he noticed (1) round and rectangular '*Chola*' or '*Chocoi*' (Emberá) houses (elevated upon posts and surrounded by extensive plantations) on a lower tributary of the river Savana, (2) 'long' and 'large' Guna houses on the rivers Canaxa and Artigarti and (3) no 'evidence of human habitation' on the lower part of Chucunaque closer to Yaviza (Marsh 1934: 45–8). The last observation, later substantiated by his expedition, demonstrates that the lower Chucunaque served as a border zone between the Guna and the Emberá, only to be settled by the Emberá three decades later (Herlihy 1986). In the course of his account of the expedition, Marsh provides us with additional information regarding the distribution of the Emberá, the lands held by the Guna, the boundaries of indigenous and non-indigenous territories, and the 'forbidden zone' controlled by wild Guna, which lay beyond the river Membrillo (a tributary of the Chucunaque).

Shamans as leaders

As they do nowadays, in the narratives of Verrill and Marsh the Emberá choose individuals with special sets of knowledge, including awareness and ability to communicate with the wider world as their representatives (for example, Avellino is presented as speaking 'considerable Spanish' [Marsh 1934: 69]). Avellino's role as 'chief'-*cum*-representative – in a time when the Emberá had no central and formalised leadership – should be understood in relation to his position as a shaman. It is worth acknowledging here an interesting pattern in the political representation of the Emberá in the times of dispersed settlement: the Swedish ethnologist Nordenskiold also relied on a single shaman, Selimo, who became his gatekeeper during his encounters with the Emberá at rivers Sambú (in Panama) and San Juan (in Colombia) (see Nordenskiold 1927, 1928; Howe 2009: 120).

Polygamy

Marsh presents Avellino as having two wives and incorrectly maintains that 'polygamy is practiced and frequent among the Chocoi Indians' (Marsh 1934: 72). It may be true that in the past renowned Emberá shamans maintained more than one wife, each living at a different river sector. This leads me to entertain an alternative reading of Avellino's marital situation: I believe that the two women introduced to Marsh as Avellino's wives were most likely mother and daughter – 'the younger wife was a buxom young girl of perhaps eighteen . . . subservient to wife number one' (Ibid.: 72). Upon closer reading of the text, I detect an attempt by Avellino to put the young girl out of reach of Marsh's crew of *kampuniá* (non-Emberá) men. If the younger girl were indeed a second wife she would be unlikely to cohabit with the first or be so evidently subservient to her. Marsh himself notes that 'in all our six weeks among the Chocoi, we never saw any indication of strife or discord among the feminine portions of the household' (Ibid.: 72). More importantly, to qualify as a wife, according to Emberá practice, she would already have been with child.

Emberá cleanness

'All the Darien Indians are very scrupulous in keeping what little clothes they wear fresh and clean, seldom wearing any garment two days in succession', observed Marsh in 1924 (Ibid.: 89). When Avellino noticed that Marsh's crew wore dirty clothes for longer than one day, he sent an Emberá woman (accompanied by her husband) to do the expedition team's laundry. The special attention paid to cleanliness is another central dimension of Emberá life, which attracted the admiration of Nordenskiold (1928: 43) who visited Darién only three years later. Contemporary Emberá do not hesitate to share pointed remarks about dirty outsiders (*kampuniá*), including *gringo* tourists who sweat too much!

The Emberá house

Marsh's description of the Emberá house resembles an anthropological account with functional overtones. He discusses the open and elevated style of the structural design – 'the most sensible for the tropics' – and appreciates the 'real architectural skill' involved in their construction, the 'ingenuity' of the high roof trusses, the coexistence of round and rectangular house plans,[1] and the house garden – or 'orchard garden' according to Herlihy (1986) – with plantain and banana trees (Marsh 1934: 78–9). We can also notice in Marsh's description several other typical Emberá preferences: (a) houses built close to the river, (b) orchard gardens, (c) floors made of strips of black palm 'which permit dust and debris to fall through to the ground below and be readily swept away with brush brooms' and (d) items (such as 'mats or rugs', 'thick bark-mats', 'hand woven cotton cloth') 'readily rolled up for house-cleaning' or stored on the 'overhanging eaves' from which they are retrieved and unravelled when it is time to sleep (Ibid.: 79, 82). Such preferences, or *imponderabilia* of everyday practice, which resonate with equivalent contemporary practices, did not escape Marsh's attention.

[1] Round houses are nowadays rare, as their construction is more difficult. With the introduction of indigenous tourism, some Emberá communities have built round houses as exhibits or fine examples of Emberá culture.

On exoticising ambivalence

Verrill's and Marsh's fascinating encounters with Otherness provide us with a good lesson in the alluring distractions of exoticisation. Among them, and the starting point of my analysis here, is a particularly ambivalent stance towards modernity and pre-modern innocence. It is rooted in the idealisation of certain forms of cultural difference, such as the appearance and practices of peoples on the periphery of Western economic power, but without challenging the superiority (and pervasiveness) of Western technologies and values. The contradictions generated by this exoticising ambivalence are often introduced by non-indigenous actors – Western explorers and tourists – who act as the 'authenticators' (Jackson and Warren 2005: 559) of other peoples' indigeneity and authenticity. In the following chapter, I refer to this ambivalent attitude, which is prevalent among contemporary tourists, as 'unintentional primitivisation': it encapsulates an uncertain, nostalgic stance about the intrinsic value of Western civilisation, but without challenging Western civilisational values. We can easily detect unintentional primitivisation in the accounts of Verrill and Marsh, and in particular in their persistent reliance on two exoticising tropes: the idealisation and denigration of cultural difference.

Eager to experience alterity, but without radically departing from Western referents, Verrill and Marsh project an idealising Rousseauian vision of a natural, noble and savage world onto their encounters with the Emberá. For a few brief moments, their ambivalent attitudes oscillate closer to a denial of modernity, a desire to identify with 'primitive' freedom and independence: no clothes, no complications. Nonetheless, Marsh and Verrill did not fully adopt the perspective of the Other. They obtained only a transient taste of Otherness, observing or mimicking local practices without fully understanding their deeper significance. In many ways, this experience resembles that of a contemporary off-the-beaten-track tourist who gives an Emberá woman two dollars to draw *jagua* designs on his body before returning to Panama City, or to New York City. Such mimicry, argues Taussig (1993), can contribute to the negotiation of alterity.

Verrill's and Marsh's negotiation with alterity in Darién involved testing the limits of their ambivalence towards Western civilisation: so close to the Indians, so far away from the marvels and destructive effects of Western transformative 'progress'. This hazy and easily manipulated distance between the Self and Other – far and away (in Darién), but also near (to the Canal and Panama City) – accentuates the identity of the intrepid explorer and legitimises the act of exploration. Placed in another spatiotemporal universe, the Other – in our case, the Amerindian Emberá – is denied coevalness (Fabian 1983) and becomes idealised and denigrated at the same time: exoticised in the context of self-discovery. The 'naked' Chokois here validate the authenticity of Western exploration and set up a contrast – so close (geographically), yet so far away (in unilineal evolutionary terms) – to the 'roaring' soundscapes of modernity in Panama City (Verrill 1921: 192).

Relaxing to the sound of the Emberá music, Verrill reveals his ambivalent attitude towards modernity in what represents a classic example of imperialist nostalgia (Rosaldo 1989): his admiration for Western achievement (technology and exploration) coexists (in an uncomplicated manner) with his longing for a lost world of innocence. As many contemporary tourists who visit the Emberá do, Verrill and Marsh saw indigenous culture as vanishing, doomed by the onward march of Western civilisation. Ironically, their 'sentimental pessimism' (Sahlins 2000) sharply contrasts with the particular juncture of Emberá history, which, as Howe perceptively observes, was marked by territorial expansion into lands in Darién abandoned by the Guna (1998: 217).

The ambivalence of the two author-explorers towards modernity is further exposed in their acknowledgement of the destructive effects of Western interference in indigenous society. Both Verrill and Marsh enthusiastically consider the natural resources of Darién as assets to economic development, yet during their more reflexive moments they nostalgically contemplate the side effects of Western penetration, which is seen as inevitable. With respect to their views of the Emberá, this ambivalent attitude is expressed in terms of patronising infantilisation, and in this respect, Marsh is one degree more explicit than Verrill. His dreams about planting rubber in Darién are combined with 'considerable worry about the harm that development could do' to the native inhabitants of the land (Howe 1998: 208). 'I did not want this lovely wild valley to be overrun by thousands of degenerate Jamaica negroes', confesses Marsh, 'I did not want its harmless and attractive Indians oppressed and exterminated.' (1934: 35)

Here we are reminded of another consistent contrast in Verrill's and Marsh's ambivalence: the idealisation of the Indians (associated with pre-civilisational naturalness) and the denigration of the Afrodarienitas (associated with the encroaching dark side of Western civilisation). Verrill (1921) presents the latter as 'apathetic' and 'lazy', and Marsh, as 'degenerate' 'negro semi-slaves' (1934: 35). In contrast, Indians are presented in terms that make their freedom and independence more noticeable. Taussig has located this contradiction within a broader Western (mythologised) dichotomy, that of the good versus the bad savage: 'the Indian and the black are the beings through which the ceaseless dilemma of labor-discipline and freedom in capitalist enterprise is to be figured' (Taussig 1993: 156). The undifferentiated Indian here stands for freedom (representing a Western spirit of independence), and the generalised black stands for 'labor-discipline' and the violent imposition of Western civilisational 'superiority'.

Yet, Marsh's (explicit) and Verrill's (implicit) racism – apparent in their pro-Indian but anti-African sentiments – becomes further complicated in their comparisons of the Emberá with the Guna. Here the mere appearance of the Guna, dressed in clothes that cover a great part of the body, encourages the two authors to jump to quick conclusions: the Guna are presented as 'more civilized' (according to Verrill) and more 'dignified' and 'superior' (according to Marsh). These early impressions are later rationalised in terms of further experiences of contact, as both Verrill and Marsh spent significantly more time with the Guna, during which they had the opportunity to discuss issues of political representation with Guna leaders. By contrast, their relationships with the Emberá did not involve politics. Their view of the Emberá is shaped by first contact: a first impression that relates to the openness of the Emberá to strangers and their talkative disposition (compared with the reserved politeness of the Guna) and, in addition, to a culturally specific perception of nudity. The 'naked', 'colourful', 'childlike' and 'joyous' Emberá fulfil Verrill's 'ideal of the primitive savage' (1921: 189) and Marsh's vision of 'wonderful, primitive, loveable, children of Nature' (Marsh in Howe 1998: 208).

Verrill and Marsh were not alone in making hasty judgements based on the appearance and dress code of the Guna and the Emberá. Nordenskiold (1928), a seasoned Scandinavian ethnologist, committed a similar mistake during his first days in Panama. At first sight, he was not impressed by the Guna men he saw in Colón: they were dressed like the whites, 'like nice gentlemen' with 'a haughty attitude' (Nordenskiold 1928: 14; c.f. Howe 2009: 120–1); in fact, he wondered if these people can think like Indians at all (Ibid.: 14)! In contrast, the first Emberá he met at river Sambú (in January 1927) captured his ethnological imagination unreservedly: instead of meeting Indians with shirts and pants – as he expected – he encountered people who were almost naked; they were painted, pleasant and amiable, as if they lived in a remote land deep in the South American main-land (Ibid.: 37). Later in his account, Nordenskiold describes the attire of the Emberá living around the rivers Sambú and Jaqué, closely corroborating Verrill's and Marsh's descriptions, before departing for the Pacific region of Chocó in Colombia. However, by the end of his journey through Panama and Colombia, and after visiting San Blas, Nordenskiold, like Marsh, identified more closely with the Guna, fascinated by their cosmology (Howe 2009: 127) and ritual wooden stat-ues (Fortis 2012a: 11). By the end of his account, the spontaneity and directness of the Emberá and the Wounaan – traits that attracted him to these people at the first place – substantiated a moderately infantilising view of simplicity and naturalness.

Less refined than Nordenskiold's, Verrill's and Marsh's narratives locate the Emberá firmly within the realm of nature: this is Darién, a wilderness presented as partially unexplored. The two North American author-explorers conceive Darién as a land with (a) resources (to be exploited), (b) inhabitants of African descent that underuse those resources (where underutilisation rationalises the civilising mission of benevolent outsiders) and (c) vulnerable Amerindian inhab-itants threatened by the encroachment of African-Panamanians (where the latter are blamed for the vices of Western civilisation). According to the same narra-tive, the Emberá – innocent, 'naked' and passive – do not appear to lay claim to any resources, unlike the Guna who are determined to protect their territory. In Marsh's and Verrill's ambivalence towards modernity – which oscillates between a corrupting (but superior) Western civilisation and a world of primordial freedom and spontaneity – the Emberá stand for naturalised innocence.

The final brush stroke on this canvas of contradictions is the element of danger that lurks behind the foliage of naturalness and innocence in the Darién jungle (see Frenkel 1996).[16] The myth of 'wild', 'dangerous' Indians is a recurring literary device in the narratives of Marsh and Verrill and is used to induce the excite-ment of their North American readership, but also to validate the purpose (and risk) of exploration. As with the 'naked' Indian – an image entirely fulfilled by the Emberá – the 'wild' Indian and the suspicion of danger it conveys (see Ramos

1991) mark the distance of the Western explorer from modernity, and provide a measure for the explorer's accomplishment. With Marsh and Verrill this distance is, once more, a grey area and is manipulated accordingly: so close to Panama Canal and the crossroads of the world and yet so far away from civilisation. The reader is led to believe that the jungles of Panama – which can be seen from the comfort of a passenger ship crossing the Canal – host dangerous Indians. Who are these people? They are the 'wild' Guna of the Bayano and the western tributaries of Chucunaque, explain Verrill and Marsh – the 'Guna *bravos*' as the Emberá of today remember them – which are not to be confused, the two authors clarify, with 'the perfectly harmless' Emberá (Marsh 1934: 24) who are 'savage only in name' (Verrill 1921: 189).

Then again, at other times in their accounts, Verrill and Marsh manipulate the ambiguity and proximity of danger to include all Indians of Darién, including the Emberá. 'They are generally not considered dangerous', maintains Marsh, 'certainly not those on the waterfronts, although a number of travellers who have ventured into the interior of their territory, among kindred people calling themselves Chocoi, have not returned' (Marsh 1934: 16). Exaggerations such as this are employed 'to turn the Darién from a backwater into a howling wilderness', cultivating 'an atmosphere of danger, mystery, and mild sexuality' (Howe 1998: 212, 213). Even Verrill (1921), who goes to great pains to advertise Panama as a safe destination for travellers,[17] cannot completely restrain himself from exploiting the alluring and sensationalist image of the wild Indian: 'within 150 miles from the busy, up-to-date port of Colon dwell primitive, savage Indians who permit no strangers within their borders' (Verrill 1921: no page numbers).[18]

It is in such terms that the conceptual distance of danger is manipulated and conveniently collapsed, repositioned in an unknown world nearby a well-known site, the Panama Canal. So many explorers who have ventured into this unknown world have died, underlines Marsh – to forewarn anyone tempted to challenge the exclusivity of his account – providing a list of failed expeditions that suffered losses (1934: 16–17), a fate that also haunted his own.[19] The idea of danger here operates as a literary trope, setting up a standard of intrepidness (of the male explorer) and authenticity (of a discovered-*cum*-undiscovered world in alluring proximity to alterity). Unsurprisingly, such old but well-crafted narratives have left a residual echo in the twenty-first century. As Velásquez Runk argues, the myth of dangerous Darién has 'facilitated taming narratives for the region via development' and a broader justification for outside intervention (2015: 129).

In an indirect manner, the exotic aura of Darién's danger has migrated, along with the Emberá, closer to routes of commerce and transportation. Inadvertently, the Emberá of Chagres – now resettled in the westernmost extreme of Emberá geographic distribution – have broadened the expansive grey area of danger established by Verrill and Marsh a century ago: 'naked' Indians who apparently live only a few kilometres from the Canal!

On a website that provides advice to expats and tourists, Richard Detrich, an expat himself, drawing from his acquaintance with the last remaining Zonians, provides us with a de-exoticising warning:

During the Canal Zone days, they were called Chocoes and they were very much looked down on, because of their traditional lifestyles and dress. People who grew up in the Canal Zone, Zonians, have told me that when they were children they were told never to leave the Canal Zone because there were cannibals out there who would eat them! (Detrich 2009)

The danger identified by Detrich is not that of wild Indians, but one much more likely to be encountered in contemporary Panama: the menace of exoticisation. We will see how the Emberá confront such idealising and discriminating expectations in the following chapters.

Notes

1 A *chicha*-festival may or may not have been triggered by Verrill's arrival. I assume that the local Emberá were preparing for the festival anyway or, knowing that the festival was taking place, invited the North American explorer to participate.
2 He mentions that he met Guna leaders from the interior, who had heard of his return to Panama from their 'San Blas tribesmen', but this meeting took place in Panama City; we also learn that he travelled to the province of Bocas del Toro in 1924 (see Verrill 1931: 214, 224, 228).
3 His 1931 account of the Guaymi – the Ngäbe, as we know them today – benefited significantly from his 'stay of many weeks' (Verrill 1931: 228), and in some respects represents a move towards an ethnographic perspective.
4 Verrill's account of the Chokois in the 1931 edition cut and pasted from the 1921 chapter 'Darien the unknown' – which reappears as 'Darien the little known' – to the new chapter 'The Indians of Panama'.
5 Marsh was born to a prominent family from Illinois, his father was a member of Congress and throughout his life he maintained privileged connections with important politicians and business tycoons (Howe 1998: 72–5); this explains how he acquired the position of first secretary of the US delegation to Panama in 1910 – which led to a brief and profoundly unsuccessful diplomatic career – and how later (in 1925) he succeeded in securing support for the Marsh Darién Expedition.
6 The particular photograph does not appear in *White Indians of Darien*, but is stored, along with other material from Marsh's expedition, in the National Anthropological Archives at the Smithsonian Institution.
7 Contemporary Emberá use the Spanish adjectives *fulo* (masculine) and *fula* (feminine), meaning 'fair', to describe those among them whose skin is lighter in colour.
8 In fact, Marsh's scientific team, which spent a few weeks at river Chico taking anthropometric measurements, reported that 'a great many of the Chocoi children had decidedly light brown hair, some all over the head and some in patches, which became dark as the children grew older' (Marsh 1934: 128). In his description of the three 'white' girls, Marsh chooses to disregard this information.
9 Reverte Coma corroborates the observations of Marsh's scientific team (see note 8) with his own from the 1960s. Reverte Coma was trained as a medical doctor and liked to add a touch of science to his descriptions. He explains that 'the hair of the [Emberá] children is silky, soft, smooth, poorly pigmented, which makes them appear blond. It darkens as they grow old and especially with the effect of [dyeing it with] *jagua*' (Reverte Coma 2002: 238, my translation).

10 We can clearly see this in one of Marsh's photographs published by Howe (1998: 208).

11 Later in his account, Marsh makes pointed remarks about the 'high-priced' black members of his crew – who originally introduced themselves as '*palanque* men' but had serious difficulty with poling canoes upstream: they are the 'crudest amateurs at that game' (Marsh 1934: 77). The clumsy canoe navigators in Marsh's crew were, without a doubt, men from Panama City, Colón or the United States, as I have seen Afrodarienita men poling canoes with skill and stamina comparable to the Emberá.

12 The carved wooden block was a *pintadera*, an Emberá body-painting stamp with prefabricated designs (see also Torres 1966: 57, 1980: 169; Reverte Coma 2002: 224–6).

13 For a detailed description of this dance and its variations, see Theodossopoulos 2013c.

14 In the past, *parumas* were worn until they wore out, as my older Emberá respondents explained.

15 In the bulletin of the US National Museum we can see a photograph of the expedition, which shows the girls dancing in single file, as contemporary Emberá women do. Two of the dancers wear single-coloured *parumas* (presumably from Marsh's cloth), while two wear multicoloured *parumas* (see Krieger 1926: pl. 34).

16 The contradiction between tropical innocence and danger in the accounts of Verrill (1921, 1931) and Marsh (1934) can be contextualised within wider idealised perceptions of tropical Panama that had developed since the late nineteenth century (Frenkel 1996). These, Frenkel (1996) explains, existed in an ambivalent relationship with contrasting perceptions of the physical danger and moral degradation lurking in the tropical jungle.

17 This is especially true in the later revision of his book republished as *Panama of Today* (Verrill 1931).

18 In his 1931 edition, Verrill plays down the same remark by editing it as follows: 'Within 150 miles from the busy, ultra-civilized, up-to-date Canal Zone dwell thousands of untamed, primitive Indians of many tribes.' (Verrill 1931: no page numbers)

19 Marsh dedicated his *White Indians of Darien* to John Baer, the Smithsonian scientist who participated and died in the course of his expedition. His dedication to Baer is in itself testimony to this particular literary style employed to manipulate danger as a measure of intrepidness and authenticity in exploration: 'This book is dedicated to Professor John L. Baer, anthropologist and ethnologist of the Smithsonian Institution of Washington, D.C. who accompanied us on our scientific expedition through Darien, who was taken sick in the unknown interior valley of Darien, who was transported by us in a dugout canoe hauled by the turbulent waters of the Chucunaque River . . . (and) who was then carried across the San Blas Mountain range in a hammock slung from a pole supported on the shoulders of eight "wild" Tule Indians, who died on the Caribbean shore at the San Blas Indian village of Acla, and who was buried wrapped in an army blanket in a grave dug with our tin eating plates . . .' (Marsh 1934: no page numbers).

5

Ghosts of Emberá present

In this chapter I will take a leap forward in time, to the beginning of the twenty-first century, to examine the exoticising view of another type of privileged outsider interested in meeting the Emberá and acquiring a short-lived experience of their culture. These are the spectres that haunt Emberá representation in the present: tourists seeking to consume the exotic. They visit Panama and the Canal in regular flows and, attracted by images of the Emberá in tourism advertisements, become interested in an experience with an indigenous culture. This is usually realised in a half-day excursion – often marketed as 'adventures in nature' or 'rainforest adventures' – to an Emberá 'village'. Photographs of the Emberá that correspond with stereotypical tourist representations of rainforest people – dressed in exotic garb, and with their bodies largely uncovered – provide a welcoming promise of excitement: a taste of wild, tropical and exotic South America. As the ghosts of Verrill and Marsh would say, here lies a world not so different from Amazonia, yet only a few miles away from the Canal!

We have already seen how scorn and idealisation were the dominant orientations in Verrill and Marsh's imaginations of the Emberá. These two exoticising orientations, the denigration and idealisation of alterity, appear as dominant tropes in the tourism imaginary (Theodossopoulos 2014). They produce contradictions that shape the negotiation of expectations during the tourist encounter (Skinner and Theodossopoulos 2011). Such contradictions range from an attitude that reflects a nostalgia for the idealised 'vanishing savage' and lost worlds unaffected by (Western) civilising processes (Clifford 1986; Rosaldo 1989; see also Conklin and Graham 1995;

5.1   The entrance of the community

Ramos 1998; Gow 2007; Berliner 2015) to an ambivalent attitude to which I refer here as 'unintentional primitivisation'. The latter attitude can be simultaneously condescending (e.g. 'they are not as civilised as we are'), but also idealising, albeit in a patronising and infantilising way (e.g. 'they are beautiful children of nature').

'Unintentional primitivisation' represents a profoundly ambivalent stance towards the intrinsic worth of Western civilisation. This ambivalence encapsulates the expectation that indigenous people may benefit from some Western values and priorities – such as education for children and hospital care – while at the same time remain unaffected by other 'corrupting' Western influences or technologies. In this respect, tourist expectations frequently oscillate between exoticism and primitivism, two visions of Otherness rooted in the 'European world hegemony' established in the age of exploration (Friedman 1994: 4). In our age of increased global flows, such pervasive and ethnocentric imaginaries persist (see Salazar 2010; Salazar and Graburn 2014) and 'are directed explicitly at consumers of the exotic, of spiritual reclamation, of jungle adventure' (Comaroff and Comaroff 2009: 3). In this respect, unintentional primitivisation shapes the tourist encounter, posing dilemmas for indigenous hosts of tourism, such as the Emberá, who make an effort to negotiate their representation in contradictory-*cum*-exoticised terms.

The coexistence of, and tension between, such diverse exoticising tropes allow us to appreciate that at any given moment several layers of exoticisation participate in and inspire a particular tourism imaginary. This realisation can help us escape from a limiting vision of indigenous hosts as passive recipients of a singular exoticising vision. The views of the tourists who visit the Emberá are far from singular; they engender perpetually ambivalent contradictions. In the sections that follow I explore this profound ambivalence in the context of Emberá tourism, paying particular attention to the exoticising images it generates. I use as a case study the tourism experience made available in Parara Puru, which is representative – in its static and essentialising simplicity – of the Emberá tourist spectacle in Eastern Panama.

The irresistible view of naturalness in Emberá appearance

Parara Puru looks at first sight like an isolated community forgotten by time and untouched by modernity. From the point of view of the Western visitor the community emerges out of the lavish vegetation of the Chagres National Park as a small island of inhabited space within a verdant ocean. Surrounded by dense rainforest and approachable only by canoe, this inhabited space gives the impression of having emerged 'naturally' out of the forest. The wooden, thatched-roof houses blend into the overwhelming naturalness of the surrounding environment, while the sounds of tropical birds mix with that of cumbia-Emberá, a welcoming first impression for incoming groups of tourists.

5.2   A Rousseauian view of the Emberá in nature

In tune with the music and the tropical birdsong, the relaxed-but-joyful disposition of the residents of Parara Puru resonates with Rousseauian representations of a seemingly true and authentic life, away from the tribulations of Western civilisation. They walk slowly to meet the tourists, dressed in traditional garb: the women adorned with hibiscus flowers, multicoloured *paruma*-skirts and long necklaces that cover their naked torsos; the men dressed in loincloths, most wearing a skirt-like belt of beads.[1] The younger children run playfully among the adults, once more in minimal clothing, while toddler boys appear completely naked (accentuating the overall impression of bareness). The geometric patterns painted on the Emberá bodies attract additional attention and add to the perception that one is encountering an authentic Amerindian group, true rainforest dwellers.

In Western imagination, the idea of authenticity has been associated, under the formative influence of Rousseau, with expectations of sincerity, primordial integrity, paradisiacal innocence and purity (Bendix 1997; Lindholm 2008, 2013). 'Tribal' or 'native' cultures – such as the indigenous peoples of the contemporary world – have been (and continue to be) perceived as being in possession of these qualities in plenty. In the twentieth century, popular ecology relied upon the appeal of earlier romantic visions, idealising indigenous communities as being closer to nature or encapsulating the primordial essence of ecological wisdom (Morris 1981; Ellen 1986; Conklin and Graham 1995; Milton 1996: 109–14; Ramos 1998; Stronza 2001; West and Carrier 2004; Carrier and Macleod 2005; Ulloa 2005). In Western discourse, romanticised images of life in the tropics often combine with the critique of modernity, the message of environmentalists, and old colonial narratives of voyages of discovery.

The tourism agencies that organise day trips to the Emberá communities in Chagres draw on such idyllic representations of life in the tropics, which they often combine with environmentally friendly depictions of indigenous communities in popular ecology. They use such images, along with the excitement of meeting one of Panama's indigenous 'tribes', to advertise the beauty of the local environment. In tourism advertisements, the Emberá are represented in a timeless manner as people with knowledge of the rainforest who live – and have always lived – in harmony with it. And indeed, the Emberá are in possession of a great deal of knowledge about the rainforest, the result of a long history of living in ecosystems similar to that of Chagres National Park. Independently of their engagement with tourism, the Emberá in Chagres are, undeniably, dwellers of a rainforest nature reserve and, in this respect, are sincere when they present themselves to tourists in these terms.

Yet, what the tourists fail to perceive – due to their exoticising predisposition, but also the short duration of their visit – is the degree of control that the Emberá, like all human groups, exercise over their natural environment. Parara Puru is first and foremost a real inhabited indigenous community, the home of approximately twenty Emberá families. The houses – all built on stilts, according to Emberá custom – and the surrounding environment bear the marks of continuous habitation, as new structures and pathways emerge organically to meet the requirements of the local inhabitants. Dwellings are continuously repaired or replaced by new ones (built on the same spot, partly by reusing the same materials), while electrical appliances are gradually incorporated into the community's family houses alongside the more traditional fire hearths. In the spaces around their houses, the residents of the community have planted trees and flowers with recognisable cultural significance or use, which demonstrate the domestication of the local environment (see Herlihy 1986; Kane 1994). But at this point let me go back one step to describe the tourist experience of Parara Puru.

The great majority of tourists who visit Parara Puru come from exclusive resorts or cruise ships passing through the Canal area. They reach Chagres by mini-bus, accompanied by tourist guides – mostly, but not exclusively, non-indigenous Panamanians[2] – who gently supervise them for the duration of the trip. The guides collect the tourists in buses or mini-buses and have an opportunity to explain, during the bus trip, the practical aspects of the tour and provide some information about the Emberá. The detail and quality of this information varies tremendously, according to the knowledge, experience and enthusiasm of the particular tourist guide. Some have visited Emberá communities many times before and maintain long-lasting friendships within them. Whereas others merely improvise – due to a lack of experience or preparation – often mixing fact with fiction, and thus contributing to the exoticisation of the Emberá. The road trip ends at Lake Alajuela within the Chagres National Park, a tropical rainforest reserve.

At this point the tourists take their first glimpse of the Emberá men, who are waiting for them at a canoe-landing area on Lake Alajuela, Puerto Corotú.[3] This canoe 'port' serves the three Emberá communities of Chagres – Tusipono, Parara Puru, Emberá Drua – and a predominantly Latino settlement, Victoriano Lorenzo,[4] located on the opposite side of the lake. During the morning, the presence of several men decorated in traditional attire adds a uniquely indigenous mark to this rather indistinctive transition point. The decorated men are the navigators of the canoes that arrive to transport the tourists. They interact with other Emberá men dressed in modern clothes (on their way to the town), Emberá women dressed in a mixed *paruma*-and-t-shirt combination, and non-indigenous residents from Victoriano. Yet, as a tourist guide once confided to me, the arriving tourists concentrate 'on those wearing traditional garb… the other locals, in normal clothes, are almost invisible!'

Dazzled by the exotic intensity of the Emberá attire, the tourists board motorised dugout canoes. The Emberá, who are legally obliged to abide by tourist safety regulations, give them bright orange life jackets to wear. The Emberá themselves are freed from this obligation – their reputation as expert canoe navigators precedes them. One Emberá man, usually the older one, controls the canoe motor, while the second stands at the prow with a long wooden pole to steer the canoe through the shallows. This is an opportunity for the tourists to admire the exceptional skill of the Emberá in poling canoes, a demanding job that they execute with performative confidence. The act of canoe poling makes visible the muscular composition and agility of the male Emberá body – bare of clothes except a bead belt and a loincloth – an exoticising image that, as we saw in the previous chapter, Richard Marsh was mesmerised by in 1924.

En route to the community, while the Emberá steer a course through the lake and the river, the tourists obtain a good view of the natural ecosystem in the Chagres Park and take photographs of the landscape, the river turtles and numerous species of butterflies and birds. The canoe ride, a couple of tourists said to me, is an added bonus to the experience, enhancing the perceived naturalness of the rainforest. This in turn creates a strong sense of anticipation for the 'remarkable' – as so many tourists have described it – encounter that follows: one with a 'truly' indigenous community in a place removed from modernity and contemporary Western society. Before entering the community, the canoe navigators take groups with more time at their disposal to the nearby waterfalls, where some tourists have the opportunity to swim and walk in the rainforest. At the end of this

5.3 Dugout canoes with tourists en route to the community

short excursion – which further blurs the perceived boundary between pristine nature and unspoiled indigenous culture – the tourists reach Parara Puru and are welcomed by its inhabitants, all dressed in full Emberá attire.

Box 5

The 'Emberá experience' in a package

- The typical tourist encounter with the Emberá at Chagres is two or three hours long, although the tourists spend approximately one-and-a-half hours travelling to Chagres, and a further one-and-a-half hours back to their hotels or cruise ships. The 'Emberá experience' on offer includes music, dance, a traditional meal and opportunities to buy Emberá artefacts (*artesania*). This cultural package is adaptable, and the Emberá are prepared to provide extras at the request of their visitors: for example, a tour in the rainforest, some guidance on Emberá medicinal knowledge or informal instruction on other aspects of indigenous life.
- There are no hotels within the park, so the very few tourists who wish to augment their indigenous experience with an overnight stay sleep in thatched Emberá houses – representative examples of traditional Emberá architecture. The traditional Emberá houses – seen by the first-time visitor – emerge from the rainforest, a view that reinforces Western expectations of indigenous life in a pristine 'natural' ecosystem.
- Although Parara Puru occasionally receives small groups of domestic (non-indigenous Panamanian) tourists, the great majority of tourists come from international destinations, mostly North America, but also Europe and, less frequently, other Latin American countries and Japan. Some of these tourists come from holiday resorts, while others are passengers on cruise ships transiting through the Canal. They respond to tourist advertisements – promoted in their hotels or cruise ships – that offer a variety of excursions, one type of which is to 'an Emberá village' or 'an indigenous community' in the Chagres National Park, an excursion that has been, as the travel agents explain, very popular in recent years.
- Images of the natural, both the rainforest and the indigenous people living in it, are highlighted in tourism advertisements. In guidebooks, tourist brochures and on the internet, Chagres National Park is advertised as an ideal setting for adventures in 'nature'. This includes an opportunity to experience an indigenous Amerindian culture in a 'pristine', 'natural', 'tropical' environment. What the tourists tend not to realise is that the overall landscape has been affected by the construction of the Panama Canal. Lake Alajuela itself is a man-made water reservoir that sustains the Canal. The establishment of the Chagres National Park in 1985 was aimed at the preservation of the natural resources – particularly the water supply that sustains the Canal – for the benefit of the surrounding human community.

- With respect to its low environmental impact and small-scale orientation, indigenous tourism – in the form developed by the Emberá – has
  some of the properties of ecotourism (West and Carrier 2004) or alternative tourism (Stronza 2001). Communicating this eco-friendly message
  to visiting tourists would, it was thought, attract them and enhance their
  appreciation of the Emberá landscape. Yet, what is not directly visible to
  the tourists is that the establishment of the national park constrained the
  traditional subsistence activities of the Emberá by imposing a series of
  environmental regulations. As we shall see in the following chapter, the
  Emberá who live within the park had no other option than to develop
  indigenous tourism, as an economic alternative with a low environmental impact.
- The Emberá of Parara Puru distinguish between the high and low tourist seasons. From December to March, a period that coincides with the
  Panamanian summer or dry season, tourist numbers are higher and
  groups of visitors tend to be larger. After April, the numbers of visitors decline and remain low until August and September. October and
  November are the rainiest months and therefore the least suitable for
  tourism. As we shall see in the following chapter, the seasonality of work
  in tourism plays an important role in decisions regarding the work priorities and mobility of the permanent residents of the community and
  related individuals.

The tourist encounter

After their arrival in Parara Puru, the tourists – slightly disoriented from their boat
trip and the journey through the rainforest – walk slowly towards the centre of the
village, taking photographs. The Emberá of communities that frequently engage
with tourism do not shy away from the camera, and they pose alone or with the
tourists for countless photographs, some of which are later posted on the internet
on social media or web pages that publish reviews of tourist experiences (such as
TripAdvisor).[5] This plethora of images enhances the visibility of the Emberá, who
become more widely known, albeit mostly depicted in full traditional attire, in a
manner appropriate – according to Emberá custom – for receiving guests.

As the tourists enter the central part of the community they are invited into
the main reception area, which comprises two long communal buildings[6] with
Emberá-style thatched roofs, where there are benches (for the visitors) and tables
covered with Emberá artefacts (*artesania*): baskets, masks and carvings made from
tagua nuts and cocobolo wood, all available for sale at prices lower than in Panama
City. The arrangement of the benches denotes that this is a space dedicated to
performance. And indeed, soon after the tourists' arrival, one of the leaders of the
community gives a short introductory speech on the history of the community, its
involvement in tourism and the various types of Emberá artefacts. In the course

5.4   Tourists arriving at Parara Puru

of this speech the tourists are given a short demonstration of the main components of the traditional Emberá costume. An Emberá man and woman stand in front of the tourists acting as live models, explaining each individual item of clothing or adornment.

The presentation of Emberá clothing to the tourist audience is a rather static explication that focuses on the normative elements of the pure – uncontaminated by modernity – traditional style of dress.[7] This is presented to the tourists as unchanging, a faithful reproduction of the past in the present, 'the way our grandparents used to dress'. In the following chapters, I will compare this static approach to self-presentation with the nuanced Emberá awareness of their clothing politics. The tourists, however, in their overwhelming majority, have no reason to challenge the authoritative, but timeless, narrative of the Emberá, although they do wonder, as I will explain in the following section, if the Emberá remain dressed – or, from a certain Western point of view, 'undressed' – 'all the time'. The overwhelming majority of the visitors attend the 'Emberá speech' carefully and respectfully.

While the tourists are seated in the communal house they are offered a taste of Emberá cuisine, a meal of fish and fried plantains served inside a folded palm leaf, in a manner that resembles how the Emberá catered for Richard Marsh when he attended a harvest festival in 1924 (see Chapter 4). In addition, and in a manner that, once more, reminds us of the experience of Richard Marsh so many years earlier, the Emberá – usually women or younger men – offer to tattoo individual tourists with *jagua* juice, while Emberá children, painted with traditional patterns, watch the skilful application with interest. The tourists are informed during the speech that designs from *jagua* last only for eight-to-twelve days and that *jagua* has therapeutic properties for the skin.

The introductory speech is usually followed by a music and dance performance, the most visually compelling part of the cultural presentation. The local women form a single line and perform a couple of dances, chosen from a wide repertoire of dances named after, and performed in imitation of, natural species: rainforest animals, birds or plants (see Theodossopoulos 2013c). These dances have a spiritual-animistic dimension and have always been danced by Emberá women with the upper part of their bodies uncovered. Such details, however, are not communicated to the tourists, who have, by that stage, already

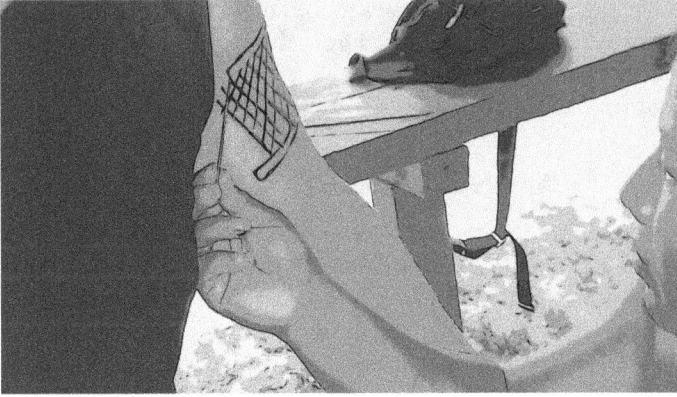

5.5 Body-painting tourists with *jagua*

been exposed to a considerable amount of information. Instead, the performance becomes progressively more joyful with the introduction of another dance, rumba-Emberá, or in some cases cumbia-Emberá, which is danced in couples and in sequence.[8] This is the traditional Emberá version of music for entertainment and celebration.

For the final stage the hosts invite members of the audience to participate, and the entertainment culminates with mixed pairs of Emberá and tourists dancing in a long merry procession. Often, when tourist groups are large, the dance presentations develop from a performance to a spontaneous 'party'. Tourists from various destinations – be it Puerto Rico, Japan, France or the United States – watch the performance, take photographs, dance with the Emberá and join in, with what looks from the point of view of the spectator, the visual consumer (Urry 1995) of the tourist performance, like an ongoing, continuous celebration. In this cheerful context, some tourists dance with Emberá adults or even children, while others record their friends or relatives with digital cameras as they follow the tune, hand in hand with indigenous partners adorned with, what seems from the tourist point of view, an 'exotic' and 'colourful' attire.

5.6 Tourists dancing with the Emberá

Eventually the tourists depart, always to the sound of Emberá music, worn out from the tropical heat, but exhilarated from the experience. 'It was like living in a dream', one tourist told me during the walk to the departing canoes, 'a journey into a forgotten place and time!'

Ambivalent tourist expectations

The tourists arrive in Chagres with varying expectations. Some of these are based on pre-existing popular stereotypes about life in the rainforest and diverse sets of knowledge about the position and relationship of indigenous communities with the wider world. As I explained in the preceding sections, tourist expectations of the Emberá range from nostalgia for the idealised 'vanishing savage' and lost worlds unaffected by (Western) civilising processes (Clifford 1986; Rosaldo 1989; Berliner 2015) to patronising and discriminatory stereotyping that caricatures indigenous difference as primitiveness and lack of cultural sophistication. In their commentary on the Emberá many tourists communicate a combination of nostalgic-idealising and patronising remarks. Even when some tourists are willing to accept – to different degrees – that their indigenous hosts are subjects of the contemporary global and interconnected world, they struggle to escape from the two main tropes of exoticisation mentioned above, the denigration and idealisation of cultural difference.

While walking around the community, tourists often discover details of the daily life of the Emberá, such as items of clothing, electronic devices or plastic toys that do not fit with their preconceptions about indigenous people in the rainforest. These small discoveries contribute to their puzzlement about the exact position of the Emberá at the interface of tradition and modernity, and usually inspire the tourists to express pessimistic statements about culture loss and the eventual disappearance of all indigenous people. The idealising nostalgia of these comments is often expressed through statements about the corrupting influence of technology and modernity on indigenous life. Some tourists adopt an extreme romantic idealism towards this issue and mourn, in Rousseauian fashion, the lost innocence of 'primitive' man, or anticipate that the culture of the Emberá will disappear due to exposure to the relentlessly homogenising forces of our global era.

A few tourists recognise that the Emberá, like other indigenous people, live in a modern world, and are confronted with change, but approach change as an undesirable inevitability. Their recognition that the Emberá 'have to' send their children to school or use modern medicine clashes with their disappointment when they discover that some Emberá houses have televisions, or when they see modern t-shirts hanging on a laundry line along with traditional Emberá *paruma* skirts. The overwhelming majority of international tourists voice ambivalent views of this type – permeated by an idealising spirit, but mixed with a slightly pessimistic, reluctant recognition of social change. This is a good example of the attitude I described earlier in this chapter as unintentional primitivisation.

There are always a few tourists who side unequivocally with modernity and caricature the Emberá with pointed comments that focus on their observable nudity and their assumed lack of knowledge of the civilised world. Domestic tourists are the most likely to caricature indigeneity in these respects. The issue of clothing or, from the tourist point of view, the bareness of the Emberá body, invites the most condescending comments. Thus, for a few tourists the sight of the Emberá in traditional attire is treated as confirmation of 'primitiveness' – or absence of civilisation – while any other evidence of contact with modernity is selectively erased. The evaluations of tourists who adopt this perspective may either remain narrowly static – 'this is how such people have always been, this is how they always will be' – or alternatively reproduce (once more) sentimental pessimism: 'I don't want to imagine what might happen to these innocent people in the future!'

Ambivalent, but (more or less) opinionated, commentary that reflects the general orientations outlined above, is often expressed by some tourists in a loud voice while they are walking around the community, or in the communal house in the presence of other tourists. On many occasions during my fieldwork I met tourists wandering in the community or, to put it more accurately, the tourists discovered me writing fieldnotes or walking in the community. Some were curious about my identity, and after I explained that I am an anthropologist, they asked questions about the Emberá, most of which reflected an ambivalence about modernity and the fate of indigenous people in the future. Many tourists explained that they had been pleasantly surprised by the 'traditional' character of the community and remarked that, unlike other similar cultural tours they had taken, this particular tourist experience was very rewarding.

Nevertheless, and as I have explored in detail in previous work (see Theodossopoulos 2013a), a small number of tourists try to discover elements of inauthenticity going on behind the scenes of the tourist encounter (see also Stasch 2014). Suspicions of inauthenticity can become more meaningful in the general context of idealistic nostalgia described above. As one tourist explained to me: 'The community looks way too good to be true!' Representative of this point of view is a question I have heard many times in the course of my fieldwork: if the Emberá do, in real life, live in Parara Puru. The same question is sometimes put in a rather clumsy manner, such as 'Do you live here in the forest all the time?'

Behind this straightforward question, however, there often lies a more complicated tourist experience. Some well-travelled tourists have attended cultural presentations by other ethnic groups that take place in locations outside the indigenous community, such as sites of historic significance (see Bunten 2011) or settings especially prepared for tourist performances. These well-travelled tourists are aware that indigenous performers often perform in designated locations where they dress in traditional costume for the sole purpose of the tourism exchange (see Kirtsoglou and Theodossopoulos 2004). This comparative dimension in the critical thinking of some tourists represents a more widespread wariness towards the commodified nature of pre-arranged cultural presentations.

This wariness is sometimes directly expressed through questions focusing on the Emberá attire, such as 'Do you wear these clothes all day?' or 'Are you dressed like this every day?' Some tourist guides welcome these probing questions and make small ironic remarks in English, which they do not translate for the Emberá: 'I am interested to know the answer to that question as well' or 'Let us see how he [the Emberá leader] answers this question.' On these occasions, the guides find an opportunity to implicitly stress their modern subjectivity – perceived as parallel to that of their clients – by adopting a perspective that challenges the exotic as represented in the tourist encounter. The implication here is that the Emberá are not expected to maintain their traditional code of dress in daily life, a point that some tourist guides will openly admit and others tactfully conceal.

Responding diplomatically to questions of this type, the Emberá leaders who deliver 'the speech' try to provide answers that are factually true without completely demystifying the tourists' exoticising expectations. They explain that the government does not allow them to venture outside of their communities in traditional attire. Non-indigenous Panamanians, they add, are also obliged (by law) to cover their body in public. They also explain that when their visitors depart, the inhabitants of the community take off their adornments (e.g. necklaces and bracelets) to carry out their daily chores in a more comfortable manner. The women, some Emberá further clarify, wear their traditional *paruma*-skirts all day, and often outside of the community. All these statements are true: as a matter of principle, the Emberá of Parara Puru do not intentionally lie to enhance their self-representation. Yet, they cautiously avoid emphasising the fact that men, women and children do wear t-shirts both within and outside the community, while men also wear shorts.

As I will discuss in detail in Chapter 7, 'the problem of what to wear' – to use an expression by Tarlo (1996: 15) – is a serious topic for debate even within Emberá society. The questions of the tourists, however, reflect a Western perception of indigenous people as inhabiting an ambiguous position at the crossroads between tradition and modernity. There are other questions the tourists ask that indirectly address this ambiguous position, for example about health and education. Most tourists are fascinated to hear about Emberá shamans (*jaibanás*) and their knowledge of the medicinal properties of plants. They are also interested to know about the degree to which contemporary Emberá rely on the shamans' care and advice, so they frequently ask relevant questions and receive honest and direct answers. Some Emberá, the tourists are told, still rely on traditional medicine – sometimes, but not all the time. To solve more serious medical problems, they take conventional medicines and, if absolutely necessary, visit a medical centre or a hospital outside the community.

Questions about the education of the Emberá, as articulated by tourists in Parara Puru, often conceal the inadvertent recommendation that Emberá children living in the rainforest should not be deprived of educational opportunities. In this respect, the tourists' admiration of pre-modern cultural lifestyles gives way to their faith in the importance of school education. The residents of Parara Puru – like those of most other Emberá communities in Panama – share very similar pro-educational values and answer these questions without any ambivalence or hesitation, proudly stating that they have a primary school in the community and that they cherish the education of their children. After all, as I discussed in Chapter 3, primary education was one of the initial considerations that led the Emberá to form concentrated settlements. An issue that is not always made directly obvious to the tourists, but that concerns the Emberá, is that primary school education is delivered (in most communities) only in Spanish, as very few teachers are qualified to teach in the Emberá language and there are currently only a few appropriate textbooks that teach Emberá.

Other types of exploratory questions asked by the tourists in Parara Puru – usually at the end of the introductory speech and before the beginning of the dances – are, for the most part, less controversial, reflecting the traveller's ethnographic curiosity. For example, tourists frequently ask: 'Are you monogamous?' (usual reply: 'yes'); 'Where do you find partners to marry?' (usual reply: 'in neighbouring Emberá communities, or in Darién, where many Emberá live'); 'At what age do young people marry?' (usual reply: 'girls at 16, boys a bit older, unless they want to continue their education'); 'How do young people have fun?' (usual reply: 'sometimes in social gatherings in neighbouring Emberá and non-Emberá communities, sometimes locally'); 'Do you have a school in the community?' (usual reply: 'yes, up the hill, you can take a walk to see it if you like'). When some of the same questions are asked by non-indigenous Panamanians, such as Panamanian students on an educational trip, the Emberá of Parara Puru might provide additional details to their answers, making more apparent to their interlocutors that they live in the same nation and are not so different from them after all. For example, in these cases it is more openly admitted that many residents of Parara Puru go to neighbouring non-Emberá communities for entertainment, that apart from their own Emberá music they like to listen and dance to popular Panamanian musical genres (such as *típico*) and that when they go to the hospital they have to show their national identity card, like all Panamanian citizens.

Contradictory images of the exotic

The tourists that visit the Emberá communities at Chagres enter what looks from the outside like a remarkably different world: a landscape of rivers, lakes and rainforest vegetation, with small villages inhabited by Amerindians who emerge out of their thatched-roof houses dressed in traditional garb. This looks like a world lost in a primordial order of existence, a journey to a land that time forgot. This experience is recreated, again and again, during short excursions that combine a trip through a magnificent natural environment, the Chagres National Park, with an opportunity to get to know an indigenous Amerindian culture. In this case, the Emberá, a people that look – when dressed in traditional attire – like postcards of Amazonian Indians emerging through the rainforest.

This is a 'touristy', performatively enhanced vision of the Emberá world – one that catches the attention of Western visitors in the first instance, and directs their experience for the rest of the trip. The success of this vision of indigeneity relies on the interplay of two major exoticising images that mutually reinforce each other.

5.7 Emberá musicians

First, a naturalising identification of the indigenous people with the natural environment, and second, a profound other-worldliness, the illusion that the indigenous hosts emerge from a primordial time, statically (or magically) preserved in
isolation from Western civilisation. The second image is a good example of what
Fabian (1983) described as a denial of coevalness, the perception that some people, such as the classic subjects of anthropological enquiry (here, the inhabitants
of the rainforest), live in another time, parallel but not identical to that of the
Western observer. From the point of view of most tourists, the Emberá emerge as
an indigenous people frozen in time, dressed in the same manner as their ancestors: a present that is the same as the past.

It could be argued that the warm reception of Emberá culture by the international tourist audience is the by-product of such an essentialising gaze, which
is based on previously established Western preconceptions of the exotic. These
revolve around static images of an innocent past and the expectation of meeting some Amerindians who have evaded – by some coincidence – the influence
of Western civilisation. The overwhelming majority of the tourists feel that this
paradisiacal state of innocence is doomed to disappear, and they mourn – in a
way that is characteristic of what Rosaldo (1989) calls 'imperialist nostalgia' – the
irrevocable changes effected by modernity on indigenous society. In this nostalgic mood, the tourists that I met in Parara Puru attempted to recapture the lost
innocence of the human experience during their short visit among the Emberá;
they attempt to superimpose their own Western aesthetic of pre-modern authenticity on the indigenous Amerindian (Conklin 1997; Ramos 1998; Gow 2007;
Santos-Granero 2009).

In the course of the tourist encounter, however, primarily through the various exploratory questions the tourists ask, we can see a slightly more complicated
view emerging. This is the recognition that the Emberá, the guardians of a natural
mythical past, exist simultaneously in the present. The static image of a rainforest
people wearing the minimum amount of clothing becomes complicated by the

recognition that another world – with schools, hospitals and marketed goods – is out there, only a few miles outside the forest. The realisation that only a short distance, to use the words of an early-twentieth-century traveller of Panama, 'separates these primitive, painted, naked Indians from the roaring trains, the busy shops, the great hotels and the teeming, civilized, modern life' (Verrill 1921: 192).

With respect to the short perceptual distance that separates the enchanted world of the Indians from modernity, tourist expectations, as they are offered to the Emberá, are diverse and often contradictory. Some tourists express a desire to see the Emberá maintaining their 'ancient' way of life, demonstrating a strong adherence to tradition to the exclusion of modernity. Others are prepared to see the Emberá as inhabitants of the modern globalised world, people who share in the benefits, predicaments and technologies of the modern era while maintaining their identity. In the end, a few, primarily non-indigenous, Panamanian visitors are happy to accept that they share with the Emberá common tastes and experiences as citizens of the same nation and are not so different to them after all. Their scorn and irony for the 'less civilised' Indians – with the simultaneous expectation that the Indians will assimilate to mainstream society – encourages the modernisation of the Emberá and sharply contrasts with the idealising perspective of most international tourists, which promotes adherence to tradition and discourages change.

The discrepancies between the different tourist expectations described above represent some general orientations but are not, strictly speaking, prescriptive. There are many foreign, but also domestic, tourists who combine in their narratives these dissimilar perspectives. They see the Emberá as 'primitive' or 'less civilised' people but are happy to think that they will remain so, guardians of an original authentic state of human existence. Other tourists state that the Emberá 'should' become 'more civilised' and benefit from education and Western medicine, but, at the same time, they are sad to see the Emberá using mobile phones and wearing Western clothes or to hear that they often disregard the medical advice of the shamans. All the above perspectives on the Emberá are equally patronising, representative examples of what I referred earlier to as 'unintentional primitivisation', an ambivalent stance about the position of indigenous people in the present, which is simultaneously idealising and infantilising.

It has become apparent so far that the expectations of the tourists who visit the Emberá – despite their common reference to a static vision of indigeneity – are far from singular. Without relinquishing the romantic vision of the naked, natural, innocent Indian, the majority of the tourists appear concerned about the future of the Emberá and their 'fate' in a changing world. Contradictory and ambivalent attitudes that range from scorn to idealisation – or from partial-integration with modernity to total isolation – coexist in the comments of the same groups of tourists, or even the very same individual tourists, adding complexity to the tourist encounter. More importantly, however, these reproduce dilemmas, which, as we shall see in the next chapter, the Emberá try to decipher and tackle. In this respect our exploration of the Western expectations that haunt Emberá tourism has opened the way to appreciate the representational choices of the Emberá and the creative adaptations that accommodate such choices.

5.8   The tourists have just departed

Box 6

The Emberá as primordial Amerindians in film

The image of the Emberá dressed in traditional attire – body-painted, adorned with beaded necklaces and dressed only with minimal cotton clothing – falls within conventional registers of indigeneity in Western imagination. In this respect, the Emberá – and the Wounaan who use similar adornments – are often seen as representative icons of the generic, undifferentiated Amerindian, a representation perpetuated by the Western film industry. In a reciprocal manner, the Emberá and the Wounaan have played a small role in contributing to this generalised Western imagery. Below I present some representative examples.

- Wounaan from the Colombian Chocó impersonated the Guarani Indians in the well-known film, *The Mission* (1986). As the director revealed in a recent director's commentary, the Wounaan received body-painting lessons from neighbouring Emberá. An Emberá woman, for example, taught a younger Wounaan woman how to paint parallel lines on Robert De Niro's body, using a painting stick with three points (see Torres 1980: 169;

Isacsson 1993: 33; Pineda and Gutiérrez de Pineda 1999: 113; Reverte Coma 2002: 225; Ulloa 1992: 181; see Chapter 2). In the particular scene, the medium of body painting is used to represent an outsider's inclusion into the tribe, in a manner that resembles Richard Marsh's mimetic transformation to an Emberá during his expedition in 1924–1925 (see Chapters 4 and 8).

- The Wounaan, including some of the same individuals who participated in *The Mission*, have also impersonated the Carib Taíno in *1492: Conquest of Paradise* (1992). Once more, their appearance becomes emblematic of the undifferentiated Amerindian, a naturalised image extended in this film to represent *indigeneity* before the conquest.

- Emberá from Chagres, including several residents of Parara Puru and neighbouring communities, participated in the docudrama *End of the Spear* (2005), which recalls the story of five American evangelical missionaries and their attempts to convert the Ecuadorian Waodani (Huaorani), played in the film by the Emberá. Here, the representational confidence of the Chagres Emberá – who are used to dressing in indigenous attire for tourism – captures the spirit of an untamed Amerindian tribe that resists contact with outsiders, despite its 'inevitable' – in nostalgic terms – evangelisation. During filming, an North American member of the film crew, Anne Gordon de Barrigón, met her Emberá husband. Anne and her husband now run a tourism agency, which is not aggressively commercial and specialises in indigenous tourism.

- In all films mentioned above, the Wounaan and Emberá speak their indigenous languages. From the perspective of the Western viewer, this particular choice conveys a sense of Amerindian authenticity. The Emberá of Chagres shared with me fond memories of their participation in the film *End of the Spear*. They are proud that they spoke their language in the film, while those who currently follow evangelical churches underlined their sympathy with the film's Christian message.

- In an episode of the television series *Man vs. Wild*, the British explorer and survival specialist Bear Grylls treks along the rainforest of Chagres National Park, accompanied by three local Emberá men from one of the communities that regularly entertain tourists. The men teach Bear Grylls how to use bows, arrows and blow darts – weapons that the Emberá stopped using several decades ago. The Emberá men adapt to the exoticising expectations of their guest, although their lack of experience with the particular hunting technologies is visible. As with most other episodes of the series, the camera lens focuses on Bear Grylls and his accomplishments. The Emberá enter the scene as secondary characters, naturalised as rainforest people, experts in survival skills. Bear Grylls mentions that 'these guys' have taught 'the first astronauts how to survive if their capsule landed in the jungle' – alluding to Antonio Zarco, the

apical settler of Chagres, who worked as a survival skills instructor for
NASA (see Chapters 6 and 9).
- The Emberá of Chagres were briefly visited by the brides and groom of the
  reality television series *The Bachelor* (Season 16, Week 6, February 2012).
  The Western visitors were body-painted and dressed in Emberá attire, as
  has become customary lately among tourists and visiting students. This
  appears to be a much older practice of 'inclusion into the tribe' as testi-
  fied by the example of Richard Marsh. I discuss further examples of such
  mimetic practices of self-exoticisation in Chapter 8.

Notes

1 Although, as I have explained before, the men in some communities that have developed
  tourism refuse to wear the skirt-like belt known among the Emberá as *amburá*.
2 The tourist guides are the employees or owners of Panamanian tourism agencies.
  Most of them are Panamanians with sufficient knowledge of at least one foreign language: English, French, German or Italian. Some are native speakers of these languages
  who now live permanently in Panama. A North American tourist guide, Anne Gordon
  de Barrigón, is married to a local Emberá man with whom she runs a small but culturally
  sensitive tourism agency that specialises in Emberá excursions.
3 Another canoe landing area used by the Emberá is at Nuevo Vigía, a non-indigenous
  community from which the Emberá of Parara Puru often buy food supplies. Nuevo
  Vigía is used primarily by two other Emberá communities at Chagres, Emberá Puru and
  La Bonga, located on the San Juan de Pequeni river. Nuevo Vigía is farther away from
  the Chagres, and the tourist groups who use it as their embarkation spot benefit from a
  longer canoe trip along Lake Alajuela and beautiful landscape views, close to the ancient
  route Camino Real (see Mendizábal and Theodossopoulos 2012).
4 The community is named after a nineteenth-century national hero and revolutionary who
  is well known in Panama. The Emberá consider it to be a Latino community, although
  it includes several Emberá households. Most of the current inhabitants of Tusipono and
  Parara Puru lived in Victoriano Lorenzo – for shorter or longer periods of time – before
  the establishment of homogenous Emberá communities.
5 They do not charge the tourists extra for these photographs. From their point of view,
  they are already prepared and dressed accordingly for hosting outsiders and representing their culture to them. Posing in traditional attire for photos is seen by the Emberá in
  Chagres as an aspect of Emberá cultural representation.
6 Parara Puru maintains two such communal buildings to entertain different groups of
  tourists simultaneously. Yet most Emberá communities who receive tourists, or aspire to
  do so, have only one.
7 I have already explained this in equally static terms in Chapter 2.
8 For a detailed description of rumba- and cumbia-Emberá and changes to, or adaptations
  of, these dances, see Theodossopoulos 2013c.

6

Representational self-awareness

For those Emberá who are actively involved in tourism, the positive attention of their foreign visitors is a new experience. The Emberá who are adults today were raised with the expectation – originating from wider Panamanian society – that they should learn Spanish, dress in modern clothes and adopt Western civilisational practices. In the context of previous discrimination and stereotyping in Panama, Emberá culture and the traditional Emberá dress code in particular were characterised as 'primitive' or 'uncivilised'. Now that Emberá tourism has taken off, the Emberá are receiving a different message. They realise that their culture is enthusiastically received and respected by individuals who come from countries more economically powerful than Panama. This realisation encourages the Emberá to identify more strongly with their culture, and in turn to project their indigenous identity to outsiders more confidently. Instead of withdrawing from the world of the *kampuniá* (the non-Emberá), an adaptation strategy that served them well in the past (Williams 2004), they are now reaching out to the international community and gradually taking advantage of the new representational opportunities offered by an increasingly globalised world (Theodossopoulos 2010b; see also Comaroff and Comaroff 2009; Strathern and Stewart 2010).

The new representational opportunities made available by tourism and, more importantly, the choices made by the Emberá about their self-representation in tourism provide us with a very good opportunity to investigate the intersections of two interrelated processes. The first of these two processes relates to the growing desire of the Emberá at Chagres to meet the exoticising expectations of international tourists who valorise certain aspects of their culture – including practices associated with the times of the grandparents – that were previously stereotyped negatively by non-indigenous Panamanians. Through frequent contact with tourists, some Emberá acquire the self-confidence to aspire, not merely to satisfy the tourists' expectations, but also to guide the tourists into their world, to teach them about all things Emberá. The second process I examine in this chapter relates to the growing concern of the Emberá at Chagres about how best to represent their culture, what aspects of it to make available for viewing and in what form. Their renewed interest in the details of their culture represents an emerging representational self-awareness; it encourages a search for new or forgotten knowledge about

6.1 Towards a more confident self-representation

one's own cultural distinctiveness and stimulates a more confident articulation of this knowledge in a form that can be presented to outsiders.

Bunten (2008: 381) has referred to this type of more confident self-representation as self-commodification: the construction of a marketable identity for the tourist encounter, but one that does not alienate the indigenous host. The wider field of the anthropology of tourism has encouraged social analysis to move away from the static view of culture commodification as culture loss, and highlight instead how the tourist encounter encourages indigenous hosts to rediscover, reflect upon and reconstitute their indigenous traditions (Abram and Waldren 1997; see also Graburn 1976; Smith 1989; Swain 1989; Selwyn 1996; Boissevain 1996; Stronza 2001; Coleman and Crang 2002; Bruner 2005; Leite and Graburn 2009; Salazar 2010). The dynamic and actor-oriented approach promoted by the anthropology of tourism informs my analysis of how the Emberá accommodate some of the representational dilemmas arising from tourism.

In the context of presentations for tourists, the established way of following older practices is augmented with the spontaneous discovery of new motifs and variations. This reorganisation of new and old cultural elements emerges organically in daily life as the Emberá adapt to new circumstances or collect new information from other Emberá. To the degree that cultural improvisation is 'intrinsic to the very processes of social and cultural life' (Ingold and Hallam 2007: 19), the Emberá representational improvisations – and the introduction of new sets of knowledge acquired by friends, neighbours or through repeated practice – emerge 'from within the local cultural matrix' (Bruner 2005: 5) and represent, to a lesser or greater extent, creative solutions to new challenges. Yet, as we shall see, different local views of authenticity – conceived as representativeness – may complicate Emberá representation as it grows in confidence.

It is time now to focus more closely on the Emberá experience of the transformations encouraged by tourism as this emerges from the bottom up. In this and the following two chapters, I will pay closer attention to the decisions and views of the

Emberá of Parara Puru, the community where I conducted my fieldwork, which is renowned in Panama for its successful engagement with tourism. Before I discuss the representational self-awareness and dilemmas faced by the residents of Parara, I would like to briefly describe the foundation of their community. Initially, it was established because of a desire to develop tourism, but in time the foundation of the community encouraged among its members the development of a more explicit indigenous consciousness, in the political and ethnic sense.

Founding a community to accommodate tourism

In the mid-twentieth century, as the Emberá population in Darién increased, small numbers of Emberá moved to uninhabited locations closer to Panama City and the Canal area (Caballero and Araúz 1962; Herlihy 1986). This is how the first Emberá arrived at the river Chagres, where Parara Puru is now located, and settled in the forested areas that now comprise the Chagres National Park. They first settled, following the old residence pattern, in dispersed settlement and enjoyed an initial period of relative freedom from external control, a time when game, fish and lumber were abundant. 'That was a good time for us', the older Emberá of Chagres remember.

Antonio Zarco – also known as Tomé – the grandfather of the founders of Parara Puru, arrived at Chagres in the years following the Second World War, a time when all Emberá lived in dispersed settlement. He lived there for several years, enjoying access to the natural resources of – what was at the time – a large uninhabited forested area. Tomé, who grew up in Darién – on the river Chico – made the most of the opportunities provided by his migration to the westernmost point of Emberá geographical distribution. His reputation spread across the Emberá world after he had worked for the US military as an instructor in jungle survival skills for several seasons. He trained all sorts of elite US forces, but also astronauts (see Koster 2005). The narratives of many contemporary tourist guides draw heavily on his achievements and personal myth: stories are told to the tourists about this amazing Indian who knew how to be invisible in the forest and taught astronauts how to survive in inhospitable environments.

Over the course of his lifetime, Tomé moved his residence to several other forested locations in the Canal area, each time inviting different groups of consanguineal and affinal relatives from Darién to live with him. They, in turn, invited their own relatives, a movement that contributed to the first wave of Emberá migration to Chagres in the 1950s and 1960s. Caballero and Araúz (1962), who studied the movement of the Emberá to Chagres in the early 1960s, trace the migration histories of particular families to particular rivers in Darién, such as the rivers Chico, Balsa and Sambú, and further corroborate the dispersed pattern of Emberá settlement in Chagres. After losing his first wife, Tomé remarried a Wounaan woman and moved closer to the Canal, to a small lake island in Gamboa where another Emberá community gradually developed, including a few Wounaan families (related to Tomé's second wife). The children from his first marriage remained at Chagres, and their children eventually became the leaders and founders of

6.2   A sketch of Tomé

Parara Puru, while his other descendants contributed to the foundation of two additional communities in the general Chagres area (Tusipono, Emberá Puru).

While the first generation of Emberá at Chagres benefited from unregulated access to natural resources – a central narrative theme of the elderly – their relationship with the land was altered by the foundation of a national park in 1985. The park imposed restrictions on hunting and cultivation (see Candanedo, Ponce and Riquelme 2003). Throughout the twentieth century, cultivation of plantains (primarily), rice and maize (to a lesser extent) and lumber provided the Emberá in Panama with cash to buy commodities from the market (see Herlihy 1986; Loewen 1975). Deprived of these economic opportunities, the Emberá of Chagres had to resort to paid labour in the non-Emberá world. Some among them moved to the outskirts of non-indigenous communities, such as Victoriano Lorenzo, located at the point where river Chagres meets lake Alajuela, and survived by taking on seasonal work for non-indigenous employers. As I will soon make clear, the experimental introduction of tourism in the early- and mid-1990s was received by the second generation of Emberá at Chagres not merely as an economic solution, but also as an opportunity to organise themselves politically.

In the meantime, the larger Emberá population in Darién was already considering the possibility of resettling in concentrated communities with elected representatives and primary schools. As I explained in Chapter 2, this movement started at a slow pace in the 1950s and took off in the 1960s and 1970s (Herlihy 1986), leading to the foundation of a semi-independent reservation (the Comarca Emberá-Wounaan). Although approximately half of the Emberá population in Panama remained outside the borders of the *comarca* (Colin 2010), the overwhelming majority resettled in concentrated villages, with political representatives, small shops (with basic commodities) and primary schools. Community formation facilitated the integration of the Emberá into national political structures (see Herlihy 1986; Kane 1994) and signalled the reorganisation of Emberá social life at the local level.

During the early 1990s, there was only one politically organised community at Chagres, Emberá Drua, founded by a group of Emberá who emigrated from Darién in the 1970s. These Emberá had benefited from the developing political awareness of broader Emberá society in Darién, an experience that guided their settlement pattern in Chagres. In comparison with this later group, the descendants of the families who migrated to Chagres in the 1950s – the Chagres-born Emberá[1] – were disorganised politically and lacked protection against the possibility of being evicted by the authorities of the national park. Evaluating this period retrospectively, the leaders of Parara Puru highlight how their previous dispersed settlement resulted in disunity and promoted individualism. It was not easy, they add, to organise themselves in communities and agree on a common plan for the future, or to establish rules. The financial rewards of tourism and the prospect of some degree of political representation, encouraged a group of Chagres-born Emberá families to overcome their initial reservations and establish ethnically homogenous communities with elected representatives. The case of Parara Puru is a representative example.[2]

In the early 1990s a group of Chagres-born Emberá started experimenting with delivering cultural presentations for tourists in an accessible forested location on the Chagres. To reach that site the tourists had to board dugout canoes, but only for a relatively short and safe ride, which added to the ambience of the tourism product. At first, the Emberá built a 'model' indigenous village[3] for the purpose of entertaining groups of tourists visiting from the city, but the park authorities, who carefully monitor and regulate human activity within the park, did not allow the Emberá to reside permanently in this new location. The success of the initial experimentation with tourism, however, was so immediate – and in line with Panama's policy towards tourism development (see Guerrón-Montero 2006a) – that this particular group of Emberá was granted permission in 1998 to found a new community on a different site farther up the river Chagres. This group of Emberá founded Parara Puru, one of the five Emberá communities within the park.[4]

For the residents of Parara, who grew up in dispersed settlement at the fringes of Emberá society surrounded by a non-indigenous majority, the establishment of homogenous Emberá communities was an issue of vital importance to the maintenance of a distinctive cultural identity.[5] During the difficult years that followed the establishment of the national park, and under the pressure of the park restrictions, several Emberá families from Chagres had moved closer to impoverished Latino settlements. Reflecting on this period, the Emberá of today describe how their children played with non-Emberá children and did not use the Emberá language, while the adults worked for non-indigenous employers. Many of them conclude that, were it not for tourism, their children would by now have become indistinguishable from their Latino neighbours, as often happens to the children of Emberá who migrate to Panama City.

Seen from this perspective, the development of tourism changed the life of the Emberá at Chagres in more than one respect. Firstly, they now have a sustainable

(a)   (b)

6.3a Sketch of señora Delia inspired by an old photograph, taken at Chagres in the 1960s (before the establishment of concentrated Emberá communities)

6.3b Sketch of señora Delia in year 2011. She now lives in Parara Puru, an ethnically homogenous and spatially concentrated Emberá community

occupation with a low environmental impact, enabling them to remain in the park without relying on readily available natural resources, violating the park's environmental regulations. In this respect, indigenous tourism is in line with the green discourse promoted by the park authorities (see Candanedo, Ponce and Riquelme 2003), an overlap that solidified the claim of the Emberá to remain at Chagres and establish new settlements. Secondly, and more importantly, the introduction of tourism opened a gateway for the reorganisation of their political and social life in ethnically homogenous communities. The coordination required to deliver cultural presentations for tourists encouraged cooperation, and gradually stimulated community spirit. To succeed in tourism, the Emberá had to bring together their individual skills, memories and knowledge in a common pool – a cooperative way of thinking that diverged from the individualism of pre-community Emberá life.

The experience of living in an ethnically homogenous community encouraged a sense of safety, confidence and independence. This allowed the Emberá of Parara to hold firm control of the tourist exchange and work towards 'the promotion of their cultural traditions', which, as they point out, are enhanced and rejuvenated by tourism. Working with tourists is a demanding job, most residents of Parara admit – it keeps them busy for most of the year and offers very few opportunities for vacations. However, almost all of them are willing to recognise that the financial rewards of this new occupation are higher than agriculture or temporary manual labour among the wider non-indigenous society. 'Playing music, dancing and talking to tourists about your own culture', several members of the community say, 'is more enjoyable than cultivating rice or plantains.' Work in tourism, they add in almost unanimous agreement, allows one to continue practising one's 'own culture' or 'traditions' without having to live in extreme poverty.

Proud of their community, the residents of Parara Puru allow the tourists to walk freely beyond the entertainment area, hoping that the tourists will realise that this is indeed the place where the Emberá live, not merely a stage for entertainment or a 'model' village. From their point of view, living permanently in a homogenous Emberá community is a sign of authenticity: like many other communities in Eastern Panama, they have their own leadership and participate in broader political initiatives, such as that of the *Tierras Colectivas*, which lobbies for the recognition of indigenous land (Velásquez Runk 2012; see Chapter 3). In addition, they do not have to travel out of the community to find work or compromise their indigenous identity by following the rules of the *kampuniá*, those who are not Emberá. It is in all these respects that the foundation of their community and their engagement with tourism have provided the Emberá of Parara with a good living and an opportunity to reconnect with their indigenous identity, politically and culturally.

Dilemmas about the authenticity of the built environment

As we have already seen, the founders of Parara Puru were born in Chagres to parents who had migrated from Darién fifty years ago. They chose the location for the community after carefully evaluating the practical implications of regularly receiving and entertaining small and large groups of visitors. For example, the community is built next to the river – like all Emberá communities – and it is located on a site where the river's flow accommodates the transportation of tourists during both dry and rainy seasons. The residents of Parara Puru frequently compare their community's position on the Chagres with that of the other two Emberá communities on the same river. For example, the community of Tusipono (downstream) is seen as being located 'too close to the lake and the main road' – in the exact position where the residents of Parara Puru in the mid-1990s built their temporary 'model' village, while the community of Emberá Drua (upstream) is 'too far away', which makes transport by motorised canoes expensive, even more so with the rising prices of gasoline. 'We are in the perfect place here at Chagres', said a man from Parara Puru while watching the boatmen from Emberá Drua struggling to pole their canoes – weighed down by tourists – upstream. 'We are neither too close to the lake, nor too far away!'

This pragmatic approach to settlement with respect to choosing a particular river sector for its potential advantages has been noted in academic literature about the Emberá and the Wounaan (see, for example, Faron 1962; Herlihy 1986; Velásquez Runk 2009). In the period before the foundation of concentrated communities, the Emberá used to choose their sites of settlement according to practical criteria, such as the availability of land for cultivation, fish and game, lumber or other resources. The Emberá at Chagres see the tourists as another available resource (see Theodossopoulos 2010a). Unsurprisingly, the Emberá communities in the wider Canal area have factored into their settlement strategies the issue of tourist access, as easily accessible locations attract greater numbers of tourists. Seen from this perspective, the new involvement of the Emberá with the economy of tourism is just another Emberá adaptation strategy.

When it comes to cultural representation in tourism, however, the flexible and pragmatic Emberá spirit of engaging with the world stumbles upon the exoticising essentialism of the tourist gaze. As we saw in the previous chapter, a great number of tourists are preoccupied with an elusive, yet static, vision of authenticity. They want to experience an indigenous culture isolated from Western civilisation, a world unaffected by modernity. The Emberá involved in tourism are aware of this particular expectation, which easily translates to the Emberá view of how their grandparents lived their lives: in dispersed settlement, using very few Western clothes and a smaller amount of market-bought goods. The communities that rely on tourism more heavily, such as those in Chagres and the wider Canal area, attempt to recapture this older aesthetic of what constitutes the 'traditional' and take it into consideration when managing their built environment and its immediate surroundings. Yet, as I will explain shortly, they often struggle to accommodate the tourist vision of authenticity because they are negotiating between two different standards of authenticity of their own.

A good example of this process is the special care taken by the Emberá to construct their houses according to the conventions of traditional Emberá architecture. Since the foundation of the community, the residents of Parara Puru have tried to respect, to the degree that this is realistic, traditional architecture, in an effort to present their visitors with yet another aspect of Emberá culture, but also to communicate indirectly their view that theirs is an authentic Emberá community. As in most ethnically homogenous Emberá communities in Eastern Panama, the houses in Parara Puru are built on stilts and have thatched roofs woven primarily from two types of palm leaf, one of which – wagara (Sabal mauritiiformis) – is rare in the vicinity.[6] The community resorts to purchasing considerable quantities of wagara from other locations in Eastern Panama at a rather high price. In applying such traditional materials at considerable cost, the residents of Parara are attempting to comply with one of the two main Emberá views of authentic representation, which identifies with Emberá customary practices in the times of dispersed settlement, or 'the times of the grandparents'.

Nonetheless, the houses in most other Emberá communities in Eastern Panama – that have not developed tourism on a full-time basis – do not match very closely with the stylistic requirements of the purely 'traditional' Emberá house. It is true that most houses in these communities are built on stilts and according to a recognisably Emberá structural pattern – a basic square with extensions built at later stages to accommodate a growing family. Yet many of these houses have corrugated-iron roofs and walls made of planks, reeds or corrugated iron (a deviation from the old principle that Emberá houses 'have no walls'). The old-fashioned traditional floors made from strips of *jira* bark are often replaced by planks, although the softer material of *jira* is still used in the parts of the flooring reserved as sitting or sleeping quarters. Furthermore, many Emberá houses in Eastern Panama organically incorporate a good number of electrical devices – powered by gasoline electricity generators located in their basements – as well as a plethora of plastic and aluminium utensils.

The adaptations described above set a second standard of what constitutes a representative Emberá house, one that is related to life in ethnically homogenous, concentrated communities. It corresponds with a more fluid view of Emberá authenticity, one that incorporates modern influences within a distinctly Emberá pattern of spatial organisation and process. Twenty-first-century Emberá houses are distinctly Emberá, not only because they are built on stilts and follow a time-honoured structural design, but also because they enable – in a fluid and adaptable way, and as in the past – the realisation of extensions and smaller transformations that accommodate the changing requirements of the growing Emberá family. More or less all of the residents of Parara Puru adopt this flexible approach, feeling constrained by inflexible, old-fashioned ideas about how 'a traditional Emberá house' should be.

In reality, all family houses in Parara Puru deviate to a smaller or greater extent from the rigid norm of the 'traditional' – where tradition is equated with the old times, incorporating elements that are common in Emberá communities that do not entertain tourists. In this case, we can clearly see two standards of the representativeness of the Emberá house competing with each other: one representing the way of life of the grandparents (who lived in open houses on stilts, with thatched roofs) and another the way of life of most contemporary Emberá (who live in houses on stilts structurally similar to those of the grandparents, but which have walls, electric appliances and often tin roofs). The residents of Parara navigate through such (partly conflicting) views of representativeness on a day-to-day basis. They know that if they overstress the traditional image of the community, they risk being accused of presenting a lie, a reenactment of their very real lives. Thus, both types of representativeness – 'we live as our grandparents' and 'we live like most other Emberá' – matter to the residents of Parara.

With respect to the architecture of Parara Puru, its residents unanimously avoid, to the degree that it is possible, corrugated iron. Tin roofs, they maintain, although cheaper than thatched roofs (and easier to maintain), make houses uncomfortably hot and spoil the appearance of the community, which relies on tourism for its economic survival. In fact, Emberá thatched roofs are appreciated and admired – not only by the tourists, who are unaware of the skill required for their construction, but also by the Emberá themselves, including those living in communities that extensively resort to using corrugated-iron roofs. Relatively inaccessible Emberá communities that do not attract sustainable numbers of tourists, take care to construct – in their hope that they may be able to enhance tourism – communal houses with beautifully developed thatched roofs.[7]

In contrast, the now-widespread Emberá preference for walled – as opposed to open – houses represents a more direct departure from the old-time dwelling ideal. All residents of Parara Puru construct walls around their sleeping quarters with planks, plywood or reeds, although sometimes they leave a side of the house open or semi-covered to allow the rare wind to enter, or to use as a balcony with a view. The old-style houses 'without walls', most Emberá of Parara agree, allowed breezes to circulate, yet they add that a certain amount of wall partitioning is necessary, as it provides welcome privacy. 'We do live here in this community', one of the leaders of the community frequently repeats to confront the expectation that all buildings and their immediate surroundings should look 'traditional' in a flawless, almost sanitised, manner.

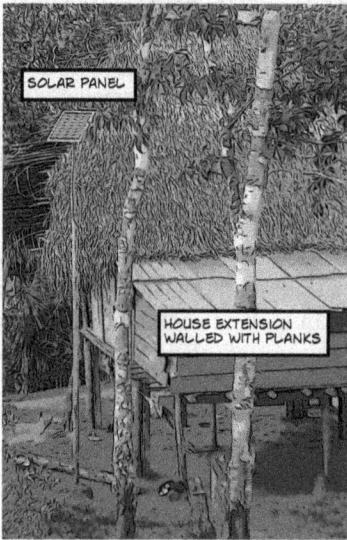

SOLAR PANEL

HOUSE EXTENSION WALLED WITH PLANKS

6.4 Indigenous-and-modern Emberá house

Thus, although the buildings constructed specifically for the tourist presentations 'do not have walls', the dwelling quarters of all local families are sheltered, or partially sheltered, from view.[8] Hidden from view are also a good number of heterogeneous items – electric devices, plastic toys and utensils, or bags of modern clothes – which are kept behind closed doors, especially during the tourist encounter. Not all Parara residents are successful in concealing modern items in their houses. Even the houses themselves, which are continually repaired or extended, sometimes diverge, to a greater or lesser degree, from the ideals set by the community. Therefore, most houses represent a compromise between the normative view of the 'traditional Emberá house' (frozen in time) and the contemporary Emberá house as seen in communities that do not receive tourists.

The leaders of the community have to continually reassess such deviations, and, in most cases, those who have digressed eventually comply, albeit unwillingly. For example in 2010, one man chose to replace the wooden posts supporting his house with cement columns erected in an Emberá fashion as if they were wooden stilts (to support a wooden house with a thatched roof). This creative adaptation was criticised by several members of the community as contradicting the 'traditional' character of the community. By the time the issue was discussed at the community meeting, some tourists had already spotted the cement columns and communicated their observation – 'We saw an inauthentic Emberá house with cement columns' – to the travel agents. The travel agents, in turn, informed the leader responsible for tourism. The next day, the cement columns were covered, from top to bottom, with reeds, creating the illusion that they were indeed poles made from natural material.

This and other similar examples – television antennae or cement bricks that had to be concealed – can help us to appreciate that only a thin line separates the two different standards of Emberá authenticity that are negotiated in everyday life. The first relates to an ethos of adapting to new circumstances, which embraces certain aspects of modernity and certain types of non-indigenous material culture. The second relates to a static view of 'tradition' as representative of an Emberá past frozen in the time of the grandparents. As I will elaborate further in the following chapter, these two parallel standards of what constitutes a representative Emberá way of life – the ways of the grandparents versus life in ethnically homogenous, concentrated communities – often overlap, creating new dilemmas and challenges for Emberá representation.

Such internal dilemmas inspire a continuous dialogue about representation within Parara Puru, yet on one general point all local residents agree: Parara Puru is first and foremost a real Emberá community, where Emberá culture is made available for observation by outsiders, but where it is also explained and respected. Thus, despite its orientation towards tourism, Parara Puru should not be viewed as a tourist enclave: the community's spaces and their aesthetics are not completely 'regulated, commodified and privatised' (Edensor 1998: 47). There is an absence of high-end tourist facilities, while the majority of houses within the community are heavily inhabited spaces and, as with all Emberá houses, are subject to continuous repair and readjustment, often reusing the materials – wooden poles, palm leaves, palm bark or planks.[9] In all these respects, Emberá culture – flexible, pragmatic and contemporary – rules over the representation of Emberá culture as statically conceived.

Emberá interest in the details of their own traditional culture

In the communities that regularly receive tourists, such as Parara Puru, the Emberá spend a great deal of time practising several performative and artistic aspects of their culture. This frequent practice has stirred a more general concern with the details of cultural representation. Month after month, year after year, the Emberá who 'work with tourists' – as many members of the community say – become more experienced artists, dancers, storytellers and guides to the Emberá tradition. Through daily practice, they share more opportunities to spontaneously improvise, introduce new patterns or designs to established motifs, incorporate new materials into traditional techniques and include additional information in customary sets of knowledge and narratives. Small fragments of partly forgotten information about Emberá history and tradition are collected and integrated into new narratives, or used to elaborate on contemporary practices.

The residents of Parara Puru maintain that tourism has provided them with an opportunity to spend more time practising their culture. They now devote more

6.5 Women in Parara rehearsing animal dances while the tourists are not around

time to manufacturing Emberá artefacts to sell to tourists, with a greater range of motifs and variations. They dance their traditional dances daily (as opposed to only on special occasions, such as shamanic ceremonies or community celebrations) and have, as a result, more opportunities to exercise their talent as dancers or musicians with a much wider repertoire of theme variations. They have also become skilled at better articulating the particularities of their culture, for instance describing or explaining artefacts, buildings, elements of the physical and man-made environment, manufacturing techniques, cultural traditions and performances. Through daily practice and improvisation, enabled by carrying out cultural presentations, they contribute new elements to the wealth of their culture, opening new possibilities for being Emberá in the contemporary world.

Frequent contact with outsiders has provided the Emberá who regularly work with tourists the know-how to anticipate some of the most common questions the tourists ask. 'Little by little we learned how to talk to the tourists', explained one of the older members of the community, 'we now have something to say for every question.' As we saw in the previous chapter, foreign tourists and Panamanian visitors have slightly different expectations and are likely to admire or criticise different aspects of indigenous life. The Emberá of Parara pay very careful attention to these subtle differentiations in the expectations of their guests and adapt their narratives accordingly, stressing slightly different aspects of their daily lives. For example they might, to some extent, underplay the differences between them and their Panamanian visitors – or stress common experiences – in an attempt to demonstrate that they too are citizens of the same nation. Conversely, they tend to accentuate their cultural distinctiveness for North American audiences.

These adaptations can help us appreciate that the Emberá are well aware that the expectations of the outside world are diverse and complex, and that this complexity can open up a whole world of possibilities for the representation of indigenous culture. For example, it is already apparent to most Emberá in Parara Puru that while, until twenty years ago, the non-indigenous majority in Panama maintained a discriminatory attitude towards the Emberá indigenous identity, international tourists, in their overwhelming majority, do not hide their appreciation of Emberá indigenous traditions. In a similar manner, an increasing number of the Panamanian middle class appear to be interested in learning more about Emberá culture, and are willing – at least at the level of rhetoric – to partly reconsider their previous negative stereotypes. Some visit Parara with their families and encourage their children to learn about the indigenous people of their country.

More generally, emerging Emberá awareness of the changing expectations of the outside world has inspired a growing interest in the subtle dimensions and details of Emberá culture. As I will explain in the following section, this often takes the form of collective introspection, a concern with the history of the Emberá tradition and the 'truthfulness' of its representation. Now that a wider non-Emberá audience is increasingly paying attention to the Emberá, they feel a growing responsibility to represent their culture in the best way they can. In the course of seven successive periods of fieldwork in Parara Puru, from 2005 to 2012, I had the opportunity to observe these nuanced changes in perspective. Year after year, as I returned to Parara for another two-to-three months, I saw new Emberá individuals – men and women – stepping forward and progressively taking a more active role in guiding the visitors, narrating the history of the community or explaining the manufacture of artefacts, the particulars of the dress code or specific elements of indigenous life. Younger men assisted the busier older men in guiding tourists around the community or the nearby rainforest, explaining buildings, artefacts and natural species. Since 2010 the women of Parara have started participating in the explanatory speech delivered by the leaders of the community to the tourists,[10] taking over the part of this presentation that explicates the art of basketry and women's attire.[11]

The increased participation of women and younger men in presentations for the tourists has meant that they have become confident speaking in front of an audience. This experience has motivated them to think about the representation of Emberá culture and invest some time and effort in developing a vocabulary – in Spanish – and their own personal style of articulating their ideas in a narrative they created for themselves and about themselves. Fifteen to seventeen years since their first encounters with tourism, the Emberá of Parara have learned how to speak about their cultural identity more fluently than before. This is a transferable skill that the Emberá gradually put into use – not merely in the context of tourism, but at any time they need to explain their culture to outsiders.

In this respect, the representational confidence acquired because of tourism has engendered the transformation of Emberá indigeneity from a liability (and an object of negative stereotyping) to a political, economic and representational asset. The gradual development of an increasingly self-assured self-representation in tourism has equipped a greater number of Emberá in Chagres with the vocabulary and the presentational confidence to insert the clause 'my culture' into a number of arguments or evaluations about Emberá practices or the practices of non-indigenous Panamanians. 'I prefer Emberá music to *típico*, the music of the farmers' (*campesinos*, used here derogatively), argued an Emberá man in the presence of two Latino friends, 'I prefer the music of my culture!' 'I like wearing my *paruma*-skirt in the town', stated a young Emberá women, raising her voice so that her modernising sisters could hear her. 'I like to wear Emberá clothes; this is my culture!'

Searching for new and old representational knowledge

Despite the confidence instilled into Emberá representational narratives through tourism, the collective pool of knowledge about Emberá culture in small communities such as Parara Puru – located at the fringes of the Emberá world – is not always sufficient to cover all potential topics of conversation or cultural practices. This is why the majority of the residents of Parara, like amateur ethnographers, have their ears open for additional pieces of information that could be gathered during conversations with Emberá from other communities. Knowledge about cultural issues can make a difference in negotiating tourist expectations, and in this respect the knowledge of neighbours and friends becomes a valuable resource (see Tucker 2011; Bunten 2011). In Parara newly acquired information is shared throughout the community at speed, between family members and from one family to another, especially when the new information in question can add to the tourist encounter.

In some cases, the Emberá of Parara introduce minor revisions to their cultural presentations, inspired by conversations they have with Emberá from other communities, or in some cases the travel agents who have visited more than one community. On one occasion, for example, I observed a small change in the daily dance presentations that occurred within less than a week. Rumba-Emberá had so far been performed in pairs, with the dancers positioned side-by-side, moving in a circular procession in a manner choreographically similar to cumbia-Emberá.[12] One day in April 2008, the inhabitants of Parara Puru started dancing the rumba-Emberá in a face-to-face position and in a freestyle manner – not in procession as before. The change described above was evidently small and involved the choreographic arrangement of the dancing couples, while the music of the dance remained the same. Given that I was concerned at the time with the details of the Emberá dance tradition (see Theodossopoulos 2013c), I was immediately struck by the changes and enquired on the issue persistently. I was given, in most cases, more or less the same answer: 'The new way is the correct way to dance rumba-Emberá.'

Considering the small size of the community, it was easy to identify the individuals who had introduced this small change in the style of the dance and their rationale for implementing it. In the Chagres area, Emberá numbers are small, and their experience dancing rumba-Emberá before the introduction of tourism was very limited. It soon became apparent that the new freestyle arrangement of the dancing couples was closer to the way the Emberá dance rumba in Darién, where dancing is more established. So the residents of Parara Puru adapted the way they danced rumba-Emberá to a more spontaneous dancing style, which was seen by several members of the community – including those born in Darién and married to local Chagres Emberá – as more authentic. Here, as we see, authenticity was conceived in terms of how the Emberá dance in other communities that have not developed tourism.

The community continued to dance rumba-Emberá according to the Darién style until 2011. However, when I returned to Parara Puru in 2012, I noticed that the community had reverted back to dancing rumba-Emberá according to the older, more rigid, 'as following a procession' style followed before 2008. Immediately, I started to investigate the rationale for this second change, only to be told that, yes, indeed, 'We have changed the way we dance rumba again.' In 2012, most of my Emberá friends in Parara avoided taking sides with respect to which style was more authentic. After persistent and repeated questions and more private conversations, they explained to me that they had discussed this issue among themselves in detail, and that the style in procession was in agreement with how the other Emberá communities in the wider Canal area danced rumba – that is, those communities that have also developed tourism. It transpired that the travel agents who had been accustomed to this particular style – 'It is more ceremonial and dignified', a travel agent argued – had encouraged the Emberá of Parara Puru to synchronise with the style followed by the other communities that receive tourists.

The rumba-Emberá is not the only type of dance that is open to change and adaptation. As older dance patterns become features of everyday dance practice, new dance moves are introduced through rehearsal and improvisation, and the Emberá dance tradition, which was declining until the introduction of tourism, is undergoing revitalisation (see Theodossopoulos 2013c). This is very much

6.6 Dancing rumba-Emberá in freestyle arrangement

evident in the Emberá animal-dances, another major type of Emberá dancing, which encourage improvisation as part of imitating the movement and attributes of native animal species. The introduction of tourism has motivated the residents of Parara to dance a much greater variety of animal dances, and to introduce a wider repertoire of dance moves to the choreography. Undoubtedly, the degree of improvisation has been accelerated by tourism, which has inspired the Emberá to explore new avenues of artistic expression.

Similar examples of improvisation and experimentation resulting in new patterns and designs can be found in the context of Emberá basketry. The wider Emberá society in Eastern Panama – not merely the communities that entertain tourists – is involved in the production of cultural artefacts that eventually find their way onto the tourist market (Velásquez Runk 2001; Colin 2013). Creating artefacts to sell to tourists is an important source of income for many Emberá who live away from the flow of tourists in inaccessible communities in Darién (see Colin 2010) or in impoverished suburban neighbourhoods closer to Panama City. With this increase in the production of material culture, new designs emerge out of older patterns, while new colours are introduced using old, but also new, dyeing techniques (see Callaghan 2002). As the art of Emberá basketry continues to evolve, new dyeing mediums are introduced to produce more colours and accommodate a greater variety of designs.[13] The residents of Parara Puru, and many other Emberá I know from communities that do not receive tourists, welcome this creative freedom and the new possibilities it engenders. Several of them argue that they prefer to spend their time constructing artefacts than labouring in the sun performing agricultural tasks.

Two further examples of 'work with tourists' that the Emberá men consider to be enjoyable work are playing the flute – which is the lead musical instrument during cultural presentations – and guiding tourists on short treks into the forest, often by providing limited or even extended information on the medicinal properties of plants. Young men in Parara Puru often go through a phase of trying to learn the flute, in the hope that one day they will lead the group of musicians that provides the music of rumba- and cumbia-Emberá.[14] These distinctly Emberá music genres (see Theodossopoulos 2013c) encompass an enormous repertoire of songs, some of which have lyrics (in Emberá), which the flute player sings when he stops playing the flute, with a percussion accompaniment. While there many accomplished flute players in Darién, where the population of the Emberá is much greater,

6.7 Practising the flute during some downtime

there is a much smaller number in Chagres, and very few sing. Yet, tourism has created a niche for this art, which encourages, as I mentioned above, several young men to practise – often while listening to recordings of the performances of other musicians. Only few persist enough to truly master the art, yet flute improvisation, tunes and styles of playing are issues that interest a growing number of Emberá men who pay particular attention to the music performed by flute players from other communities.[15]

In comparison with Emberá music, ethno-botanical knowledge is an area of expertise claimed by a great number of men, even in communities at the fringes of Emberá society. Most have learned about plants and animals from a young age, particularly during hunting trips, and are very articulate when describing plant properties and their medicinal potential. Some are even confident enough to advise on medical treatments, although they clearly distinguish between the role of the 'botanist' (el botánico) and the 'shaman' (el jaibaná). The first, explain the Emberá, 'cures only with plants', while the second 'uses plants, but also sings [to the spirits]', using the spirits as a curative medium. Parara Puru does not have a shaman, yet on a few occasions visiting shamans from Darién have cured in the community (see Chapter 8), while some residents of Parara have also travelled out of the community to seek their aid.

The botanical knowledge of several Parara men is good enough to impress the tourists, some of whom entertain the expectation of having an exotic and mystical encounter with an indigenous shaman. En route to the nearby waterfalls, or during short walks around the community, younger men would identify particular plants and say a few words about them, practising their guiding skills. In other communities that have developed tourism, the walk in the rainforest is a customised activity offered by an experienced botánico and is often included in, or added as an extra to, the tourist package. The leaders of Parara Puru have even contemplated preparing a trail specifically for a botanical walk – one that meets safety regulations – but this plan has been put on hold. Closer to the community, and in the cleared spaces around their houses, the Emberá have transplanted trees and plants that have a specific practical or medicinal use. This is an established Emberá practice that marks the domestication of the immediate environment and the claim of particular families on a piece of land (see Herlihy 1986; Kane 1994). Such trees and plants in Parara have grown enough to reveal the (seventeen-year) history of the community and in some cases provide readily available opportunities to demonstrate snippets of ethno-botanical knowledge to visitors.

I will offer yet another example that can help us appreciate the Emberá search for new and old representational knowledge. On each successive fieldwork period to Parara Puru, I took with me one ethnographic monograph about the Emberá. At the beginning I felt that an anthropology book would provide me with an opening to describe what anthropologists do, so I carried with me in successive years the work of Kane (1992), Tayler (1996), Torres de Araúz (1966) and Vasco Uribe (1987). The Emberá searched the pages of these books for photographs with excitement, and asked me to read or translate short extracts. Encouraged by this reception, I started sharing on my computer screen scanned photographs from

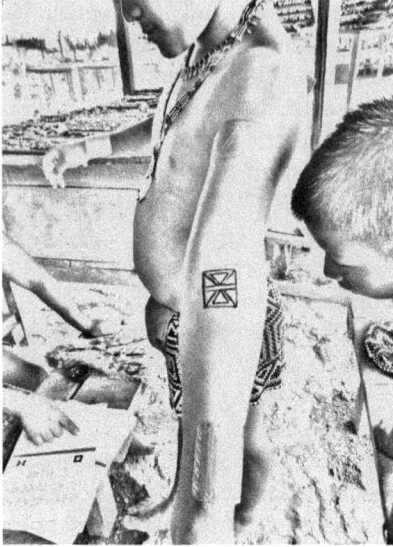

6.8 Practicing body-paint designs from
Ulloa's book

a variety of ethnographic sources. The Emberá were interested in the captions and offered their own interpretations of the clothes or objects in the old ethnographic photographs.

This more general search, and the growing interest of the Emberá in information about their own culture, can be easily contextualised within the broader context of the Emberá emerging representational self-awareness. As more Emberá have the opportunity to articulate a narrative about their culture and its history, information from ethnographic sources is received as a welcome addition. It is therefore not surprising that on several occasions during my fieldwork I was asked to translate and summarise ethnographic facts, or to share my views about declining cultural practices, historical events and comparable informa-tion about other Emberá communities in Eastern Panama or Colombia. Aware that I read 'all those books', my friends in Parara expected me to reciprocate the knowledge I received from them – by sharing my knowledge from sources that were inaccessible to them. I responded to their interest enthusiastically (see Theodossopoulos 2015), following the call of an emerging engaged approach in anthropology (Sillitoe 2015).

A final, but representative, example of the Emberá willingness to experiment with ethnographic information about their own culture was their willingness to learn new body-painting designs from Ulloa's (1992) monograph on Emberá body decoration in Colombia. The residents of Parara asked me to laminate selected pages from Ulloa's book, which they used while body painting the tourists. With the frequent demand to body paint foreigners, the Emberá in the communities that entertain tourists on a day-to-day basis are on the lookout for new themes. On some occasions the laminated pages were used as a 'menu' of designs for the tourists to choose from. In this, and other unanticipated respects, information from anthropology books has enhanced Emberá representation in Parara Puru.

From entertaining others to guiding and educating others

When the residents of Parara Puru founded their community they simply relied on cultural knowledge that was readily available – that is, what most Emberá know. This knowledge was enough to make a start in the tourism industry and an impression on the tourists. A general Emberá conception of how to entertain important guests-*cum*-outsiders was available from previous eras. We have seen how in the early-twentieth century Marsh and Verrill were invited to participate in Emberá festivities that included music and dances, during which the Emberá decorated themselves (and their guests) with body paint and adornments.[16] Dances as cultural demonstrations had previously been performed in the indigenous conferences of the 1970s and 1980s (see Kane 1994: 166–7), while in later years several communities maintained dance troupes of schoolgirls who trained during their extracurricular activities. Emberá music and dance was periodically performed at intercommunity festivals and celebrations, which also provided a context for Emberá flute players to polish their skill in virtuoso improvisation. In each individual community in Eastern Panama lived men who knew how to build houses in the traditional way, or how to talk to the visitors about the local fauna and flora or the medicinal properties of plants. One community in Darién, Mogue, located within reach of cruise boats approaching from the gulf of San Miguel, started receiving and entertaining tourists in the 1980s (Herlihy 1986: 247).

In the early- and mid-1990s, when indigenous tourism was developed for the first time at Chagres, the local Emberá had a general idea about how to entertain their guests. They knew for example that they should welcome their guests dressed in full Emberá attire – as appropriate for receiving visitors – and present them with a meal, some explanation of their culture and a demonstration of Emberá music and dance. These choices corresponded to a more widespread pattern of entertaining foreign guests in Eastern Panama, and are common to communities that receive visitors very rarely (see Theodossopoulos 2007). Frequent cultural presentations presented the Emberá hosts with opportunities to augment their representational choices, acquire a good selection of adornments, improve and improvise in dancing or body painting, and learn how to explain the construction of traditional artefacts in a more detailed or enticing way, which would encourage more visitors to buy them.

As a result, in a relatively short period of time and through frequent work with tourists, the Emberá of Parara Puru and other communities at Chagres have built up a certain degree of expertise in cultural matters. To cement this experience, they also started to refine their skill in presenting and representing Emberá culture. This led to subtle, but significant, changes in the self-representational awareness of those Emberá who work with tourists on frequent basis. While initially the Emberá attempted to provide their guests with an indigenous experience, a spectacle (see Urry 1990), with the passage of time they started guiding the tourists into and around their culture instead. This confidence in cultural representation came slowly and after some years of practice and experimentation.

In this gradual manner, the task of explaining Emberá culture to outsiders became a common aspect of life in Parara Puru and other communities that work regularly with tourists. Interaction with foreigners may take place in a variety of contexts, which may be less structured or staged than the cultural presentations. As some younger Emberá learn a few words of English, and with increasing visits from Spanish-speaking tourists, the Emberá communicate with their guests more frequently and spontaneously: for example, while transporting visitors in a dugout canoe, guiding them through the rainforest or chatting with them while waiting for the regular presentations to start. The increasing representational confidence that emerges from such spontaneous interaction encourages an increasing number of Emberá to see themselves as guides to Emberá culture, who lead the tourists around the local environment or 'teach' the tourists basic Emberá concepts. As I have already described, an increasing number of Emberá in Parara Puru take turns delivering speeches to the tourists. In Parara, the art of articulating a narrative about Emberá culture is not merely the responsibility of community leaders.

This gradual transformation in the representational confidence of the Emberá at Chagres reflects their ambition to move beyond the initial hesitant experimentation with merely entertaining Others. After fifteen years of interaction with tourists an increasing number of residents of Parara express the idea that their work in tourism can be described as a type of education. 'We are like schoolteachers (maestros)', one of the leaders of the community explained, 'we teach the tourists what Emberá culture is . . . we work for the education of the tourists and we learn how to do this better and better every year.' 'And we are happy to see that the tourists want to learn', added his wife. This realisation encourages the Emberá to see their role in tourism as more akin to that of a teacher who educates an audience, rather than that of a performer (cf. Bunten 2008).

Now that a wider international audience of tourists is paying attention to the Emberá, the Emberá of Parara Puru wish to become better-informed and more articulate tourist guides. They want to be able to describe a wider variety of cultural particularities that might interest a larger variety of foreign guests, including those who are more knowledgeable and inquisitive. It is in this respect that the manner of the presentation to tourists, as well as the explanation of the presentation, become acts of ever-increasing consequence. This is why the Emberá who work in tourism are so interested in collecting information about their own culture, comparing their practices with those of other communities. As I explained earlier, they even welcome information that I – 'their anthropologist' – collected by comparing older ethnographic accounts (see Theodossopoulos 2015). Such knowledge informs new, fluid strategies of representation, adapted to cater for audiences of national and international tourists who share contradictory – idealising and also stereotyping – expectations.

The dilemmas set by the contradictory expectations of Others encourage concern with the issue of authenticity, which leads the Emberá to negotiate different standards of representativeness. As we have seen in this chapter, not all local choices comply with the narrow – and static – view of the authentic as equivalent to old-fashioned. A parallel standard of representativeness is provided by the practices of Emberá in communities that do not entertain tourists. For the Emberá of Parara Puru it is very important to demonstrate that they do actually live in an authentic, homogenous Emberá community, in 'authentic' Emberá houses that follow the general principles of Emberá architecture but are also real living spaces that expand organically to accommodate the needs of their families. Here, authenticity defined as 'the way any other Emberá live' identifies rather uncomfortably with authenticity as 'the way our grandparents lived'. We will soon see more contradictions of this kind.

6.9   Dressed and ready to go and pick up the tourists

Notes

1 As I explained in Chapter 3, the descendants of the first Emberá migrants to Chagres in the 1950s often refer to themselves as 'natives of Chagres' (*nativos de Chagres*). According to the regulations of the national park those – indigenous or not – who are born in Chagres have right of residence in the park. Emberá men and women born in Darién can only remain in the park if they marry an Emberá from Chagres. The residents of Emberá Drua, despite their later arrival in the area, have right of residence, as they established their community before the foundation of the park. It should be noted that the right to reside in the park must not be confused with the provision of legally approved land titles. The Emberá in Chagres do not have ownership of their land and have to abide by the regulations of the park authorities, which retain ultimate control over the whole area.
2 Parara Puru's neighbouring community, Tusipono, followed the example of Parara Puru two years later. The founders of both communities came from related Emberá families who had for some time been residing at Victoriano Lorenzo and the surrounding area.
3 The idea of creating a model village was introduced by non-indigenous advisors – travel agents and other tourism professionals – who helped the Emberá during their initial steps into the tourism industry in the 1990s. At the time of writing, an example of such an uninhabited 'model' Emberá village is still visible on the premises of the Gamboa Rainforest Resort in Panama, a site where Emberá from the neighbouring communities at Gamboa island come to perform and to sell indigenous artefacts. In recent years, the positive feedback of tourists participating in excursions to inhabited Emberá communities in the Canal area has been so overwhelming that the practice of staging indigenous

performances in model villages has fallen out of fashion. The Emberá of Gamboa prefer to entertain tourists in their own community, rather than the model village.

4 There are five Emberá communities within the Chagres National Park: Tusipono, Parara Puru and Emberá Drua at river Chagres, and Emberá Puru and La Bonga at river Pequeni.

5 By the 1960s, Caballero and Araúz (1962) had already reported that the Emberá of Chagres – who lived closer to a non-indigenous majority – adopted non-indigenous habits at a faster rate than the Emberá living in relatively inaccessible locations in Darién.

6 For more information about the harvest of *wagara* and related issues, see Potvin et al. 2003.

7 This sometimes includes houses built in a circular design with circular roofs. Circular houses are rare nowadays, but most Emberá maintain that their roofs are impressive examples of Emberá architectural artistry. Nordenskiold reports that his key respondent, Selimo, believed (in 1927) that all Emberá houses were once circular (1928: 64, 69).

8 The buildings without walls include those dedicated to hosting the occasional visitor who is prepared to stay overnight. After all, as the Emberá indicate, sleeping in a house 'without walls' provides a good experience of the Emberá way of life in the old times, which is, from the Emberá point of view, what tourists desire.

9 Wooden planks are either bought from outside the national park or made out of fallen trees by the Emberá themselves (who use machine saws as efficiently as axes and machetes). The park regulations do not permit the Emberá to cut down trees. Nevertheless, the Emberá are allowed to use fallen trees (or trees submerged in the river) as firewood or to make canoes, wooden poles, planks and, depending the quality of the wood, sculptured artefacts (for sale to tourists).

10 Although the leaders of the Emberá are usually men, women have also occasionally been elected to political office. For example, the leader (*nokó*) of the community of Ella Puru in Gamboa is, at the time of writing, a woman, and I am aware of two other female leaders who held such a position in the last ten years in other Emberá communities in Panama.

11 Despite the exceptions mentioned in the note above, the Emberá attach importance to a clear-cut gendered division of labour. As Emberá women increase their participation in cultural presentations – from dance performers or producers of artefacts to guides and narrators of Emberá culture – they feel more confident talking about cultural practices that relate to women's work and experience.

12 For a detailed description of rumba- and cumbia-Embera and the significance of improvisation in Emberá dance, see Theodossopoulos 2013c.

13 For comparative examples of indigenous arts, new designs and older patterns, see Graburn 1976; Smith 1989; and, among the Guna, see Salvador 1976; Tice 1995; Fortis 2012a.

14 A well-organised group of musicians – such as the ones formed in Chagres – can have a flute (*chirú-droma*[E]), which is the lead musical instrument, a large drum (*el tambor grande* or *caja* or *chim-bom-bom*), a smaller drum beaten with sticks (*la requinta*) and some (or all) of the following percussion instruments: *churuca* (*chogoró*[E]), maracas and turtle drums (*chimpigí*[E]). The flute player introduces the main musical theme and also engages in virtuoso improvisation, often repeating the refrain several times.

15 In fact, Parara Puru has only one highly skilled flute player, so during the high season the community invites an additional flute player to work on a short-term basis, usually for as long as the tourist numbers are high enough to support his wages.

16 See Chapter 4 and Howe 1998; see also Verrill 1921, 1931; Marsh 1934.

7

Shifting codes of dress

Questions of dress or 'the problem of what to wear' (Tarlo 1996: 15) are not confined to people with a rich wardrobe, though nowadays most of the Emberá of Parara Puru do have a considerable amount of both 'traditional' and 'modern' clothes.[1] Their mere availability generates choices, dilemmas and new potential combinations. Some of these are inspired by the material properties and practicality of particular types of clothing items, while other choices relate to considerations regarding the degree to which a certain individual wishes to accentuate (or not) an indigenous identity. In this respect, clothes may challenge or uphold a 'cultural allegiance' (Tarlo 1996: 17) and proclaim, but also conceal, a particular identity (Delaney 2004: 353; see also Schneider and Weiner 1989).

I would however like to resist the temptation to see Emberá clothes merely as a superficial cover for a hidden identity (Miller 2005b). The clothes themselves play a role in shaping the identity of the Emberá. In the previous chapter, for example, we saw how wearing the traditional attire in the context of tourism has provided the Emberá performers with a renewed representational confidence. Similarly, wearing modern clothes substantiates and reinforces the Emberá claim to a modern, contemporary vision of indigeneity. Interestingly, in the communities that have developed tourism the Emberá wear, in the course of a day, 'modern' *and* 'traditional' clothes – or, as the Emberá say in Spanish, *'ropas modernas'* and *'vestidos tradicionales'*[2] – a coexistence of different dress codes that provides scope for choice between, and unexpected combinations

7.1 Two men go to pick up tourists (dressed in Emberá attire), and a younger one to attend high school (wearing the school's polo shirt)

of, different dress elements. In this respect, emerging choices or combinations of clothes play a role in the negotiation of Emberá identity.

In fact, as the Emberá of Parara Puru maintain, they enjoy wearing both 'modern' and 'indigenous' clothes; from their point of view being modern is not necessarily 'incompatible with being indigenous' (Conklin 2007: 25). A point of view that may encourage the uninitiated Western observer to assume – with a certain degree of nostalgia (see Clifford 1986; Rosaldo 1989; Berliner 2015) – that the Emberá have reached the end of their traditional society, following a singular, uniform pathway towards a deculturating modernity. The ethnography that I am about to present in this chapter attempts to complicate such a limiting unilineal vision of change. I will discuss instead how Emberá dress codes often shift in the course of the day, or in the course of an individual's lifetime, coming closer to or further away from indigenous aesthetics and practices. I will further explore various dress combinations of 'modern' and 'traditional' elements, the adaptation of some 'traditional' clothing items to accommodate non-indigenous rules of modesty – yes, even traditional clothes can change! – and the spontaneous, often accidental, re-emergence of old dress styles in the present. The latter will provide me with an opportunity to reassess my ethnographic nostalgia, and to learn how to appreciate the complexity of Emberá dress choices.

Dressing up and down in the course of the day

Parara Puru wakes up at dawn.[3] The local residents have between three to five hours before the tourists arrive, which they devote to the completion of a variety of chores that vary from one day to another. Standard morning duties include clearing the central area of the community for the arrival of the tourists. Several women dressed in *paruma*-skirts and modern tops work together on this using rakes in preparation for the arrival of tourists (for which they receive day-wages

7.2   Dressed to work in the forest

from the communal earnings from tourism). Similarly, women dressed in *parumas* – a very versatile garment for manual work – clean the fish that the tourists will later consume.[4] They usually do this work at the riverbank, where a few women sometimes stay topless – as in the old times, but in all-female company. If an unfamiliar man or outsider approaches (on foot or by canoe), they cover the top part of their bodies with another *paruma*. Outside tourist presentations, the women of

Parara Puru, as those in most other Emberá communities, wear a *paruma*–skirt combined with a modern top most of the time (a t-shirt, vest top, tank top or cropped top).

Men start the day dressed in Western clothes, such as shorts and t-shirts. On those less frequent occasions when work involves more arduous tasks, such as carrying wood, clearing or walking in the rainforest, they prefer to wear long trousers, long shirts and rubber boots, as they do when they go on hunting trips.[5] Before the arrival of the tourists, both men and women take a shower under the cold-water pipes located close to each family's house.[6] When there is no running water, due to the frequent failure of the pipes, they revert to the old practice of bathing in the river. Adults and children arrive at different points – often holding plastic soap dishes containing soap – to wash alone or in small groups. Adults in Parara Puru never bathe completely naked in public view. Men keep on their shorts, swimming trunks or equivalent, and women wear their *parumas* because they can wash themselves underneath these. All the Emberá I know are meticulous about cleaning their bodies, a feature noticed (and admired) by early-twentieth-century observers (see Verrill 1921; Nordernskiold 1928; Marsh 1934).

Cleaned and refreshed, all men and women who participate in the cultural presentations dress up to welcome the tourists. They put on their traditional attire, following the standard 'traditional' dress code, as described in Chapter 2. Those few residents of the community that do not work for tourism – due to old age, illness or other reasons – or those Emberá guests (usually relatives from other communities) who stay in Parara Puru temporarily do not appear before tourists in modern clothes. This is a formal decision of the community and is communicated to newcomers. 'We want to show the tourists what Emberá culture is', explained one of the community leaders defending this particular rule, 'to welcome our guests in our *own* clothes, the Emberá clothes'. The Emberá who stay at home during the tourist encounter are free to dress as they like, although usually adult women still wear the *paruma* combined with a modern top. Visiting Emberá men from other communities often hesitate to wear a loincloth. The *guayuco*, as the loincloth is referred to in Spanish, is a heavily stereotyped item of clothing in Panama, as we shall see in the next section (see also Chapter 2).

Every morning the children who attend the local primary school – like all children in Panama – dress in school uniform. Wearing shoes and carrying colourful (but inexpensive) schoolbags they walk to the school, which is located on a hill at the rear of the community. When they return from school, they throw off their uniform and shoes, don more traditional clothing and join in with the tourist presentations, dancing with their parents, interacting with the tourists or playing with each other (and occasionally with tourist children) in the central area of the village. Emberá boys under four years of age remain completely naked for the greater part of the day (see Reverte Coma 2002: 235, 237). Older boys wear a loincloth, while Emberá girls wear mini-*parumas* and sometimes necklaces and simple strings of

7.3   Children of Parara in school uniform, waiting
for the teacher to come

beads or metal ornaments. The afternoon is spent playing around the community or swimming in the river, so a loincloth or little *paruma* are as convenient as shorts and t-shirts, but easier to wash.

The older boys and girls of Parara Puru who travel out of the community to attend high school also dress in the appropriate school uniform.[7] They often have to carry their shoes and socks when they walk on the muddy riverbank to reach the dugout canoes, and endure the seasonal challenges of travelling (for a part of their journey) by river. Yet, they try to appear at school well-presented with their uniforms in good order. They return to the community exhausted in the afternoon. If the tourist presentations are still underway, they are sometimes tempted to change their school uniform to traditional attire to join the buzz of social activity at the centre of the community.

For the duration of the tourist encounter the Emberá who participate in the cultural presentation stay dressed in their traditional attire. Some individuals are body-painted when sufficient amounts of *jagua* fruit are locally available.[8] Most men in Parara wear the *amburá* over their loincloth, a traditional wide belt which conceals their buttocks. Similarly, most women wear an *ubarí* or, in Spanish, *pulsera de plata*, a heavy necklace with layers of coins that partly covers their chest. The Emberá of Parara say that these two clothing items provide them with the comfort of not having to appear before the tourists completely naked (see Chapter 2). I will discuss the politics, adaptations and aesthetics of these two articles of clothing later in this chapter.

In the afternoon, usually between two and four, the last group of tourists departs, and Parara Puru becomes noticeably quieter. The Emberá return home and take off their formal adornments. The men carefully put their beaded strings, arm cuffs and *amburá*-belts aside and replace their loincloths with shorts. They are more likely to wear flip-flops close to home, rubber boots when clearing the forest or hunting and shoes or sparkling white trainers on their ventures to the town. T-shirts are used extensively, and young men may have some with bold designs, which are reserved for going out of the community. Light short-sleeved shirts are preferred for more formal occasions, such as visiting a government institution or attending worship at an evangelical church. Obviously particular types of jobs require the use of heavier clothes such as long-sleeved shirts and long trousers (e.g.

7.4 Three Emberá men departing from Parara. Rafael is dressed in full attire, on his way to collect tourists. Anel and Naldo are dressed in modern t-shirts, on their way to the city

for cutting and carrying palm leaves or repairing roofs), while for others lighter clothes will suffice, for example topless with a pair of shorts (e.g. while digging a ditch, chopping wood or repairing a canoe on the riverside).

After returning from the tourist presentations, the women replace their beaded strings, arm cuffs and beaded necklaces with modern t-shirts and tops. Most women remain dressed in *parumas* for the remainder of the day. For trips to the city – to visit relatives, a hospital, or a government institution – they might temporarily replace the *paruma* with a non-indigenous skirt, or they might continue wearing their *parumas* irrespective of the destination. Young unmarried or married women might also wear shorts (instead of a *paruma*) to go to a birthday party, a date or an outing outside their immediate community, while other young women dress for the same occasions with a *paruma* and t-shirt combination, but replace their ordinary top with a newer or slightly more expensive one.

Later in the afternoon, usually after yet another shower under the cold-water pipe – or, in the case of the children, after another dip in the river – the majority of the residents of Parara Puru put on fresh clothes. Those who plan to go out of the community for a walk or fast-food meal in one of the neighbouring Latino settlements prepare more carefully. The men put on their newest t-shirts (often with elaborate designs), cropped shorts and bright white sport shoes, while the women wear their *parumas* and a matching newly acquired top, or sometimes dress fully in Western clothes, with a skirt or shorts and a top. Dressed in their newest Western clothes, married couples with or without their children, or groups of adolescents – with inexpensive but fashionable clothes – share a canoe ride to the world outside Parara and an opportunity to mix with Emberá from other communities or non-indigenous friends and acquaintances, usually from the neighbouring community of Victoriano Lorenzo.

To attend church worship, the Emberá of Parara follow a variety of dress codes (see also Chapter 8). For such occasions, some men – usually married and over thirty – dress according to more conservative Latino fashion, in long trousers held up by thin leather belts. Yet several other men – usually younger or unmarried – feel comfortable attending church dressed in cropped trousers and colourful shirts. Some older women may wear modern skirts to go to church, yet the majority still rely on their *parumas* which, despite their indigenous character, are considered modest. When children are taken to the church, they are allowed to attend the service or play in the surrounding area. They are dressed, as in most cases outside the community, primarily in modern clothes, with the exception of school-age girls who often wear their *paruma*-skirt – which can be seen as an ethnicity identifier in a mixed-ethnic crowd – combined with a modern cotton top.

Churchgoers, older individuals and families with children usually return back to the community before dark or shortly after. To go to sleep they prepare their 'bed', which in most cases, and according to Emberá tradition, is merely the floor or, more often, a slightly raised extension of the floor. Although in recent years I have seen some beds in the community, most local residents use only thin mattresses and cover themselves with a light cotton sheet. Yet, some Emberá insist on sleeping on the floor, especially if it – or part of it – is made of the soft bark of the *jira* palm.[9] During the day, mattresses and sheets are folded or rolled up – according to old Emberá practice – and stored on the beams that support the roof, only to be brought down when preparing for sleep the following night. Groups of adults without children or couples who go out of the community in the afternoon often return back in the dark. They may interrupt the tropical-night soundscape for a brief moment, telling a joke that can be overheard in the nearby houses. A half-asleep neighbour might reply with another joke or a flash of a torch before the community is submerged in the tranquil sounds of the night once more.

'In-between' dress codes and ethnographic nostalgia

I will start this section with a confession. On several occasions during my time in Parara Puru, I caught myself reproducing the very same idealising, exoticising views I set out to criticise. I found myself victim to an irresistible anthropological inclination: the tendency to celebrate the re-emergence of the 'traditional' – or the 'indigenous' – in juxtaposition with the modern. Every time I saw the Emberá enacting practices that were – or could be anthropologically read as – distinctively or representatively Emberá, I felt reassured that Emberá culture was resisting the pervasive influences of the wider non-indigenous culture. Obviously, my 'ethnographic nostalgia', rooted in the view that Emberá culture was 'alive' and 'strong' – as if Emberá culture was about to be 'lost' – was founded on an old-fashioned, exoticised perception of 'tribal cultures' as vulnerable remnants of a lost world (Berliner 2015: 22–5). Such a static view – that denies the Other coevalness

(Fabian 1983) – has only hindered the project of anthropology. Yet, as I hope to demonstrate here, when ethnographic nostalgia is put under an analytical and self-critical lens, it may provide insights that allow us to appreciate the intimate nuances of social change.

7.5 Francisco working on his new canoe, inspiring the author's ethnographic nostalgia

In the first place, ethnographic nostalgia may encourage us to see an Emberá working on his new canoe – dressed in a loincloth and using an axe – as a fragment of the past in the present. We may forge a romantic connection with the past while we observe the repetition of a structuring pattern identified by ethnographers who worked with the Emberá in previous decades. In this respect, our reading of previous ethnographic descriptions may contribute to our ethnographic nostalgia by adding a veil of romantic mystique to an image we observe in the present: an Emberá working on his new canoe – dressed in a loincloth and using an axe. The more we know about the Emberá, the more likely we are to appreciate – with some implicit idealisation – an old cultural pattern when this reappears in the present. And indeed, as many ethnographers of the Emberá corroborate, the dugout canoe has compelling symbolic associations (see Isacsson 1993: 92).[10] According to the old Emberá tradition, making and owning a canoe is a credential that qualifies 'a man to live with a woman' (Kane 1994: 69). Many contemporary Emberá are aware of this now outdated idea. They may communicate this knowledge to tourists who are curious about Emberá marriage customs. Reading the expectation of the tourists, the Emberá may choose to provide the tourists with the type of Emberá knowledge that meets the exoticising expectations of the tourists.

Nonetheless, the contemporary ethnographer knows that nowadays the Emberá make their dugout canoes dressed in shorts, not in loincloths, and that for a great part of the job they rely on machine saws, which they use with admirable precision, along with axes and machetes. In fact, it is the modern elements of contemporary Emberá canoe-making that frame, in juxtaposition with the past, the image of 'the man dressed in a loincloth' as representative of Emberá tradition. It is the very contrast of the old and new form that emplaces the image of the Emberá

7.6   Brenio, repairing a canoe with an ax, wearing shorts

canoe maker in a broader context of meaning. Thus, for the ethnographer, the sight of an Emberá man making a canoe dressed in a loincloth may signify a deeply embedded Emberá pattern – one that the ethnographer can corroborate through scholarly study and comparison. But how much can this underlying pattern tell us about the present? On its own, very little. For example, it may reveal continuities in process, but not necessarily a continuity of intentions.

It is more likely that the recognition of a scholarly construct as a process reenacted in the present may trigger ethnographic nostalgia, encouraged by the recognition of what may seem a normative, static view of authenticity, defined in terms of past referents. This view may entertain the deception that the old form re-emerges from within the pages of a book. For instance, my ethnographic nostalgia in figure 7.6 was triggered by my memory of a drawing of an Emberá canoe maker wearing a loincloth and wielding an axe in Kane's monograph – the caption says 'Dzoshua wielding an axe' (Kane 1994: 68) – which provides a good example of how influential the previous ethnographic record can be in shaping ethnographic nostalgia (see Theodossopoulos n.d.).

Let us now return to the renewed confidence of some Emberá in Parara Puru to carry on doing some of their chores dressed in a manner that meets the aesthetics of the old times. This inevitably triggered my curiosity and nostalgic gaze. Considering that the reintroduction of the traditional Emberá attire at Chagres was initiated for the sake of tourism, one would expect that the Emberá would rush to put on their Western clothes immediately after the tourists leave the community, and especially so since (a) the 'traditional' dress code has been stereotyped by non-indigenous Panamanians as 'uncivilised' and (b) so many Emberá see the traditional attire – especially the use of the loincloth by men – as a bit old-fashioned. In fact, some Emberá do rush to put on their Western clothes, especially when they have to go out of the community for a job in the city, or to any destination farther away from their familiar social environment at Chagres.

However, as we shall see, there are a few instances when some residents of Parara may keep on elements of the traditional dress code even after the tourists depart. Such instances can be seen as representing a temporary in-between stage in the

7.7 Claudio, in full traditional attire, carrying plantains he bought from outside the community

shifting dress code of the Emberá, one that should not be seen as liminal – in Victor Turner's (1967, 1969) terms – as it does not bring about disorientation, intensity or transition between different identities. On the contrary, these in-between dress adaptations occur silently and spontaneously, triggered by practical considerations. Yet, though they do not result in an identity crisis, the particular dress combinations comprise examples that can help us contextualise the ambiguity regarding the use of (more or less) traditional and/or Western clothes by the Emberá, and the shifting nature of their dress transformations.

We saw in the previous section how the Emberá of Parara change into various types of dress over the course of the day. Although all of them put aside their adornments – *amburás*, arm cuffs, beaded strings, *ubarís* and other types of necklaces – after seeing off their last visitors, a few, and in particular those still involved in labour-intensive tasks, may find the relative clotheslessness of traditional dress more convenient. So they may delay putting on Western clothes (or covering their torso). There are usually several jobs to finish, such as cleaning or maintaining the reception area, cooking, cutting wood, repairing houses or clearing the areas surrounding family houses. Most of these jobs, and especially those closer to the river, are more comfortably performed in fewer clothes. Thus, it is not surprising to see Emberá men in Parara repairing canoes wearing a loincloth or, more frequently, Emberá women cleaning fish topless on the riverbank, wearing only a *paruma*-skirt.

In these instances, when the Emberá leave their torsos uncovered and wear only a loincloth or a *paruma*, an intermediate dress code is marked out, which has elements of the old 'traditional' form – understood as what the grandparents did or 'as in the old times' – but does not fully reproduce the static conception of formal, traditional attire. After finishing their work in tourism, some of the residents of Parara Puru dress more informally by putting aside the adornments that were in the past reserved for celebrations, but they may choose to keep their loincloth on (in the case of men) for a bit longer or remain topless (in the case of women) to complete the odd job. In this way, they free themselves from clothing items that complement the formal, traditional attire, but may temporarily retain other items or elements that resonate with the dress code of the everyday – as opposed to the ceremonial – dress of their grandparents.

In communities that have developed tourism, the use of the loincloth by men is encouraged by the simple fact that the Emberá do have to put on the full traditional attire for part of the day, and also the availability of loincloths in a man's possession. As loincloths are now used much more frequently in Chagres – in comparison with the 1980s and early 1990s when they were almost abandoned – they have regained their reputation as versatile clothing items. Nowadays, they are sometimes used in conjunction with other types of clothing – such as a t-shirt or shirt to protect one from the sun during outdoor work in the area surrounding the community, or on a long canoe ride (for example, on the way to collect tourists and bring them to the community or on the way home after the tourists have departed). While the loincloth was reintroduced in Chagres as a formalistic element complementing the traditional attire, it has now recovered part of its original informal functionality – a result of the fact that it is indeed, like the *paruma*, a very comfortable and versatile item of dress.

In the community upriver of Parara Puru I have seen men wearing a wide unbuttoned long-sleeved shirt on the top of a loincloth, a hybrid modern-indigenous dress style that was common in the past (see Torres de Araúz 1966; Reverte Coma 2002).[11] In Parara, men dressed only in a loincloth may perform a manual job, or they may jump on a departing canoe to do some last-minute shopping at the outskirts of the national park, wearing only a t-shirt on top of the loincloth. As I mentioned before, and as I will further discuss in the next section, the loincloth is an item of dress heavily stereotyped by the Latino neighbours of the Emberá. Those Emberá who feel comfortable wearing the loincloth for a bit longer, even outside the community, maintain that the traditional dress is 'now' tolerated by their Latino neighbours in the general Chagres area. 'They know that we work for tourism', the Emberá explain, so 'they understand' or 'they don't bother us anymore'.

7.8 Donardo with non-traditional *jagua* designs on his right arm and t-shirt

Another example of in-between dress codes concerns the old tradition of painting one's body with *jagua*. This does not involve only the presentation of the Self in tourism, but also mixed indigenous-and-non-indigenous dress combinations in daily life within or outside homogenously Emberá communities. Body painting with *jagua* is a normative constituent of the formal attire and is considered by the Emberá to be a type of dress, one that stays imprinted on the body from eight to twelve days (depending on exposure to water). In this respect, the practice of *jagua* body painting evades the distinction between formal and informal contexts of dress. When the Emberá dress down by either putting their adornments aside or covering their bodies with modern sleeveless tops, the *jagua* designs remain visible, as we see in the photograph below. Many Emberá at Chagres and in Darién – including adolescents and young adults – go out of their community (entering ethnically heterogeneous neighbourhoods) wearing their *jagua* designs, often beautifully combined with the latest t-shirts. In such cases, *jagua* unmistakably communicates an indigenous identity which is not hidden from view, but projected to the non-indigenous world.

But let me return once more to the issue of ethnographic nostalgia. With respect to Emberá clothing, my idealised and enthusiastic identification of old patterns of dress in the present led me towards two distinct possibilities. The first was the recognition of traditional cultural patterns through a unidirectional connection with the past: the delineation of a continuity, a potentially deceptive and exoticising conceptualisation. The second was the appreciation of traditional cultural patterns as part of a wider nexus of parallel practices: continuities, contradictions, new cultural adaptations that may engender a number of – to use an expression by Kane (1994: 41) – 'authentic discontinuities'. The first possibility comes with the risk of denying our ethnographic subjects coevalness, the acknowledgement that they too inhabit the same time as the ethnographer and his readership (Fabian 1983). The second possibility engenders an advantage, the recognition of the multidimensional exotic as 'a challenge to understanding' (Kapferer 2013); in the case of the Emberá, the recognition that within dress choices contradictions and hybrid forms are implicated.

I can see now that my initial ethnographic nostalgia for the traditional Emberá dress encouraged me to pay attention to particular in-between dress codes, which I might have otherwise very easily taken for granted or failed to notice. In turn, recognition of this led me to appreciate the complexity of mixed indigenous and non-indigenous aesthetics in Emberá clothing practices. In time, my exposure to the complexity of Emberá clothing practices encouraged me to deconstruct the previous static conceptions that framed my nostalgic feelings. It is in this respect that exoticisation may potentially facilitate – if assisted by a healthy dose of reflexivity – its own critique. But this observation comes with a disclaimer: I don't entertain the illusion that I am cured, once and for all, from my nostalgia for the old Emberá clothes. This may wait for me at the next ethnographic corner. As with ethnocentrism, an author's battle against ethnographic nostalgia is never entirely resolved.

Indigenous accommodations of non-indigenous modesty

The loincloth – *guayuco* in Spanish; *andeá* in Emberá – is a heavily stereotyped clothing item in Panama. It communicates a prejudiced non-indigenous perception that certain indigenous groups or individuals live outside (or are lagging behind) the values and aesthetics of Western civilisation. In Panamanian popular imagination the loincloth is paired with the undifferentiated representation of the generic Chocó (Emberá or Wounaan) man in particular, as the other Panamanian ethnic groups do not use this clothing item. Until the second half of the twentieth century, the loincloth was used widely in several communities in Darién, and the figure of 'an Indian wearing a *guayuco*' is not merely a pejorative non-indigenous caricature, but also a childhood memory of many contemporary Emberá who have now entered the second half of their lives.

Thus, while for many non-indigenous Panamanians the loincloth stands for primitiveness or ignorance of 'civilised' life – reproducing an image of the Indian as a wild man living in the forest, for many contemporary Emberá the image of a man dressed in the loincloth can trigger the recollection of a biological grandfather or a reminiscence from childhood. More widely, and especially among younger generations of Emberá, the use of the *andeá* is associated with adherence to the old ways and with a view of 'tradition' as representativeness located in the past. Unsurprisingly, during the last two decades of the twentieth century, the *guayuco* – a direct target of Latino contempt – fell out of fashion, and most contemporary Emberá men – in communities that do not regularly entertain tourists – will think twice before being persuaded to wear it.

These old-fashioned, stereotypical connotations of the loincloth have more recently been mediated by an emerging sense of pride in upholding an Emberá identity, regardless of the scorn of non-indigenous Panamanian neighbours. In the context of presentations for tourists, the reintroduction of the loincloth as a component of the full traditional attire engenders an indirect identity statement: 'I am an Emberá and I am not embarrassed to wear an *andeá*', a declaration that is sometimes voiced by men who were self-conscious about wearing it before, but have now partially overcome their initial hesitation. In the course of my fieldwork, usually following activities or conversations that indicated my enthusiastic identification with the Emberá point of view, the Emberá teased me encouragingly with the remark that 'tomorrow' or 'next time' I should 'wear a *guayuco*'. In the next chapter I will discuss mimetic appropriations of the Emberá dress (or other cultural practices) by non-indigenous admirers, which are usually welcomed by the Emberá as signs of acceptance and respect for the Emberá identity. Such mimetic appropriations by Westerners exorcise the old stereotype by reversing the stereotyping gaze.

Despite its status as an indicator of upholding, or desiring to identify with, Emberá tradition, the loincloth is used nowadays primarily on occasions that involve a cultural presentation (in particular, although not exclusively, to foreigners). Emberá men in Parara Puru who do not work for tourism or are temporary visitors tactfully remain out of the tourists' sight (usually dressed in shorts and t-shirts). From their point of view, there is no obvious reason to wear a loincloth, as they do not participate in welcoming and entertaining the tourists. Some of these men, however, will not refuse to wear a loincloth to receive tourists in their own communities, provided that such an opportunity arises and is economically rewarding. Although Emberá friends from large Emberá communities in Darién have reported the rare example of the odd old man who still wears an *andeá* – mostly while cultivating land outside of the community – it would be fair to say that contemporary Emberá men in communities that do not rely on tourism only wear a loincloth for occasional performative contexts.[12]

The Emberá men from Parara Puru who are between thirty-five and forty-five years old admit that back in the 1990s, when they first started working for tourism, they felt embarrassed wearing the loincloth. 'We were shy to wear the *andeá*', they say, 'we grew up wearing trousers and shorts', 'our skin [in those areas] was white!' One man in particular confessed his humiliation when his young (at the time) Latino friends saw him wearing a *guayuco* for the first time. 'I did not know how to wear it', he said, 'my father showed me how, and I was embarrassed. We did not have our own [homogenous Emberá] community back then and we all had Latino friends.' After a short reflection he added, 'Now the Latinos know that we are working for tourism and do not bother us', 'we can dress like our grandparents within our community every day. When they [the Latinos] see us on the other side of the lake [wearing a loincloth, usually while meeting the arriving tourists] they know that this is our job.'

To reduce the overall impression of nakedness communicated to non-indigenous audiences by the use of the loincloth, many men of Parara Puru use another item of the full Emberá attire, the *amburá*, a belt made of glass beads woven in colourful, mostly geometric, designs (see Chapter 2). The use of this traditional clothing item comes with an additional advantage: it hides his buttocks from view. Seen from behind, a man wearing a loincloth (but not an *amburá*) looks almost completely naked, remarked Reverte Coma (2002: 213), reflecting on his fieldnotes from the 1960s. The same observation was apparently made by some of his contemporary tourists. The Emberá of Parara Puru responded by adopting the *amburá* enthusi-astically; almost every adult male in the community has one. 'Some elderly *gringas* [American women] did not like our buttocks!' a younger Emberá man humor-ously explained, and his father agreed: 'It is better this way [to cover them with the *amburá*]', he said, 'So many tourists come here every day. Some from the cruise ships prefer to see us that way [with the *amburá*].'

However, as I soon came to realise, wider Emberá views concerning the *amburá* are more controversial. The men from another Emberá community at Chagres – Emberá Puru – that has similarly developed (and relies heavily on) tourism refuse to wear the *amburá*, even if solely for the entertainment of tourists. During my first visit to the community, I politely enquired why the men do not wear an *amburá* 'like the men in Parara and Tusipono do'. They responded that they feel more com-fortable wearing only the loincloth. Yet, on my return to Parara, I was told that the men of Emberá Puru do not like the *amburá* because 'it looks like a skirt'. On a later visit to Emberá Puru, and after a longer conversation, two local men corrobo-rated this point of view, highlighting that they find the *amburá* womanish. In their eyes, the *amburá* looks more like a skirt than a belt, a point that has not escaped the attention of some Latino men in neighbouring communities, resulting, I was told, in some pointed remarks.

In a subsequent conversation with a young Emberá man from Darién who lives in Panama City and aspires to become a professional tourist guide I found myself in the middle of an argument. When he saw photographs of men in Parara Puru on my laptop screen he remarked with derision in his voice that he does not like the *amburá* and that this item of dress 'is not traditional'. Provoked by his rather absolute statement and as I had my laptop on the table, I produced early-twentieth-century photographs of Emberá men proudly posing with an *amburá*. 'Here you can see that this is a truly traditional item of clothing', I remarked, overwhelming my younger interlocutor with an authoritative but static view of authenticity that derives its legitimacy from the past. However, when I looked into the matter more closely, through careful comparison I came to realise that the *amburás* that the Emberá wear today in Parara Puru are approximately three to four centimetres wider than the ones used in the past. If the latter can be described as broad belts, the former could be described disparagingly as very short skirts!

The ambivalence of the Emberá towards the *amburá* revolves around different Western expectations about modesty and nudity. While some outsiders are offended by the naked bottoms of the Emberá men, others see the *amburá* belts as mini-skirts: a few tourists have described them as carnivalesque (or suspect that they are inauthentic, touristy decorations), while Latino neighbours see them as effeminate. In response to such evaluations by outsiders, different Emberá communities have adopted different solutions. The increase in width of the *amburás*, and their enthusiastic adoption by most men in some communities, is an adaptation that aims at decreasing the overall minimalism of the male attire. The refusal to wear the *amburá* by some other communities reflects concern for the aesthetics of masculinity in wider non-indigenous society.

Another indigenous item of clothing, which has lately been adapted to accommodate the non-indigenous aesthetic of covering the upper body, is the *ubarí*[E] (*pulsera de plata*[S]), a heavy beaded necklace that extends over the chest with lines of coins hung in layers. In the last twenty years, the beaded components of this item have expanded to such an extent that the *ubarí* looks more like a top than a necklace. This adaptation provides some cover to the otherwise topless female body of Emberá women dressed in traditional attire and – as with the extension of the *amburá's* width – comprises an example of another indigenous accommodation of non-indigenous aesthetics and principles of modesty. In fact, the *ubarís* of most women in Parara Puru are so heavily built that they effectively mask the general perception of female toplessness, all the while without compromising their commitment to upholding an indigenous etiquette.

Outside of contexts within which the use of traditional attire is appropriate, the most significant adaptation of Emberá dress in accommodating Western standards of modesty is the combination of a *paruma* with a modern top. This is the standard dress code followed by the overwhelming majority of Emberá women and, as I will describe in more detail in the next chapter, its popularity relies on two factors. First, the freedom it provides in matching colours or using different types of tops (t-shirts, vest tops, tank tops or cropped tops), and second, the creative articulation of non-indigenous standards of modesty (the *paruma*, when wrapped around a woman's body, is after all a skirt) with an indigenous identity (the *paruma* is seen in Panama as an undeniably Emberá-Wounaan item of clothing). The particular dress combination allows women to cover their upper body – thus confronting the stereotype of primitiveness or immodesty conveyed by the toplessness of the traditional attire – and to do so by using contemporary or fashionable items of non-indigenous clothing.

Embarrassment, pride and individual dress choices

Despite the relative uniformity of the dress styles followed by the Emberá in Panama, particular individuals identify to different degrees with elements of the modern or the traditional dress codes, such as the extent of upper body nudity (overall) or use of the *parumas* (in the case of women). Potential changes of this type do not always follow the same direction or pattern, along the lines of a unilineal path that leads away from tradition (conceived as identification with the past) and towards modernity (conceived in terms of Western aesthetics and rules of modesty). Many Emberá women conform to the Western preference of covering the upper body (all or most of the time), while others, especially in communities that have developed tourism, have increased the overall time they remain topless, not merely during the tourism presentations, but also, to a lesser degree, during everyday activities in the vicinity of the domestic compound (in a manner that resembles the dress code of their grandmothers).

It is easier to trace those nuances in the life trajectory of particular individuals. Deborah, a thirty-five-year-old woman from Darién who used to live in Parara[13] with her Chagres-born husband, often remained topless in the close vicinity of her house, even after the tourists' departure. She and her husband were proud and very articulate about their identification with Emberá culture. Her sisters, however, live in a non- indigenous small community in Darién, where the Emberá are a very small minority. When I visited the sisters on a long field trip I was surprised to realise that not only did they avoid toplessness, but they also wore skirts instead of *parumas*. They explained that they 'like *parumas*, but . . ', they emphasised, 'live in a predominantly Latino community'. The decision to wear skirts was related to the social pressure of adapting to life among an overwhelmingly non-indigenous majority.

Immediately after my return to Parara Puru, I visited Deborah to give her news and photographs from her relatives in Darién. While we were looking at the photographs I pointed out that her sisters were wearing 'skirts' (*faldas*) – as the Emberá refer to all Western skirts, in contradistinction to their own *parumas*. Deborah, who had recently adopted a strong identification with Emberá culture, explained to me how difficult it was to live in a *kampuniá*-town – that is, among people who do not appreciate 'her own culture'. For many years, she confessed, she was dressed 'like her sisters'. She only discovered the benefits and importance of the 'Emberá type of dressing' after moving to live with her husband in an all-Emberá community in Chagres. 'Here in Parara', she said, 'I learned how to wear the *paruma* and dance with the other women [dressed in traditional attire and with the chest uncovered]'. 'In the beginning', she added, 'I was shy, but later I became accustomed to it. Now I prefer the Emberá clothes.'

Amelia is also originally from Darién and is married to a man from Chagres. She is twenty-nine years old and also identifies enthusiastically with Emberá cultural practices. She always wears a *paruma* – even in the town, she emphasises – but to avoid complete toplessness she always carefully combines her *paruma* with a cotton top or, when dressed in full traditional attire, with a heavy coin necklace (*ubarí*[E]). She feels very content that tourism has provided her with opportunities to wear traditional attire, which is – she has recently come to realise – 'very beautiful'. However, in her childhood her father tried to make her believe otherwise and did not allow her to dance or wear earrings and beaded necklaces. 'My parents raised me like this because my father became Christian', she explained.

Amelia's exposure to Christian principles from an early age is evident in the careful manner she covers her body. Unlike Deborah, she does not do household jobs topless, and she puts on cotton tops immediately after the end of her work in tourism. In contrast with her parents, she dresses her daughter in *parumas* and allows her to participate in Emberá animal dances, which revere animal spirits. Yet, as Amelia explained to me in a confidential tone, the dances for her are a 'cultural thing' or 'something of our culture', rather than a religious practice. Her identification with evangelical Christianity has fluctuated over the years, but has become stronger recently, after the death of her father. So far, she has succeeded in negotiating the contradictions between indigenous practices and Christian belief, by compartmentalising the two into different contexts of her life: her work in tourism, when she is dressed according to the traditional code, and the rest of her life when she covers the top part of the body more carefully.

Let me now trace a similar pattern of dress choices in the life trajectory of Amelia's aunt, Ubertina, who is approximately twenty years older than her niece and the wife of the community's leader (*nokó*[E]), Claudio. Ubertina has always maintained a close relationship with the evangelical church that helped her family migrate to Chagres from a community in Darién close to the Colombian border, which was, at the time, under threat from Colombian guerrillas and paramilitaries. During the early stages of the introduction of tourism, Ubertina helped her Chagres-born husband and the other women in the community learn about many traditional practices. Nevertheless, as her husband remembers, she used to wear a skirt in the early 1990s, when she met Claudio. Following the foundation of Parara Puru she always wears a *paruma* (in the community) and remains a source of inspiration in matters of Emberá tradition and language.

Since the recent loss of their younger son, Claudio and Ubertina have strengthened their relationship with the church and dress more conservatively to attend church services, which they go to more often than before. To go to church out of the community, Claudio wears long trousers and a shirt, while Ubertina combines her *paruma* with a modern top (although sometimes she wears a skirt). This is obviously not the first time Ubertina's and Claudio's dress choices have shifted slightly closer to or further away from a heavier reliance on modern clothes. In the 1970s, as a young girl in Darién, Ubertina was accustomed to the old dress code. But when her family started following evangelical Christianity in the 1980s, she fully adopted modern clothes. Much later, in the mid-1990s – as a married woman at Chagres – she started to use the full traditional attire for tourism, and a *paruma* combined with a t-shirt outside tourist performances.

The involvement of the Emberá of Chagres with tourism is for Claudio an important moment that shaped his life and that of his family. 'Work for tourism', he maintains, did not merely encourage him to learn about and practise the culture of his parents, but also motivated several families of locally born Emberá to establish a community, within which it became possible to practise Emberá culture without subjecting oneself to the ridicule or criticism of non-indigenous neighbours. 'A few years ago', he said, the Latinos were staring at us when we were painted [with *jagua* designs]. Now they know that this is part of our culture.' Then he continued:

> We, the Emberá who are native to Chagres, grew up wearing shorts. The women used to wear skirts, and the young ones, shorts. When I met my wife we lived at Victoriano with the Latinos. Then we started working with tourists. Little by little, we started to learn all the things we had forgotten. We did not have many trad- itional clothes, and some women did not want to paint themselves with *jagua*. My wife helped me improve my Emberá, and I helped her improve her Spanish. If it weren't for tourism, we would all, by now, be speaking only Spanish; we would all be wearing only modern clothes!

Several other Emberá men and women from Parara Puru explained to me that tourism presented them with acceptable opportunities to wear, and become accustomed to wearing, traditional clothes. They stressed that they appreciate this opportunity and enjoy wearing traditional clothes, yet when the tourists depart, they also enjoy wearing modern clothes. For most, the freedom to wear traditional clothes without being subjected to scorn from outsiders is complemented by the alternative option of wearing their newest modern clothes when they go out of the community. This is because most individuals in the community, and especially the younger ones, enjoy wearing both traditional and modern clothes. Dari and Erika, two young women raised in Parara Puru by families born at Chagres, put this into perspective.

Dari, who is twenty-one and mother to a young child, dresses in modern outfits to go to the city, but unequivocally prefers the traditional clothes. They are very comfortable, she says, and she is used to wearing them. Besides, she adds, the trad- itional dress is 'more striking (*más llamativo*), and [in this respect] is better.' She also prefers seeing her husband in traditional attire: 'He is more handsome (*más hermoso*), more attractive (*más atractivo*).' Her friend Erika, however, who is three years younger and – at the time of writing – still unmarried, has a preference for modern clothes. They are more comfortable and simple, she says. Yet, she is not embarrassed to wear the traditional clothes, she emphasises. When she goes out of the community she prefers modern clothes, although occasionally she does wear a *paruma* in the city. Some Latinos, she explains, like the Emberá clothes, but others 'are racist' (*son racistas*).

More than one woman in Parara Puru voiced the opinion that 'some Latinos are racist' to me. Some described how they disliked the intense, almost rude, gaze of Latino men, as they have experienced it focusing on their *paruma* or *jagua* designs while they travel on the bus or walk in the street. In spite of this, most women believe that this type of racism is nowadays abating. 'Some Latinos', clarified an Emberá girl who goes to high school, 'like our culture and do not ask many ques- tions when they see us wearing a *paruma*', and after a brief reflection she added, 'when they ask, I explain to them, so that they learn.' Clearly, the performative confidence that comes from presenting Emberá culture to foreign audiences has contributed in a new sense of pride in identifying publicly with Emberá culture and has helped some Emberá in Parara Puru, especially the younger ones, develop a vocabulary for doing so. While older women are more likely to admit that they were once inhibited when wearing traditional items of clothing (but are no longer), younger women declare much more emphatically that they are not embarrassed to wear *parumas* (outside the community) or the full traditional attire (inside the community).

The converging point of all local narratives regarding choices between traditional and modern clothes is the issue of freedom to shift between established dress codes. Wearing the traditional attire without being scorned is considered an accomplishment, from the result of their growing reputations as professional hosts of tourism. A corollary of this success was the establishment of a homogenously Emberá community, a safe context for occasionally departing from the formalistic code of the full attire by adopting mixed or in-between dress codes that rely on selected clothing elements. A young man, for example, may choose to paint his arms with *jagua* designs that match his latest t-shirt, while an older man may choose to apply the *jagua* juice only on those parts of his body that will be hidden when he wears a t-shirt or shirt. Yet what is valued by the Emberá of Parara Puru is having the option. One married woman in her late twenties encapsulated this freedom with following words:

> I like modern clothes . . . but I like the Emberá clothes more. It makes me happy to see that my children use the *parumas* and the loincloth. I wear the *paruma* every day, as you can see, but sometimes I like to wear trousers. In our community we are free to dress in modern clothes, but in traditional clothes too!

Box 7

Women's clothes as an index of indigenous authenticity

- The Emberá and Wounaan women can be easily recognised by their colourful *parumas*, in a similar way that Guna and Ngäbe women can be identified by their own distinctive modes of dress. With most Panamanian indigenous groups, female dress is emblematic of indigenous identities (Howe 1998, 2009; Salvador 1997: 151; Tice 1995; Martínez Mauri 2012; Margiotti 2013; Young 1971; Karkotis 2012). It is also interesting to note that when the Guna, Ngäbe, Wounaan or Emberá men are dressed in Western clothes, it is often only the dress of a wife or a daughter that will identify the ethnicity of an indigenous man who is walking in the town with his family. Thus with respect to dress codes and practices, indigenous women in Panama, like elsewhere, are 'icons of contemporary ethnic tradition' (Knauft 2007: 103; see also C. Hendrickson 1995). As

I discuss in the following chapter, a majority of Emberá husbands and parents in Chagres and Darién insist that their wives or daughters wear the *paruma* and comment with unreserved irony that girls who do not wear the *paruma* look like *gringas* or *Latinas*.

- It must be also noted that during the times of dispersed settlement, Emberá men wore more indigenous adornments than women and took greater care of their appearance (see Nordenskiold 1928; Torres de Araúz 1966; Pineda and Gutiérrez de Pineda 1999; Riverte Coma 2002; for more details, see Chapter 2). In those days, it was the men's dress that highlighted indigeneity and cultural difference. It appears that with the resettlement of the Emberá in concentrated communities – which signalled a greater exposure to national education and participation in wider political processes (Herlihy 1986; Kane 1994) – men abandoned their previous styles of adornment, while women took over the responsibility of representing an indigenous identity. In the 1980s, Kane described an emerging gendered incongruity in the Emberá dress code as it was revealed during an indigenous congress: 'The men wear factory-made, imported shorts, pants, and shirts' and conduct politics, yet 'women are not vocal participants in most congressional dialogue'; they cooked for the men, washed their clothes, and a few danced bare-breasted traditional dances silently embodying indigeneity (Kane 1994: 167–9). With the establishment of concentrated communities we see a new pattern unravelling according to which Emberá men represent indigenous identity in political terms, wearing non-indigenous clothes, while Emberá women are valorised by Emberá society as nurturers of indigeneity, wearing *paruma*-skirts predominantly in domestic and indigenous spaces.
- But let us compare the traditional dress of the Emberá with that of their neighbours the Guna. The dress codes of both groups are distinctive and have caught, as we have seen, the exoticising attention of early-twentieth-century ethnologists, travellers and explorers. Nordenskiold, who eventually identified much more closely with the Guna, was initially attracted by the indigenous association of the Emberá dress code and, in particular, their avoidance of Western clothes (1928: 37, 42–3). His impression of the Guna as deculturated and snobbish was based on a superficial view of Guna men dressed in Western clothes (1928: 14; see also Howe 2009: 120). Verrill (1921) and Marsh (1934) associated the relatively uncovered Emberá body with 'nakedness' and 'primitiveness', and remarked that the Guna, who covered the greater part of the body with clothes made from fabric, were, in comparison to the Emberá, more civilised and refined (see Chapter 4).
- Yet, it was the dress of the Guna women that became the target of assimilating policies, while the desire of the Guna men to defend that style of dress sparked the Guna revolution in the early-twentieth century (see Howe 1998, 2009). Following the revolution, and throughout the

twentieth century, Guna women received the brunt of negative stereotyping by the Panamanian national majority, due to their determination to wear indigenous dress in non-indigenous spaces, even in the capital. In this respect, they have opened the way for the women of other ethnic groups, such as the Emberá, the Wounaan and the Ngäbe, to wear their distinctive dress in the presence of Latino neighbours or in the city.

- In comparison to the female attire of the Guna, the traditional dress of the Emberá, which relies less on fabric garments and more on body painting and adornments, has not inspired revolution or any political opposition by non-indigenous majorities. It has been largely perceived by outsiders to represent an absence of clothes, a 'problem' that can be potentially rectified by the advance of Western civilisation, which from the perspective of the vanishing savage is seen as inevitable (see Clifford 1986; Berliner 2015). Approached from such a viewpoint – that echoes a nostalgic view and unintentional primitivism – the recent reintroduction of the old Emberá dress code as a tourist attraction is not considered threatening, but is tolerated by non-indigenous majorities: a further exotic addition to Panamanian multiculturalism (see Horton 2006; Howe 2009; Velásquez Runk 2012).

- If the Emberá dress, with its minimal fabric garments, was rendered less threatening for the nation as it was easily replaced with 'Western', mass-manufactured clothes, the embeddedness of Western fabrics into Guna culture, and their transformation into emblems of Guna identity, was apparently seen as more conspicuous. Taussig (1993: 141) has referred to the distinctive dress and appearance of Guna women as the alteric *sine qua non* of Guna identity, while Howe (1998: 17) has stressed that it was the Guna women 'that visually displayed the distinctiveness of Guna society and its separation from the world'. The latter have developed in time a rich cultural tradition of making their own clothes from Western fabrics, while one clothing item in particular, the *mola*, a panel that forms a part of a traditional blouse, is now considered a quintessential icon of Guna culture and a distinctive type of art (see Salvador 1976, 1997; Tice 1995). Guna women invest a great part of their lives making and recycling clothes, and, as Margiotti (2013) persuasively argues, the experiential dimension of their relationship with their clothes impacts on the materialisation of Guna sociality. Although the Emberá also recycle and alter certain types of 'traditional' clothes and adornments, they do not, in general, alter Western fabrics. Their concern is mostly focused on the interface of indigenous and non-indigenous clothes, or the potential combination of the two.

The flow of change

As we have seen in this chapter, the changes in Emberá dress codes cannot simply be explained in terms of a unilineal progression that moves in one direction

A. (a view of Emberá cloth transformations, as a unilineal line of progression in time)

traditional attire ──────────▶ modern clothes ──────────▶ traditional attire
                                                               (only for tourist presentations)

B. (a more nuanced view of Emberá cloth transformations, as series of changes in the course of the day)

traditional attire, for tourist presentations   →   in-between dress codes, part of the body uncovered

                                                       mixed combinations of modern and traditional dress

mixed modern and traditional dress   modern clothes, to work in or around the community
                                                       modern clothes to go out of the community
                                                  ←

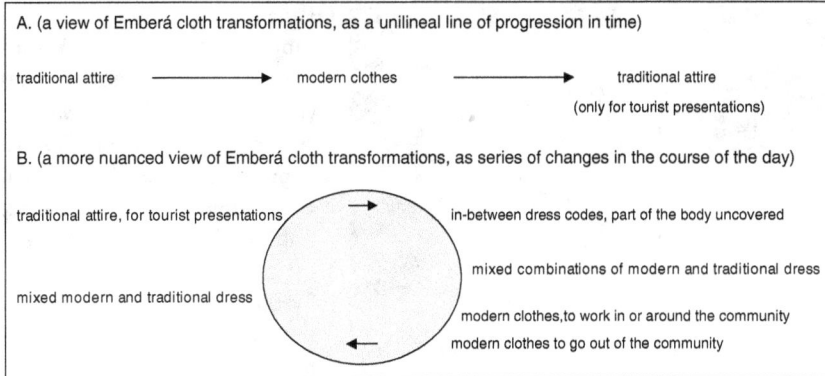

7.9 Unilineal vs. non-unilineal dress transformations

(i.e. away from traditional attire and closer to the complete adoption of Western clothes). The decline of the traditional code of dress was followed by its partial reintroduction in some communities that developed tourism and a more general revaluation of tradition in Emberá society. Yet, even this process, when described as a unidirectional development – see option A in the table below – fails to account for the complexity of Emberá dress choices. These may include styles of dress that include certain traditional elements (for example, the *parumas* or body painting) while exclude others (for example, beaded necklaces and belts or bracelets) and the overall mixing of indigenous items of dress with modern clothes. Different styles – or different combinations of styles – of dress may be deemed appropriate for different contexts of everyday life, especially in communities that entertain tourists. In the latter, the mere availability of a greater number of indigenous clothes and adornments provides a greater scope for mixed, or other spontaneous and unpredictable, dress combinations.

These observations may help us to appreciate that the dress practices of the Emberá show a remarkable ability to adapt to new circumstances and incorporate new elements. In the communities that entertain tourists, for example, we may see a series of dress codes unravelling in the course of a single day, as depicted by option B in figure 7.9. These can be understood, as I have argued elsewhere (Theodossopoulos 2012a, 2013a), as transformations based on previous transformations (Gow 2001a: 127), instilled with local meaning (Veber 1996:156). They may accommodate the exoticised expectations of others (Conklin 1997; Theodossopoulos 2011), but also address considerations stemming from everyday social relations (Margiotti 2013). The various dress codes adopted by the Emberá – indigenous, Western or mixed – represent the choices of the Emberá, who decide what is appropriate to wear at home, in the forest, in the city and in the presence of non-indigenous Panamanians (who tend to stereotype indigeneity) or tourists (who tend to idealise the exotic).

As with other cultural practices, the meaningfulness of Emberá clothing choices is context specific. In the early 1980s, Emberá women danced bare-breasted for

7.10 Emberá protesting in Panama City dressed in traditional attire

Panamanian officials, while Emberá men negotiated politics in factory-made clothes (Kane 1994:167). Nowadays, several Emberá men in Eastern Panama will consider (even if with some initial hesitation) putting on the loincloth – a garment heavily stereotyped by the wider society – to join the women in performances for tourists. The reenactment of tradition in this symbolic form – repeated and performatively re-embodied in the communities that entertain tourists – has instilled some Emberá with an emerging sense of confidence (Theodossopoulos 2011, 2014). Here, wearing particular clothes engenders the consolidation of pride and a more explicitly articulated indigenous identity. In 2009, groups of Emberá from Chagres participated, along with other indigenous peoples of Panama, in pro-indigenous-rights demonstrations in Panama City, where they danced, dressed in traditional attire, in the streets of the capital. Such acts of indigenous identification in public would have been unthinkable – at least for the Emberá of Chagres – in the early 1990s. In this sense the choice of dress in a particular context – such as going to the city with body-painted arms or wearing a *paruma*-skirt in Avenida Central (the central commercial street of the capital) – becomes a statement of indigeneity (see Conklin 1997; Gow 2007; Ewart 2007; Santos-Granero 2009), and the clothes themselves, remembered in the embodiment of a daring act, constitute part of the integral indigenous person (Miller 2005b; Keane 2005).

Notes

1 Although sometimes they receive donations of 'modern' clothes by North American friends of the community or evangelical churches, the Emberá of Parara Puru mostly buy their own clothes – *parumas* and fabric to make loincloths, beads to make *amburás* and necklaces, or Western mass-produced clothes – at the market.

2 Here the choice of the Spanish noun *vestidos* highlights the formal and presentational nature of the full traditional attire. Even in the past, before the Emberá started extensively using 'modern' clothes, they decorated themselves with their full complement of available adornments only for special occasions – celebrations or ceremonies that usually involveddancing, guests and the consumption of alcohol. In everyday life they used a minimal dress code that involved usually only a loincloth

(for the men), a *paruma*-skirt (for the women), sometimes a simple, short necklace and commonly *jagua*-body-paint designs, which were often, but not exclusively, applied for special occasions, but remained on the body for several days afterwards.

3 With the exception of mornings after big national or religious holidays during which many men had consumed significant quantities of canned beer. Drinking heavily during celebrations is an old Emberá custom, which in the past involved the consumption of locally produced alcohol, *chicha fuerte*, produced in the context of shamanic curing ceremonies or independently. In the twentieth century, evangelical missionaries have worked hard to discourage heavy drinking, though not always successfully.

4 The cleaned fish are later cooked by the *cocinera* (the cook) or, depending on the size of the expected tourist group, two or three female cooks who undertake the responsibility of preparing the 'traditional' meal of fish and plantains for the tourists. They are dressed in full traditional attire (that is, with *parumas* but topless, with their chests covered by a heavy *ubarí*-necklace). This job is rewarded at a higher rate on the local pay scale for work invested in tourism, and women take turns performing this and most other duties.

5 At Chagres, the park authorities have discouraged hunting as a subsistence strategy. Nevertheless, they allow the Emberá to hunt on a limited number of days every year, and many Emberá men take full advantage of this opportunity, organising long hunting trips to the most remote areas of the park that may last two or three days.

6 The community has pipes of running water connected with a water source higher on the forested hills that surround the community. Very often the pipe breaks, and a group of men, dressed in long trousers, undertake the demanding task of fixing it.

7 Not everyone completes the full course of secondary education, due primarily to the cost of travel, uniforms and books. Yet in the last five years a few were successful – two young men and three young women, some of whom took further foreign-language training in the city, aiming, as they say, to 'help their community with tourism'. The cost of these extra studies was very heavy for the respective families.

8 In Parara Puru there are not many mature *jagua* trees (*Genipa americana*), and the local residents often have to buy *jagua* from other Emberá or even Latinos (usually at the price of four fruits per dollar). When they do not have enough *jagua* juice they reserve their supply to body-paint the tourists for a small payment. Other Emberá communities at Chagres that receive tourists have a greater supply of locally produced *jagua* and apply the jagua-juice on their bodies more frequently and freely.

9 The bark of *jira* palm (*socratea exorrhiza*), which represents, according to Emberá convention, the ideal flooring material, is nowadays more difficult to find and expensive to buy and transport if it is not locally available. This is why nowadays the floor in the majority of contemporary Emberá houses in most Emberá communities in Panama are made of planks. The floors of some houses have a portion of the floor made from *jira*, usually the house extensions used as sleeping quarters, and another portion of the floor made from planks. As houses are periodically rebuilt or renovated, older *jira* bark is reused to floor the corners (or extensions) of the house where the Emberá sit or sleep. For more information about traditional and modern elements of the Emberá house, see Chapter 6.

10 Emberá canoes have their own spirit, and they are emblematic of the concept of the family (Isacsson 1993: 92).

11 In Darién, the Emberá still use long-sleeved shirts extensively, especially during long canoe trips or work in the forest, but they have replaced the loincloth with shorts.

12 For example, community celebrations that involve Emberá music and dance, or political gatherings or demonstrations with a performative element – for example, a dance – to accentuate an indigenous identity.

13 She has since moved to another community with her children. Her husband remains in Parara and is one of the new leaders of the community.

8

Three authentic Emberá discontinuities

'Of all the aspects of life in the upriver forest . . . the most authentic', says Stephanie
Kane in *The Phantom Gringo Boat*, are 'the discontinuities that present themselves'
(1994: 41). Discontinuities, in Kane's analysis of Emberá social life, emerge from
the intrusion of the market economy into peripheral indigenous worlds. They
highlight inequalities and inconsistencies – similar to what Appadurai (1996)
calls disjunctures – that arise when peripheral actors attempt to connect with a
wider economy of expectations, albeit at a slower speed and with limited control.
The discontinuities of the Emberá case make visible a 'fractured context', argues
Taussig: the anthropologist – for example, Kane – collecting pagan myths from
respondents who are lectured by a priest (Taussig 1993: 18); a dedicated Christian
Emberá woman sitting on a shaman's stool, wearing non-indigenous clothes, but
refusing to speak non-indigenous languages; or an Emberá man dressed in traditional attire to entertain tourists, texting via his mobile phone the date of an
indigenous protest.

Taking inspiration from Kane's focus on contradictions, in this chapter I present three examples of discontinuity authentically embedded in Emberá everyday life. In the first example, I focus on a 'traditional' item of dress made in
Asia specifically for an Emberá audience in Latin America: this is the cloth of the
paruma-skirts, a clothing item – or better, a 'lived garment' (Banerjee and Miller
2003: 1) – considered by the Emberá to be an authentic mark of indigeneity. In the
second example, I follow the members of an Emberá family as they put aside their
indigenous clothes – without putting aside their Emberá identity – to go to church
in an 'authentic' Emberá canoe that excites the author's misplaced ethnographic
nostalgia. And finally, in the third example, I present a mimetic appropriation
that represents a reversal of the exoticising gaze: Westerners who put on Emberá
clothes to embody indigeneity – reconstituting the authenticity of the imitation
and the imitated (Taussig 1993).

Paruma fashion, materiality and versatility

One summer day in early February 2011 I met a middle-aged married couple from
Colón who were spending a few days in Parara Puru with one of the local Emberá

8.1   *Parumas* hanging loosely on shop floor

families. The husband was
an Emberá himself, and a
relative of the host family,
but his wife was a Latina
from Chiriqui (in western
Panama). When I pointed
out that she was wearing
a *paruma* although she
was not indigenous, they
explained: 'The *paruma* has
become very popular in
the last three or four years',
said the man, 'you can see
Emberá women wearing the *paruma* in the city.' 'The success of the *paruma*', said
the woman, 'is that they are colourful (*llamativas*)'; the various colours (in the patterns) facilitate 'many combinations' with a variety of tops. Recently, she added,
women who are not indigenous have started wearing *parumas*, 'as I do now here
in Parara, where I am taking a few days off work to relax.' 'In Colón, I have even
seen black women wearing the *paruma*', her husband added, 'they look good in the
colours of the *parumas*.'

I should not mislead the reader in believing that non-indigenous Panamanians
have started wearing indigenous dress; those few non-indigenous women who
might occasionally wear a *paruma* do so as an exotic diversion. They are con-
scious of the fact that the *paruma* is a distinctively Chocó – Emberá-Wounaan –
type of dress, though it has more recently become a popular and fashionable
one. Similarly, women from other Panamanian indigenous groups, such as the
Guna and Ngäbe, stick to their own style of dress. As I discussed in the last
chapter, indigenous women's dress is seen in Panama as an identifier of ethnicity (see Young 1971; Salvador 1976; Tice 1995; Taussig 1993; Howe 1998;
Margiotti 2013). Although indigenous men appear in public dressed in modern
clothes, indigenous women are expected – by parents, husbands and indigenous leaders – to dress more traditionally. Yet, if some younger women show
some occasional discomfort with the preference for the *paruma* in Emberá
society, it is not an exaggeration to admit that the Emberá fondness for the
paruma, and women's pride in wearing them, has evidently increased in recent
years. The emerging status of the *paruma* as a fashionable item of clothing has
played a role in all this.

To help the uninitiated reader understand how a rectangular piece of cloth used
primarily as a skirt can acquire a distinctive fashion, I should clarify two or three
descriptive details. It is important to note that a critical majority of Emberá and
Wounaan women have always worn the *paruma*, a preference that survived the
decline of the traditional Chocó code of dress.[1] At the turn of the twentieth century the last *parumas* made from bark-cloth (see Chapter 2) were for the most part
replaced by *parumas* made from ordinary cotton cloth bought at market. Since the
1970s synthetic cloth, mass-produced in Asia, gradually replaced other varieties

of cloth. In the 1990s a particular type and style of Asian cloth – with colourful designs – became especially popular among the Emberá and the Wounaan. In the first decade of the twenty-first century this new type of *paruma*-cloth became very popular and is now recognisable by indigenous and non-indigenous Panamanians as a distinctively Emberá and Wounaan item of dress.

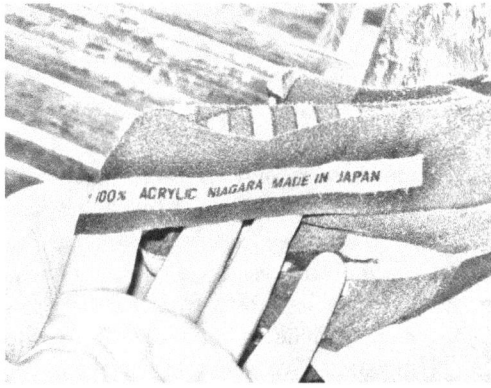

8.2   The most common *paruma* maker's mark

A second issue that deserves clarification is that *paruma* fashion does not affect the overall shape and length of the cloth used as a *paruma*-skirt. What changes from season to season is not the size of the *parumas* or the way of wearing them, but the patterns and, more gradually over the years, as the Emberá observe, the quality of the cloth. Each new set of multi-coloured patterns is printed in different combinations of colours, providing the women with a choice. Season after season and, more recently, almost every other month, a new design – in a variety of colour palettes – is introduced to the market on a pre-announced date. As I will describe below, a great number of Emberá and Wounaan, women as well as men, come to Panama City to buy the new *paruma*, either for their own use or to resell to friends and neighbours in their communities all over Eastern Panama.

A newly released *paruma*-cloth is referred to by the Emberá and the Wounaan in Panama as the 'new *paruma*'. The new patterns are usually naturalistic depictions of leaves, flowers or birds, but bear absolutely no relationship to the distinctive and elaborate Emberá art of drawing *jagua* designs on the human body (see Chapter 2) or on pieces of wood used by Emberá shamans in healing ceremonies.[2] In fact, the designs of the new *parumas* look stylistically Asian – which is where they are produced – but the Emberá insist that they are manufactured specifically for them. As the new *parumas* are used by the overwhelming majority of Emberá and Wounaan in Panama, and have become increasingly popular in recent years, they are now unquestionably accepted (and presented) – by the Emberá, the Wounaan, other Panamanian indigenous groups and non-indigenous Panamanians – as representative of Chocó culture and tradition, and, in turn, their Asian origin is ignored. But let me, for now, turn to the noisy streets of Panama City and the anticipation of the Emberá for yet another 'new *paruma*'.

The day after I returned to Panama in 2012 coincided with the release of the latest *paruma*. As I was already in the city, I thought it would be a good idea to buy two or three to augment my collection of presents for my Emberá friends. At Avenida Central, a commercial street in the centre of Panama City, I met with

8.3 *Parumas* on display in the entrance to a shop in Avenida Central

a Peace Corps volunteer, Sara Taylor, who was working at the time in a neighbouring Emberá community at Chagres, Emberá Puru. We visited the shops that sell the *parumas*, which trade fabrics for a primarily Emberá and Guna market (see Salvador and Howe 1997: 42). On the wall of a more central shop we saw the pattern of the *paruma* to be released a month later, displayed in a variety of colours. However, 'the *paruma* of the month' was only available in another shop on the busy side street of La Bajada de Salsipuedes.[3] Although it was early in the morning, we saw a very long queue of Emberá – mostly women, with a few men – extending out of the shop and to the street. We were told that the queue had started to form hours ago.

While standing at the queue I saw a friend from Parara, Jorge, walking out of the shop with a big plastic bag full of new *parumas* he bought for the women of 'our community'. The queue had started at two in the morning, he said: 'I had to wait for many hours to buy these *parumas*.' As Jorge had beaten me to it – and he would, at this rate, be the first to arrive at Parara with the new *parumas*, I decided not to wait anymore. I left the shop impressed by the sheer magnitude of the Emberá crowd: people who had travelled from their communities all over Eastern Panama to buy the 'new *paruma*' while the price was still at its highest. Some make this trip frequently, and they can often make a small profit by selling the new *parumas* at slightly higher prices to their communities. Throughout Emberá society in Panama many women wait with excitement for the latest *paruma* design!

I started to wonder whether this desire was manipulated, to a certain extent, by the non-indigenous vendors of the *parumas*. The release of every 'new *paruma*' is always well planned, announced and anticipated. I had visited the shops that sell the *parumas* many times before, but on random dates, and I had never encountered such a big crowd. On my previous visits I had persistently asked the non-indigenous employees of these shops to provide me with information about the *parumas*' designers or production processes. They always refused to provide further information, for fear that I might be a commercial competitor. Yet, as several Emberá from Chagres and Darién had told me, two or three individuals were spotted – 'a Guna and a Latino man' – soliciting Emberá opinion regarding the designs and colours of the *parumas*. The manufacturers employed them, I was told, to ask the Emberá women what they prefer, and to design patterns for the new *parumas* accordingly.

Sara told me of an accidental encounter that corroborated this information. As is the case for many other female Peace Corps volunteers who work in Emberá communities, she had been using the *parumas* a lot and maintained a good collection of those released during the two years of her service. She also used to wear a *paruma* in the city. One day in 2011 a non-indigenous Panamanian gentleman at the supermarket made a remark about the fact that she – a *gringa* – was wearing a *paruma*. It is not surprising that the sight of a North American women wearing a *paruma* was noticed by a non-indigenous Panamanian, since the *paruma* is recognised as first and foremost an indigenous item of dress.[4] Nevertheless, it transpired through conversation that the man in the supermarket was one of the people employed to design *parumas* and to collect information about Emberá preferences, and, in this case, his interest was sparked by a *gringa* choosing to wear a *paruma*. Regrettably, Sara, unaware of my efforts to come in contact with the *paruma* designers, did not take this gentleman's contact details.

In time, my repeated attempts – which invariably met with disappointment – to unravel the secrets of *paruma* production made me more aware of the international, globalised dimensions of indigenous cloth trade.[5] Western cloth has been circulating widely for centuries without inhibiting the creative sartorial innovations of non-Western people (Schneider 1987: 433–41; Craik 1994: 26), a case made more evident by ethnographic studies in the Pacific (see Colchester 2003; Küchler and Were 2005; Bolton 2003, 2007). Asian textiles, in particular, have been present in Latin America since the sixteenth century, and their influence in inspiring local styles of dress has been, so far, underestimated (Tinajero 2005: 67). In Panama, the Guna represent one of the most revealing examples of an ethnic group that has historically incorporated Western materials to generate a distinctively indigenous dress code (see Salvador 1976, 1997b; Sherzer and Sherzer 1976; Hirschfeld 1977a, 1977b; Swain 1989; Tice 1995; Howe 2009; Margiotti 2013). Nowadays, factory-made textiles for the Guna, the Emberá and the Wounaan are often sold in the very same fabric shops. The international producers, however, are well aware of the requirements of their clientele. For example, they produce cloth for Guna head-cloths and wraparound skirts different from that they produce for Emberá and Wounaan *paruma* skirts. This demonstrates that the internationalisation of cloth production adapts to indigenous specifications and creative adaptations, which in turn resulted from the indigenisation of industrially manufactured cloth in previous eras.

In sharp contrast to my fascination with the manufacture of the contemporary Emberá *parumas* in Asia, the Emberá women at Chagres and several other Emberá women I met during my trips to Darién did not appear to be concerned about the international dimension of *paruma* production. From their point of view, the *parumas* are, and always have been, a quintessentially Chocó – Emberá-Wounaan – item of clothing. In fact, the new *parumas* that are produced in Asia are made only for the Emberá-Wounaan, I was told, and this particular *paruma*-cloth is not for non-indigenous Panamanians or other indigenous groups. Unlike *parumas* from older times, which were cut out of ordinary pieces of cloth, the new *parumas* are seen as emblematic of an Emberá – or more accurately,

Chocó (Emberá-Wounaan) – identity. Over the course of many conversations, this particular identification was presented as one of the primary reasons why the *parumas* are so well liked by the women themselves, but also by Emberá-Wounaan parents, husbands and community leaders.

The Emberá recognise two additional characteristics of the *parumas* which account for their popularity and widespread use: first, their similarity to skirts, which conforms to wider, non-indigenous views of modesty, and second, their versatility as practical, comfortable and multipurpose items of dress. Although the *paruma* is merely a three-yard-long piece of cloth, when folded around a woman's lower body it looks like a skirt. Combined and matched with a t-shirt or other type of modern top, the *paruma* provides the basis for a style of dress that looks modest from a non-indigenous point of view, but is still recognisably Emberá (or Wounaan). Even schoolteachers, missionaries and Christian pastors – to refer to non-indigenous actors who tend to promote the modernisation of Emberá dress – are likely to agree that the *parumas* allow for modest dress combinations. After all, and as many Emberá women would stress when reflecting on this issue, 'the *paruma* is like a skirt (*como la falda*).'

The materiality of the *paruma*, which conforms to a medium-length-skirt aesthetic, puts the *paruma* wearer at an advantage. The Emberá and Wounaan women can easily shift from purely indigenous to mixed (indigenous-*and*-modern) dress codes without much effort, merely by adding a light top to match the *paruma* that they happen to be wearing at any given moment. The simplicity of this transformation is very convenient when the *paruma* wearer is confronted by the sudden arrival of unfamiliar men, and it allows for frequent and effortless shifts in one's dress code in a variety of contexts in everyday life. This relative ease – in accentuating or underplaying the indigenous tone of a woman's appearance – sharply contrasts with the female Guna attire. In comparison, Guna women, whose indigenous dress relies on a more complex combination of garments, cannot change so easily between indigenous and modern sartorial practices and aesthetics. It is not, thus, surprising that Guna female dress has stirred up so much resistance and opposition in the Panamanian politics of indigenous representation (see Howe 1998, 2009).

As I mention earlier in the book, an overwhelming majority of Emberá parents, husbands and community leaders explicitly advocate their preference for this item of clothing. As a general rule, in Chagres, and even more frequently in Darién, community elders encourage the use of the *paruma* – sometimes in public forums such as community meetings – and criticise with derogatory remarks the wearing of shorts by adolescent and young-adult women.[6] Similarly, most parents of young girls and husbands of young women express a dislike for shorts and an enthusiastic preference for *parumas*. In all cases where I addressed this issue in conversation with parents and daughters together, the latter were quick to stress that they liked the *parumas*, while the former, usually with a touch of irony, made remarks about their daughters' use of long or short trousers.

In one conversation in Parara Puru, the issue of wearing the *paruma*, as opposed to shorts, cropped up spontaneously in the presence of a mother, her married daughter and son-in-law (an Emberá man from Darién), but also her younger unmarried daughter. This was for me a unique conversational context as it included a complex constellation of gender-age subject positions between individuals that I had known well for several years. In the following extract from my fieldnotes, I have replaced the names of the subjects with kinship descriptives to protect their anonymity:

> The mother made the first remark commenting on the bright colours of her married daughter's new *paruma*, 'the latest one', that her son-in-law had bought and brought from the city. The son-in-law continued to reflect upon the rising popularity of the *parumas* and how their price is steadily increasing. 'Now, you can see more women in *parumas*', he said, 'in the city, at Avenida Central.' Seizing the opportunity I addressed the two daughters who were listening (the older with her baby son on her arms, and the younger making a basket). I asked them how often they wear the *paruma* in the city. Instantly, the mother and her son-in-law looked at each other and smiled with a touch of irony indicating their silent agreement in contradiction with the views of the two sisters. They had both shared with me their pro-*paruma* position in several previous but separate conversations. Their moderately ironic smile provoked the married daughter to come forward and depart from her usual diplomatic position ('yes, I like the *paruma*') to a more complicated view: 'I use the *paruma*', she said, pointing at the new *paruma* she was wearing, 'here in the community, I wear the *paruma* all the time, but when I go to the city I want to wear trousers.' She further admitted: 'I like to wear trousers sometimes, not only shorts, but long trousers as well.' At this point, her younger, unmarried sister who was listening, dressed in shorts, entered the discussion: 'I like the *paruma* more than my sister', she said, 'but I like to wear shorts too. When I go to the city in the morning I wear a *paruma*, but sometimes when I go out with my girlfriends I wear shorts.'

Following this conversation, I systematically pursued opportunities to discuss Emberá preferences for the *paruma* with as many Emberá women as I could, preferably without parents or husbands present. Adolescent girls and young women offered the most complex opinions. The majority liked the *paruma*, but they also liked wearing shorts. Almost all girls from Parara Puru – whose confidence in wearing indigenous clothes has grown as a result of increased tourism – clarified that their penchant for shorts did not represent embarrassment at their Emberá identity; in fact, they pointed out that they do not feel shy or intimidated when wearing a *paruma* in the presence of non-indigenous outsiders (*los latinos, los kampuniá*). They stressed that they wear shorts because they are comfortable and because they like them and they do so not only when they go out of the community, 'but some days also at the house'.

In comparison with adolescent girls, Emberá women in their mid- or late-twenties rely to a much greater extent on *parumas* in their everyday life and wear them more frequently outside the community. In addition, they are more likely to report that sometimes they feel embarrassed by the way non-indigenous Panamanians look at them when they walk down the street with a *paruma*. On the whole, my discussions with women in Parara Puru indicate that those in their late teens or early twenties are much more confident about wearing the *parumas* outside the community, despite their frequent use of shorts. The confidence of the younger women may represent a generational shift that reflects the increasing popularity of *parumas* as an indigenous fashion, and the slightly more tolerant attitude of the non-indigenous Panamanian society towards indigenous dress. Middle-aged and old Emberá women almost never wear shorts. They use *parumas* combined with cotton or synthetic tops for most of their daily life; however, they may wear normal, non-indigenous skirts to go to church.

8.4   Protecting oneself and others from the sun

Young and old Emberá women are unanimous in praising the versatile properties of the *parumas,* which mostly relate to their simple form and materiality. Apart from being worn as skirts, the *parumas* can be used as protection from the sun or the cold, when put on or wrapped around one's shoulders.[7] They can be easily transformed into hammocks for babies by tying two strings on either side. They are often used as a readily available cloth to cover the chest of a topless woman's body, for example when unrelated or unknown men approach. The *paruma*-cloth also allows for creative adaptations and recycling. Although the Emberá reuse old cloth to a much lesser extent than their neighbours the Guna (see Margiotti 2013), old or damaged *parumas* are often cut up and reused for a variety of purposes, such as, for example, to make mini-*parumas* for young girls or sheets for babies.[8]

The overwhelming majority of Emberá women in Panama – and here I can generalise with confidence, based on a large number of conversations I had in Chagres and Darién – see the *parumas* as a very comfortable item of dress. They are light and stretchy, the women say: ideal to wear while cooking or carrying out household chores, when clearing the forest with machetes or when sweeping the land surrounding the Emberá house and community spaces with rakes. As *parumas* are easy to clean and dry, they are appropriate for work close to water, such as cleaning fish or washing clothes at the riverbank or closer to home. When taking a shower under a pipe of running water or bathing in the river, the women do not take off their *parumas*. The *paruma*-skirt is thus also used as a flexible body covering that allows one to wash underneath. As with the sari in India and the sarong in Indonesia, the *parumas* have acquired an intimate connection with the female body and can be seen as 'lived garments', indispensable parts of an Emberá (or Wounaan) woman's life (Banerjee and Miller 2003; Allerton 2007).

Overall, and as I have stressed previously in this book, the materiality of the *paruma* facilitates combinations with most inexpensive acrylic or cotton tops, which is a quality the Emberá women underline and appreciate. Their colourful and elaborate designs match a wide variety of monochrome tops and provide a wide range of opportunities for quick but complementary colour combinations, a good solution for women who possess only a limited collection of clothes. To paraphrase what Banerjee and Miller (2003: 1) say about the sari, the way Emberá women wear and combine their *parumas* expresses 'their personal aesthetic and style' and also an identity statement 'about what it is to be a woman' – indigenous and specifically Emberá or Wounaan – in contemporary Eastern Panama. Closer to home, but also in some all-Emberá gatherings of relatives and close friends, women wear a *paruma* and a bra (usually black or white), a combination that provides a convenient compromise between the older practice of keeping the torso uncovered and the contemporary preference for covering a woman's chest.

One additional potential combination comprises the use of *paruma* with *paruma* ('*paruma con paruma*', as some Emberá say), which is becoming more popular in communities that have developed tourism, where women are not allowed to wear Western tops in the presence of tourists. The first *paruma* is used as a skirt, while the second is wrapped around the chest – at times tied at the back or kept in place by the upper arms held tightly to the ribcage – providing tempo-rary cover for a woman's breasts (yet without resorting to non-indigenous items of dress). This practice predates the introduction of tourism, as Reverte Coma observed during his fieldwork in the 1960s:

> When visiting a town in Darien such as La Palma, Pinogana, Chepigana, Yaviza or El Real, the Indian woman wears a shawl, which she casts on the shoulders and drops down to the breasts to hide them, by order of the authorities, from the curi-ous view of non-Indians, who are not accustomed to seeing their women in this way, and sometimes they observe them too intensely. (Reverte Coma 2002: 235, my translation)

Apart from the frequent occasions during which women use a second *paruma* as a shawl – or temporary cover of their torso – during the tourist encounter, I had opportunities to observe similar uses of the *paruma*-cloth in daily life. For example, Señora Delia, the oldest woman in Parara, usually starts her day wearing a *paruma* combined with a cotton top. Yet, as the day gets warmer, and while she is alone in the house, she takes the top off and stays bare-breasted, wearing only a *paruma*, as in the old times. When a familiar but unrelated man approaches, she may cover her chest with an offcut from an old *paruma*. This she places on the front of her chest, the frayed sides of the fabric under each arm, held into place by holding her upper arms tightly to her ribcage, keeping her forearms free. This leaves her back uncovered and thus keeps her cool in the heat of the day. To go to the church out of the community, as she does many afternoons, she wears a Western skirt and a top.

When discussing *parumas*, some women make comparisons with or remember the *parumas* that they wore in the past. For the older women, these were mostly

8.5   Choosing a *paruma* to match with a top

pieces of monochrome cloth, although they did also use cloth with patterns. Progressively, multicoloured cloth became cheaper and more easily avail-able – especially so in the 1990s, when the contemporary style of multicoloured *parumas* from cloth produced in Asia (specifically for the Emberá and the Wounaan) became popular.[9]   In   several conversations that I initiated in 2010, 2011 and 2012, the women of Parara Puru were in unanimous agreement that the *parumas* from the mid- and late-1990s were cheaper and lasted for longer. In contrast, they said, 'the new ones have bet-ter designs', 'more vivid colours', but 'are more expensive'. 'At home I have one that I bought for three dollars', said one of the older women in Parara, 'while the one I am wearing now cost me eighteen!'

Most Emberá women have individual collections of *parumas* that stretch back in time. Thus, a particular *paruma* may elicit memories of a certain period in a woman's life or specific moments in the history of her family and the com-munity. In this respect, layers of *parumas* in a woman's house envelop layers of time, which may become visible again on the laundry line, where *parumas* from different years dry alongside each other outside almost every Emberá house. On several occasions, I pointed to particular *parumas* on a washing line, asking questions about their price or year of manufacture. Their owners had difficulty remembering the exact year, and referred instead to moments that were mean-ingful to them: 'This is from the time my son was very small' or 'This one is from the year we built this house.' 'The *paruma* I am wearing today is from the year we founded the community [1998]', remembered one woman. 'Look, it looks like new! The old ones were better, their fibres did not falter . . . and they cost less, something like seven dollars.'

Dressing up to go to church

We have seen in previous chapters how those Emberá communities in Panama that have developed tourism, such as the communities at Chagres, have signifi-cantly strengthened their identification with Emberá cultural practices. With respect to the traditional Emberá code of dress, this increased identification can be seen as performative confidence – during presentations for tourists – but can also be attributed to a more relaxed attitude towards older Emberá codes of dress, which has resulted in numerous informal and 'in-between' – traditional mixed with modern – dress possibilities in everyday life. During my fieldwork, and as I described in Chapter 7, I identified such in-between dress practices with idealistic enthusiasm, treating them as small victories of (indigenous) tradition over (occidental) modernity, or examples of how Emberá culture can corrupt external, Westernising trends from within.

That this particular nostalgic attitude towards indigenous cultures is simplistic and exoticising is a topic that I have already discussed, and one that I will develop further in the conclusion of this book. In anticipation of this broader discussion, in this section I would like to present an example of Emberá inclination towards modern dress. This is the dress code followed by the Emberá when they go to church, which provides us with opportunities to identify the limitations of juxtaposing modernity with tradition in simple binary terms. Emberá dress choices shift from the valorisation of tradition to a preference for modernity, and vice versa, very often without any particular tension, as the same individuals claim simultaneously an indigenous and a modern identity.

When the Emberá go to church, as well as when they go to the city, they rely to a greater extent on modern clothes and non-indigenous styles of dress, a clothing style that covers more of the body. This clothing aesthetic contrasts with the 'traditional' – pre-1960s – preference of the Emberá to leave a large part of the body uncovered. In the early stages of my fieldwork, I falsely interpreted the Emberá preference for a non-indigenous dress etiquette – which they adopt to a greater extent in particular contexts, such as that of the church or the city – as indicative of the weakening of Emberá culture. Although critical of imperialist nostalgia – the coloniser's tendency to mourn the perceived cultural loss effected by colonisation (see Rosaldo 1989) – I could not contain my disappointment when I saw examples of what I conceived to be an Emberá willingness to assimilate to mainstream Panamanian culture. Even though I criticised tourists for reproducing the pessimistic rhetoric of the vanishing savage – anthropologists, as I explained to some of them, do not believe that cultures are lost – I described the modernisation of Emberá social life in my fieldnotes with a tinge of melancholy, as the by-product of an unequal relationship with more powerful, non-indigenous Others.

It took me a long time to fully accept that the Emberá do not merely imitate modern practices but that they seek to become modern Emberá or, in some cases, modern Christian Emberá. One non-indigenous element that some Emberá desire to introduce to their lives is Christian belief, and in particular Christian practices inspired by North American evangelical Christianity. From the point of view of those Emberá who identify with evangelical practices, this does not negate in any fundamental respect their identity as Emberá. Similarly, and as a Christian Emberá friend confided to me, wearing modern clothes does not transform an Emberá into a non-indigenous person, a *kampuniá*. Step by step, fighting with my initial tendency to view the adoption of Christianity by some Emberá as a non-indigenous project of assimilation, I started to accompany my Emberá friends to some of the activities organised by a local church.

In time, the change in my attitude was noticed by my Emberá friends who
started confiding to me, at an increasing rate, their religious experiences. Here is
an extract from my fieldnotes:

> First day in Parara after ten months. Anel, a young Emberá friend [who was at
> the time almost twenty years old], stopped by my house to welcome me. He wore
> long trousers and a white shirt, holding a tie in his hand. The trousers cost ten
> dollars, he pointed out, the shirt seven, and the tie two. I showed him how to put
> his tie on. Then he revealed to me – before I even had a chance to ask – that a
> change had taken place in his life while I was in England: he had now come closer
> to Jesus. I asked what triggered this change, as I had known him since he was fif-
> teen and I had never before noticed any particular religious inclination.
>
> A few months ago, he explained, a snake bit him on his thigh. It was a small
> snake, and Anel did not ask for help or go to the hospital immediately. This delay
> led to a serious infection and poisoning and he almost lost his leg. He stayed at
> Santo Tomas hospital for a long and painful time, facing serious problems with
> his renal system. During his time at the hospital Anel reconsidered his life. He felt
> the need to come closer to Jesus. He now [2012] goes to church twice or thrice
> a week, and spends lots of time with his uncle and aunt talking about the bible.

Three days later I joined Anel and the family of Claudio, his uncle and the leader of
the community, for a pre-Easter vigil in the neighbouring settlement of Victoriano.
We boarded the family's canoe at dusk, but we did not use a motor engine. Claudio
steered a course with his traditional Emberá oar, while his two sons took turns
punting at the bow. In full idealising mood, I felt as if that particular moment was
cut and pasted from the Emberá past, before the Emberá started to rely extensively
on outboard motors: as I enjoyed nightfall on the tropical river and the rhythmic
splash of the oar, I kept thinking about what Kane (1994) would have called an
'authentic discontinuity': an Emberá family going down the river – in the ancient
Emberá way – this time not to join a shaman's ceremony, but instead to attend the
vigil of an evangelical church.

But then a sudden splash interrupted my ethnographic nostalgia, framed in
terms of the work of a previous ethnographer and my idealising imagination of
an undifferentiated Emberá past. Claudio's old canoe was particularly narrow
and unstable – much like the canoes of the old times, before the Emberá started
transporting plantains and tourists in wider, longer canoes. I was now wet and on
my way to the church, where I felt I should be presentable. My Emberá compan-
ions were better prepared. They kept most of the clothes they intended to wear to
the church in plastic bags. After arriving at Victoriano we walked to the house of
Claudio's mother to change into more appropriate clothes. Claudio and his sons
changed into long trousers and shirts, while Anel put on the white shirt and tie he
had been wearing three days earlier. Claudio's wife and daughter-in-law exchanged
their *paruma*-skirts – which they wear every day in Parara Puru, but also for other
less celebratory church services – for normal non-indigenous skirts.

Claudio's mother had always presented me with contradictions that I found difficult to reconcile until, after years of struggle with my ethnographic nostalgia,
I accepted the dynamic and fluid intersections of indigenous modernities. By 2012

she had lost her husband, but she preferred to live alone in Victoriano, despite the constant requests of four of her children and her numerous grandchildren to move and live with them in Parara Puru. Her most frequent explanation for refusing was that she wanted to be close to the church. I knew very well, from the word of others, that she had a long relationship – longer than thirty years – with more than one evangelical church. Yet at the same time, she was a woman who refused to speak Spanish, a steadfast icon of Emberá identity. Despite living in a nonhomogenous Emberá community, her house had many elements of traditional Emberá architecture: a traditional log ladder, a floor of *jira*-palm leaves, a traditional hearth and, as I noticed that particular night, a traditional carved stool of the type often referred to by the Emberá as 'chair of the shaman' (*silla del jaibaná*). For me, the 'chair of the shaman' in the house of a close follower of the church posed an interpretive contradiction. For her, it was simply 'an Emberá chair'.

At the church we met a large mixed Emberá and Latino crowd. Around the church, and for the duration of the night, people were meeting friends, chatting and eating the food that was prepared for those attending the vigil – which for many in that impoverished region was a good reason to come. Yet, unlike in other intercommunity gatherings, such as football or basketball matches, no alcohol was consumed. Many Emberá had come – men, women, children and babies – from all three communities on the river Chagres, and the coming together of families related by kinship contributed to a collective effervescence. In the church four pastors each delivered a speech, including one who was Emberá, from the community upriver of Parara. Performances by Christian rock bands were had in between these speeches, in Spanish, performed by Latino-Christian youth with electric guitars, electric basses and drums. At various points during the vigil, individuals from the congregation – Emberá and Latino – stepped forward and danced to the music until they fell to the ground in a trance.

I must clarify that not all evangelical churches in Chagres use Christian rock music during worship or follow the same experiential and expressive approach. Many Emberá do not attend evangelical worship and declare themselves to be simply 'Catholic'. According to my observations, these 'Catholic' Emberá tend to be rather uninterested in the details of Christian belief and very rarely go to church. They are also, as I will explain below, more likely to rely on the healing and advice of Emberá shamans (*jaibanás*). Despite the efforts of Catholic missionaries to proselytise the Emberá – which started at least three centuries before the latter's ancestors migrated to Panama (C. Williams 2004; see also Isacsson 1993) – Catholicism never succeeded in attracting a large Emberá following. For the most part, the Emberá dealt with the occasional pressure of the Catholic church by avoiding direct confrontation. When priests and missionaries departed – exhausted by life in the rainforest – the majority of the Emberá returned to the guidance of their shamans.

Evangelical Christianity, however, expects greater commitment and more regular worship. During the early part of my fieldwork in Parara Puru, a number of (primarily young) Emberá asked me repeatedly if I was a Christian. In most cases I replied diplomatically, highlighting that in my native culture people are not often confronted with this dilemma; they are just put in a baptismal font when they are babies and declared Christians for life. Notwithstanding this explanation, my cultural affiliation to Orthodox Christianity – which I presented as the tradition of the people of Greece – was not always received as sufficient evidence of Christian commitment. Everybody could clearly see that I was not attending any church. On the contrary, my lukewarm self-presentation as a Christian resembled that of those Emberá who say they are Catholic but depend on the services of shamans.

In 2010 and 2011, after returning from trips to Darién, I shared my travel impressions with my friends in Parara, including details about shamans that I happened to meet on the way. Information about Darién shamans attracted the keen interest of the overwhelming majority of the Emberá at Chagres. Some of these shamans were renowned figures in the Emberá world, and being able to mention that I met them, while the local Emberá had not, gave me some kudos as an outsider-insider who knew about things Emberá. Nevertheless, a few of my friends in Parara Puru who followed (more closely) evangelical worship were not particularly thrilled by my involvement with shamans. This became more evident when, in 2011, I invited a Darién-born shaman to perform a cure for a North American friend. This shaman had cured in Parara a few times before, and was in fact the father of a Parara resident, but my association with him provoked mixed responses: a clear majority were intrigued and wanted to know every single thing the shaman (*el jaibaná*) said or predicted, while a small minority of Christian Emberá declared that they were unhappy with the 'witch' (*el brujo*) and his presence in the community.

My concern not to alienate this minority of very committed Christian Emberá encouraged to me to attend Christian worships at Chagres. I also met a few North American pastors and missionaries, and I travelled with them to Darién, witnessing their attempts to provide aid for Emberá communities afflicted by the 2011 floods. I also met Christian medical volunteers, whose efforts to set up temporary medical stations in Emberá communities and provide free dental and medical care are undoubtedly admirable. These experiences gradually led me to appreciate the amount of practical help offered by religiously motivated Westerners to Emberá society. I soon realised that not all missionaries and pastors desired the eradication of traditional Emberá practices, although all appeared explicitly hostile towards shamanic practices. In fact, some pastors encourage the Emberá to worship in their own language, while a few speak Emberá with admirable fluency, or, during their attempts to translate the bible, were among the first to formulate an Emberá alphabet.[10]

It must also be acknowledged that Christian missions and churches, along with schools, provided the first impetus for departing from dispersed settlement and founding concentrated Emberá communities in Darién – a development which the contemporary Emberá see as a positive change, as it enhanced their political organisation (Loewen 1975; Herlihy 1985a, 1985b). Herlihy tracks the presence of the first North American missionaries in Darién to the mid-1950s (Herlihy 1986: 151). One of them was the missionary, linguist and anthropologist Jacob Loewen (1922–2006)[11] – a Canadian Mennonite of Eastern European origin and author of numerous short articles on missionary dilemmas which are illustrated with examples from his work among the Chocó (see Loewen 1975). In the 1950s and 1960s, as Loewen (1975) highlights, many Chocó women were driven closer to the church by their dislike of the traditional custom of Emberá men to drink excessively. During that period, banana and plantain cultivation provided the Emberá of Darién with significant profits, but a great part of these were spent on liquor. As a result, Loewen remarks,

> . . . the women didn't even get the piece of cloth for a wrap-around skirt, or the couple of pounds of sugar they expected as a reward for their part in the family effort of raising bananas and plantains. (Loewen 1983: 249)

A similar dislike for men's excessive drinking has partly stimulated many Emberá women to identify with the evangelical churches in the Chagres area. Yet, according to my observations, one of the most important reasons for closely committing oneself to a church is the death, illness or accident of a close family member. The year 2011, for example, brought a great deal of pain to Parara Puru. In a short period of time local families experienced two deaths – including that of a young boy – and two serious accidents. These events intensified the devotion of the most committed evangelical Emberá, who received regular emotional support from members of their church (including non-indigenous pastors). During the same period a few other members of Parara Puru expressed the view that the community would benefit from the intervention of a shaman. Almost everyone suspected that evil spirits had something to do with the bad luck of the community, but the Christian Emberá argued that the presence of a shaman would make the situation worse by inviting additional malevolent beings in. After all, Emberá shamans fight against undesirable spirits by soliciting the help of other spirits.

One day in 2012, approximately two weeks after the Easter vigil I described above, and after much debate within the community, a shaman was finally invited and arrived in Parara. The shaman was asked to perform a cure for the whole of the community. A good number of Parara residents helped him decorate a house for the ceremony, cutting palm leaves and soft wood (from which the shaman made ceremonial dolls). Several of the individuals who volunteered to help had participated in the Christian vigil a few days earlier. When night fell, the community gathered in the decorated house for the ceremony. It was then that I realised that eighty per cent of the community was in attendance, including Emberá who frequently attend church worships. Only the most committed Christians abstained; some left the community before the ceremony began to spend the night in the houses of relatives in neighbouring communities – an act interpreted by most as disapproval (or fear) of the presence of the shaman.

The Emberá of Parara are very closely linked by kinship ties, and this intimate relationship facilitates the quick dissolution of disputes – such as, in our case, disagreements about the shaman's visit. Yet, on the night of the shaman's community cure I could not help but notice that the brothers and sisters of some of the most zealous Christian Emberá had attended the shamanic-curing ceremony. With discipline and concentration they resisted the temptation to sleep, aware that the ceremony would last for hours and that those in attendance were not allowed leave after the first invocation of the spirits. Covered with blankets, cotton and synthetic jumpers, and many other heterogeneous, 'warmer' non-indigenous clothes, they endured the cold night breeze of an unusually windy night. For me this was an opportunity to see a number of thicker clothes that the Emberá rarely use, including colourful pyjamas with cartoon designs sported by two pre-adolescent girls. They hugged their parents and slept on the floor, hypnotised by the monotonous chant of the shaman.

Provoked by the shaman to stay awake – who teased me, in the breaks between different chants, by repeating the words 'England is now sleeping' – I indulged in unruly ethnographic nostalgia. There I was, I wrote in my fieldnotes the day after, participating in 'a quintessentially Emberá animistic ritual'. Overwhelmed by the participation of so many Emberá from Parara, including many who regularly go to the church, 'makes me feel that Emberá culture will not become eradicated by the onslaught of Christianisation', as I wrote in my notebook. Then, embarrassed by this unacceptable – for an anthropologist – commentary I added a parenthesis: 'of course I know that Emberá culture cannot be eradicated, and that the Christian pastors are good guys . . . but I cannot help it . . . I do find the shaman more fascinating!'

Only a few days after the shaman departed, the evangelical church from Victoriano organised one of their regular worship-visits in Parara Puru. Once more a majority of the Parara residents participated, including many of the attendees of the shamanic community cure. Most women wore their *parumas*, but three or four appeared in a non-indigenous skirt, while a couple of middle-aged Emberá men were dressed 'like the pastor' – that is, with light long trousers supported by a thin leather belt and a short-sleeved shirt (in conservative light-brown or grey colours). We all sang religious songs, and – given that the worship was taking place at the home of the Emberá – a couple of women sang Christian songs with Emberá lyrics. Enthused by the Emberá lyrics, which I saw as a sign of the resilience of Emberá culture and its ability to remerge and corrupt non-indigenous practices, I entered into discussion with the non-indigenous Panamanian pastor, advocating for the importance of using Emberá language and music during Christian worship. I knew well by that stage that if I couldn't overcome my nostalgic admiration for everything Emberá, I could at least acknowledge the emergence of an Emberá Christianity, one of the many faces of Emberá modernity.

When Westerners undress to dress up as Emberá

I would like to focus here on a particular temptation in the encounter with alterity that entails the potential of reversing the exoticising gaze, yet one that is heavily grounded in exoticisation. This is the desire of Western travellers to throw off their clothes, dress as natives and escape momentarily the decorum of a heavily clothed existence – for example, the burden of being a well-dressed northerner in the overpowering tropical heat. Such a desire may entail a temporary escape from the confines of a well-trodden identity: a fleeting, playful flirt with the possibility of being Other. It involves, in the case I will examine here, a double metamorphosis from the appearance of the Self to that of the Other and back to the appearance of the Self. Western clothes stand here – in a Rousseauian manner – for the restrictions of Western civilisation, while the light dress code of the Emberá, which exposes a great part of the body to the naked eye, stands for freedom and a primordial, naturalised innocence.

The traditional dress code of the Emberá has on many occasions inspired such self-exoticising transformations. An early example, spectacularly staged in front of a camera, was provided by Richard Marsh (see figure 8.6). During the early stages of his expedition in Darién, he received an invitation from shaman Avellino to attend an Emberá celebration on the river Chico (see Chapter 4). Tired from the canoe ride, Marsh and his crew of North American scientists succumbed to the temptation of taking off their wet clothes to receive a thorough body painting by their Emberá hosts. They stripped to 'make-shift gee-strings' made from face towels and were painted in 'various designs' by the Emberá women who studied 'the effect produced on their living canvases with much artistic attention', as Marsh remarks (1934: 93–4). He intuitively understood that the body decorations with *jagua* were necessary in order for him and his crew to be 'formally adopted into the tribe' (Ibid.: 93).

Despite being aware of the importance attributed by the Emberá to the careful decoration of the body (in preparation for an impending celebration), Marsh appears overwhelmed by the excitement of dressing as a 'native'. Taussig (1993) and Howe (1998) detect in Marsh's narrative a self-constrained sensationalism that ambivalently flirts with the possibility of adopting the ways of the Other. Hidden behind Marsh's colourful description, the reader feels Marsh's temptation to relieve himself of his Western clothes, to become exposed to the physicality of the rainforest, like the Emberá whose uncovered bodies he sees, as Howe aptly observes, as 'disconcertingly powerful and attractive' (Howe 1998: 215). Yet, this is certainly a short-lived transformation; Marsh's Western readership is left with no doubt: revitalised by his brief, exotic diversion, the explorer will eventually put his Western clothes back on – cleaned and dried by the Emberá women – to continue his relentless advance through the impenetrable forest.

Participating in a parallel process of identity negotiation, the Emberá, for their part, imprinted the motifs of their culture onto a white man's body: they transformed alterity – dangerous, white, non-Emberá power – to Emberá-ness, a transformation effected through the medium of Emberá body designs. In Emberá language, *Emberá* stands for a human being. From this point of view, we can see the 'painted' Marsh as being transformed to fully human, stripped of the colonial power that he represented. Being body-painted with *jagua* Emberá designs signifies – as several contemporary Emberá have pointed out to me – acceptance by the Emberá community. These views corroborate Isacsson's observation that 'the painting signifies much more than a plain decoration of the skin . . . It constitutes a necessary complement to the identity of the individual as complete member of society' (1993: 32). Thus, as Marsh correctly presumed, body decoration was

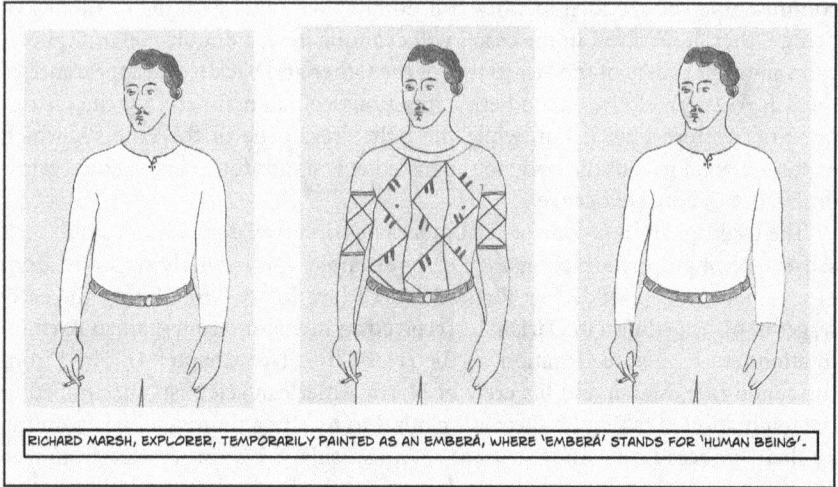

RICHARD MARSH, EXPLORER, TEMPORARILY PAINTED AS AN EMBERÁ, WHERE 'EMBERÁ' STANDS FOR 'HUMAN BEING'.

8.6   Marsh relieved of his Western clothes and body-painted in Emberá style

indeed a form of adoption 'into the tribe': the socialisation of the *kampuniá torro* (white, non-human Other) into Emberá society.

In the early-twenty-first century, body painting with *jagua* is – unsurprisingly – available as part of the Emberá tourist experience. The standard pattern of cultural presentations for tourists, as this is adopted by most Emberá communities in Panamá, presents an opportunity for the visitors to receive a '*jagua*-tattoo', which is usually a geometric Emberá *jagua* design applied on the guest's arms or legs. In this manner, the visitors can experience an indigenous cultural practice without having to completely strip themselves of their clothes. The designs applied are recognised by the Emberá with names (see Chapter 2), and have been applied to the bodies of other tourists and Emberá many times before. They are chosen by the Emberá individual who is painting, although sometimes, and in particular when the guest to be body-painted is a child or adolescent, the Emberá may deviate from traditional designs and instead draw naturalistic figures, such as leaves, flowers or birds.

Pleased with their freshly painted *jagua* designs, many visitors proudly pose for photographs, which are disseminated to friends and family via digital social networks. In this way, the Emberá decorations are treated as embodied exotica bearing evidence of one's contact with Otherness. Various tourists described the Emberá art of body painting as 'cool', 'beautiful' or 'fascinating' and were thrilled to return to their hotel or cruise ship with a small *jagua* painting. 'My friends who didn't dare to take this trip kept on asking me about my new tattoo', remarked a North American visitor, 'I was so pleased to remind them what they missed!' Within Panama, tourists and backpackers can be spotted with increasing frequency in public spaces – the streets, the markets, in restaurants – with *jagua* designs, contributing to the visibility of Emberá-Wounaan culture.[12] As a seventeen-year-old urban Panamanian once told me, 'The designs of the Emberá go so well with black shirts and gothic t-shirts!'

For their part, the Emberá are pleased to see the *kampuniá* – the non-Emberá Others, both tourists and Panamanians – practising one of their traditions. The *jagua* designs on the white people's bodies are seen by some as an advertisement for their identity. 'When other *gringos* see our designs', an Emberá from Parara said, 'they will come here and ask to be painted as well.' 'And some Panamanians too', added his brother, 'the young (*muchachos y muchachas*) like *jagua* [body painting] too!' Unsurprisingly, and as I described in previous chapters, an increasing number of Emberá men and women are now willing to appear 'painted' in the non-indigenous world. It is in this respect that the tourists' fondness for body painting – however exoticising or seemingly superficial this may be – has facilitated the gradual penetration and acceptance of one indigenous practice into non-indigenous contexts.

If the Emberá are pleased to see the *kampuniá* merely body-painted with their designs, they like to see their visitors dressed in full Emberá attire even more. Such opportunities occur, from time to time, in communities that frequently receive tourists. More regular examples involve group visits of Panamanian schools or higher-education institutions. Of the visits that I was fortunate to observe in Parara Puru from 2007 to 2012, some of the visitors – usually two young women and two young men – volunteered, under the enthusiastic encouragement of their teachers and fellow students, to put on Emberá clothes. Dressed in loincloths or *parumas*, beaded strings and, in the case of the girls, *ubarí*-necklaces (covering their breasts), they faced the cheery reception of friends and fellow students. The particular act was welcomed by all sides as an exercise in strengthening multiculturalism, an attitude supported by Panamanian national education. Local primary schools, especially in areas with mixed indigenous and non-indigenous populations, such as Chagres, organise cultural events, during which students from different schools compete in educational games and dance and dress in each other's costume. At such an occasion hosted in Parara (in 2009), a group of Emberá girls reciprocated by wearing the non-indigenous Panamanian folk dress, *la pollera*, only to take it off and dance their 'own' animal dances along with a non-indigenous girl.[13]

The following and final example provides us with a more dazzling case of dressing in the Other's clothes. During a hot and busy summer day in February 2010, a couple of French tourists who had been captivated by their encounter with the Emberá asked if they could get married in the community. The Emberá of Parara, who are in general prepared to accommodate most of the tourists' requests, started making preparations. They cut strips of palm leaves and tied them on the wooden poles of a communal house and then added hibiscus flowers to the decoration, in a manner appropriate for a shamanic ceremony. In the meantime, the bride and groom willingly submitted themselves to their own process of transformation. They removed their Western clothes and put on the standard adornments of the full Emberá attire: the groom used a loincloth, an *amburá*-belt, a small necklace and beaded strings across his chest, and the bride a *paruma*, two small necklaces

8.7 The wedding of a French couple in Parara Puru

and a heavy *ubarí*-necklace that covered her chest. Barefoot, the French couple stood in the middle of the communal house, surrounded by the Emberá dressed in full traditional attire.

There was some initial hesitation on the part of the Emberá that hosted the occasion, as there is no prescribed wedding ceremony in Emberá custom (see Pineda and Gutiérrez de Pineda 1999: 198). At some point during the preparations, I introduced this issue, but I was told by one of the women that what the Emberá understand as 'the wedding' is the particular moment when the man has completed building a new house and invites his wife to live in it. Such an occasion is sometimes marked by decorating the house with designs of *jagua*, flowers and palm leaves, an all-purpose pattern of house decoration also followed in preparation for shamanic-curing ceremonies. As there was not a sufficient amount of *jagua* available at that moment, the women used only flowers and palm leaves. Antonito, the leader of the community responsible for tourism, undertook the task of delivering a few words, enacting the role of an Emberá father who talks to the young man that marries his daughter.

Throughout the occasion Anne Gordon de Barrigón, a tourist guide, and I were facilitating communication by translating and explaining the details to the soon-to-be-married couple. Anne is an American woman married to an Emberá man from another community in Chagres. With her husband she runs a small and culturally sensitive tourism agency and, unlike other guides, she has a deep understanding of Emberá practices. Two years later she facilitated another similar wedding ceremony, but this time in the community of her husband, Emberá Puru at river San Juan de Pequeni. Once more, the Emberá dressed the tourist couple in Emberá clothes, although in this case, the groom did not wear an *amburá*-belt, as the men of Emberá Puru refuse to wear this item of dress (see Chapter 7). However, unlike Parara, Emberá Puru has an abundant supply of *jagua*, so the tourist couple was body-painted accordingly on the back and front of their torsos.

Pictures and videos of this second wedding were posted on the internet under the headings 'Our Emberá wedding' and the more exoticising 'Topless Emberá village wedding'. To avoid misunderstanding, I should underline that only the Emberá present at the ceremony were topless, and not the woman getting married. As in Parara Puru, the chest of the bride – and that of another tourist woman from the same group that dressed in Emberá clothes – were carefully covered by *ubarí*-necklaces. In both *gringo* weddings, the Emberá ended this improvised ceremony with Emberá animal dances, as would have been appropriate, according to Emberá tradition, if a new house was inaugurated. In both cases, the Western desire to embody indigeneity was accommodated by creatively adapting recognisable Emberá practices.

The reversal entailed by these examples encourages us to think about what Taussig (1993) calls the 'magical power' of imitation. The Western visitors put aside their Western clothes to dress up as fully decorated Emberá, where my use of 'dress up' stands for both dressing smartly (in full Emberá decoration) and dressing as somebody else. This impulse to become the Other, argues Taussig (1993) drawing from Benjamin (1936), often entails some conceptual distance that separates and reconstitutes the imitation and the imitated. In our case we see not only some *gringos* imitating the Emberá, but also the Emberá staring back at the *gringos* imitating the Emberá. In Taussig's words, 'the representation shares in or takes power from the represented', while the image affects 'what it is an image of' (1993: 2). Through this process both parties – the Emberá and the Westerners dressed as Emberá – obtain a new vantage point in their relation with alterity.

Petra Kalshoven, in an ethnography of western Europeans – the Indianists – who dress as North American Indians on a regular basis, draws from Taussig (1993) to highlight the contribution of the mimetic process to the renegotiation of self-identity. Through the enactment of the Other, Kalshoven argues, the Indianists become more aware of their normal, modern lives (Kalshoven 2012: 242). In this respect, the engendering of what is imitated provides some distance, a measure of conceptual clarity, to reconceptualise the point of departure before imitation.

In a similar manner, the awkward caricature of the tourist mimicking the Indian provides the Emberá with a spectacle that encourages self-reflection. To the degree that the Emberá *jagua* designs and adornments mediate to re-socialise the foreign body, cultural difference is framed from within a culturally intimate context. In this process the Emberá have an opportunity to see themselves in the Other, to blur the exclusiveness of indigeneity and to humanise the *kampuniá*. The Westerners dressed in Emberá clothes, stripped of their (post-)colonial power,

stand humble, painted and barefoot, emplaced within an Emberá world of meaning. The magic power of imitation has turned Emberá culture from the target of
caricaturing to the object of desire.

Notes

1 I would like to acknowledge that the *paruma* is as much an Emberá as a Wounaan item
    of dress. The ethnography that follows privileges Emberá narratives that describe the
    paruma as Emberá dress, without the deliberate intention of excluding their cultural
    cousins, the Wounaan. I progressively revert to this generalised use, as I do not want to
    overuse the descriptive *Chocó*, which includes both groups but is seen by many Emberá
    in Panama as a derogatory term (see Chapter 1). When I address general issues, such as
    the Emberá anticipation for the new *paruma*, I refer indirectly to both groups.
2 In contrast, some of the patterns of Guna *molas* bear, as Salvador (1976, 1997b) indi-
    cates, some resemblance to old body-paint designs.
3 La Bajada de Salsipuedes descends from Avenida Central towards the Chinese quarter.
    It is said in Panama City that the name of this street – 'leave if you can' – echoes its repu-
    tation as a dangerous neighbourhood in past centuries.
4 As I will discuss further in the last section of this chapter, the sight of foreign-
    ers dressed in *parumas*, or more frequently painted in *jagua* designs, is becoming
    increasingly frequent in Panama City. Non-indigenous Panamanians usually assume
    that the *gringos* using Emberá dress or body decoration are either tourists or Peace
    Corps volunteers.
5 Caroline Knowles (2014) has traced the international trail of flip-flop production and
    distribution in a fascinating study of global interconnectedness. Reading her book has
    inspired me to consider the idea of investigating the international aspects of *paruma*
    production. Such a project, however, will inevitably have an entirely different scope and
    require substantial time and resources.
6 In some communities in Darién, young women who prepare to go out of the commu-
    nity wear a *paruma* over their shorts, so that parents, neighbours or community leaders
    do not notice the shorts. After exiting the community they take off and fold their *paru-
    mas*, ready to use them again on their return. It remains to be seen whether the recent
    fashion for the *paruma* will render such practices of concealment obsolete.
7 'When it's cold, when it's sunny, like a parasol' rhymed a male friend from Parara Puru
    (*quando hay frio, quando hay sol, como un parasol*).
8 For a similar use of old *sapurret*-skirts among the Guna, see Margiotti 2013: 399.
9 Although cloth produced in Asia was used by the Emberá women before.
10 Two dedicated missionaries, Sara Watkins and Edel Rasmussen, have been involved
    in missionary work with the Emberá since the 1960s and have made groundbreak-
    ing contributions to the Emberá translation of the bible and the establishment of
    the Emberá alphabet. They also worked in the Chagres area, and during the 1970s
    provided support to the families of the two most prominent leaders of Parara Puru.
    The mothers of the two Emberá leaders now follow a different church, but retain a
    strong Christian devotion.
11 Jacob Loewen was involved in missionary work first in Colombia (1947–1953) and
    later in Panama (1959–1984). Because of his role as a missionary, he was not welcomed
    by traditional anthropology. This led him to pursue his PhD in linguistics and make a
    significant contribution to the study of Chocó dialects (see Loewen 1963a, 1963b).

12 Non-indigenous Panamanians understand body painting with *jagua* to be a representative Chocó (Emberá-Wounaan) cultural practice.

13 It must be acknowledged that schools in Chagres, as in Darién, apart from the homogenising mission of cultivating a national consciousness, also promote multiculturalism at the superficial level of expressive cultural traditions such as dance, dress or food. In many communities in Darién that do not entertain tourists, school cultural performances are an opportunity for Emberá girls to learn how to dance and dress in the Emberá way.

9

Indigenous-*and*-modern Emberá clothes

NOTHING EVER STAYS THE SAME ; OTHER WATER CONTINUALLY FLOWS IN

NOSTALGIC PREDILECTIONS ABOUT CHANGE...

9.1 The author at his favourite contemplation spot at river Chagres

'You cannot step into the same river twice', I say to myself, hoping to contain my nostalgia for the Emberá past. And I keep repeating the same phrase in my mind as I think about the Emberá and social change. So I put my feet into the river Chagres, in the shallows, to feel the strength of the current – to sense how the flow of life overtakes me. Heraclitus of Ephesus made a similar observation many centuries earlier: ever-newer waters flow over those who step into the same river more than once. If this were true – that nothing ever stays the same – should we celebrate or grieve? And what a profound contradiction it would be if we did decide to celebrate, but instead we find ourselves mourning nostalgically for what has been lost?

Past tense is more appropriate now that I come to the conclusion of this book. But my use of the ethnographic present – the most fiercely debated of all tenses – is deliberate. In its allochronic, caricaturing simplicity (Fabian 1983), such an improper use works as a reminder: despite critical deconstruction, the possibility of nostalgically privileging the Emberá past – sanitised, orderly and articulate – lurks behind the project of writing this book. Every new ethnography structures nostalgia and authenticity – not merely via the authority generated by the writing process, but also by extending the bibliographical 'record' further into the past. In this respect, nostalgia and the search for a singular indigenous authenticity, the ghosts that haunt the Emberá present and past, wait for me just around the river bend. These are the temptations – the Sirens – that have enticed me on my ethnographic journey (and continue to do so). But without them – and without the exotic recognition they have provoked, the challenge of new knowledge (Kapferer 2013) – I would not have had, as the poet Kavafis said, 'the marvellous journey'.[1]

To the degree that the nostalgic search for an authentic past in the present re-emerges in concentric circles, confrontation with it seems more like a continuous journey than a battle. Here, my nostalgia is not merely framed by the previous ethnographic record, but also by my own recording of Emberá culture: the sanitisation and categorisation of knowledge that I have struggled to construct. Writing about contemporary cultural practices is by definition an unending project – a process 'intrinsically incomplete' (Geertz 1973: 29): the practices that make up our ethnographic object are likely to transform faster than our search for underlying patterns and meaning. The resulting feeling of incompleteness – the realisation that we cannot actually contain change in our writing – inspires ethnographic nostalgia, but also facilitates its demise. Every new social process we learn to recognise can be as representative, it seems, as the last. How can we prioritise one narrative we recorded – one authenticity – over the many that unravel in an incomplete form in front of our eyes?

9.2 Sketch based on a photograph of Tomé standing at river Chagres in the late 1950s

With more than one overlapping narrative about Emberá authenticity in mind, I choose to return to my favourite contemplation spot on the Chagres, upstream of Parara Puru. Here in my allochronic imperfect present, I see the Emberá canoes – filled with tourists – struggling against the current. The noise of their outboard motors troubles my mind, and I choose to escape momentarily into the past: 'an Emberá time without motors, only the sound of poles and paddles', I say to position myself deeper in a timeless zone. I stand in the shallows at the same point where Tomé (Antonio Zarco), the first Emberá settler in Chagres, stood before (see figure 9.2). I imagine that he looks to the future – as I now look to the past – searching for opportunities in (what was then) a sparsely populated land. 'This is the Emberá way', I say, trying to establish a comforting continuity, 'what the Emberá have always done, moving to new lands, exploring opportunities'.

So, here I am clinging to the past, like many anthropologists before me, focusing on what I try to see as an unchanging pattern – 'a form of structural nostalgia in itself, the pervasive presence of which in our own thinking might help to explain why we find the phenomenon so hard to spot in the field' (Herzfeld 2005: 40–1). While writing this book I struggled with my desire to see the ethnographic object through the lens of the previous ethnographic record, my inclination to identify underlying cultural patterns while disregarding the intentions of the present moment, and exoticising. If we cannot 'eliminate nostalgia from cultural theory' – and I believe we cannot – then perhaps, argues Strathern (1995: 110) paraphrasing Robertson (1992), we can 'thematize it as an object of cultural analysis'; 'its forms, meanings, and effects shift with the context' and are everywhere, comprising a cultural practice, not a particular content (K. Stewart 1988: 227). 'Analyzing nostalgia in context, locating it richly within the landscape of the present, seems a task especially well suited to ethnography' (Bissell 2005: 239). And there are so many lessons we can learn from our own nostalgia, and that of Others (see also Angé and Berliner 2015; Berliner 2015).

At Chagres, nostalgia may be a means – 'a vehicle of knowledge' (Battaglia 1995: 77) – to think about representation and identity. Tomé is remembered fondly by his many children and grandchildren who inhabit the Emberá communities close to the Panama Canal. Some of his grandsons, who are now indigenous leaders in Chagres, talk about the challenges he faced when he arrived from Darién, how he opened the way for the others to follow. The story of his life is testament to Emberá expansion and settlement in that part of Panama, a connection to the land that deserves recognition and titles. Tomé is also remembered as an important and respected man. I am told not to forget that he was, after all, the Emberá who trained the astronauts (see Chapter 6), a teacher of *gringos*. Nostalgia for Tomé's many exploits – how he could hide and surprise the US marines – reverses the exoticising gaze: an indigenous man, 'an Emberá', once employed by the US elite forces to teach them survival skills. 'We too are like teachers', say Claudio and Antonito, the leaders of Parara Puru, grandchildren of Tomé, 'we explain our culture to *gringo* tourists.' Then, in the time of the grandfather, as it is now, Emberá culture has been a valuable asset to the world.

No single authenticity to discover

If there were one singular authenticity hidden within the cultural matrix of Emberá culture, I would have managed by now – after so much nostalgic searching for underlying meaning – to capture it. I would hold it as a precious truth and incarcerate it in a singular (uncontested) narrative. But fortunately – for me, and for the Emberá – I have found nothing of the sort: no inner Emberá authenticity hidden beneath the surface (or behind the scenes) of social relations, neither an ancient nor a pre-modern indigeneity masked by (or unearthed through) the use of various types of Emberá clothing. The search for a real, or more real, Self beyond superficial appearances suspiciously reflects a rather Western presupposition (Miller 2005b; see also Strathern 1979), rooted in a particularly European history (Trilling 1972; Handler 1986; Bendix 1997; Lindholm 2008, 2013). When one sets out on such a quest into the past of contemporary indigenous societies, it usually reproduces yet another version of 'imperialist nostalgia' (Rosaldo 1989).

My ethnographic nostalgia – limiting and accidentally enabling – led me to entertain the wrong questions: Who are the true Emberá after all? Those dressed in traditional or modern clothes? Those who embrace change or those who resist it? Trapped with such a limited view of what the authentic may be (see Theodossopoulos 2013a) I have struggled, again and again, to redeem my nostalgic (well-hidden) preference to see the Emberá in 'traditional' clothes: 'proud, resisting, uncompromised', as I once wrote in my notes. As if the traditional costume represented the essence of a deeper indigeneity, untarnished by the temptations of the wider non-indigenous world. And if such a deeper cultural essence existed, what would be my role? Would I become 'the recorder and interpreter of fragile customs', the 'custodian of an essence', an 'unimpeachable witness to an authenticity' (Clifford 1986: 113), an authenticity isolated from the rest of the world? Anthropology is now past the crisis of the representation era; the pursuit of timeless meaning, now visible in neostructuralist accounts, is once again more popular. 'The spectre of authenticity can still be found at the anthropological banquet: if not at the table, then at least as ghostly presence in the room.' (Fillitz and Saris 2013: 8)

Unravelling one layer of nostalgia after the other, eventually I learned how to ask a somewhat more nuanced question – to de-exoticise: 'Can we see the reintroduction of traditional clothes – or better, the practice of wearing them – as an emerging Emberá modernity?' The residents of Parara Puru, with whom I discussed the practical dimensions of this general question, provided me with short and direct answers: they are Emberá, they say, independently of the clothes they wear, 'their own traditional clothes' or the clothes they call 'modern'. They feel Emberá despite having embraced modernity. They are, after all, contemporary citizens of Panama, indigenous and modern and they wish to be respected by their non-indigenous neighbours and recognised as indigenous Panamanians. In Chagres, non-indigenous neighbours are accustomed to seeing the Emberá dressed in traditional attire, and recognise that indigenous practices are part of a modern enterprise – indigenous tourism. From this point of view, the indigenous attire is another dress code followed by modern, indigenous tourism entrepreneurs.

All this leads me to argue that the reanimation of the old Emberá dress codes for tourism is not merely an imitation of the past, even if this were its original intention. 'There is no simulacrum' here, Bruner would say, as 'there is no original'. A single normative and prescribed Emberá dress code has never existed before. If we look to the past we can identify formal and informal styles of dress, but also periodic and local fashions: popular *jagua* body-paint designs and haircuts, and favourite types of garments and adornments. But even in the present, where a normative traditional dress code has been typified as a costume – a measure for a prescribed, static authenticity – its application in real life evades the singularity of an ideal authoritative code: certain traditional clothing items have been enlarged to cover a greater part of the body to accommodate contemporary concerns about modesty. Other types of traditional clothes, such as the *parumas*, have gained popularity that goes beyond representational contexts. It is therefore fair to argue that every time the Emberá put on their attire, they give their 'traditional' clothes 'new life' (Bruner 2005: 5, 257); and, in a reciprocal manner, the 'traditional' clothes allow the Emberá wearer to relive – and to embody – their relationship with a fluid and changeable Emberá tradition. Dress practices, creative and sometimes unpredictable, evade the static representation of a normative view of authenticity. Even costume can become a medium for expressing a self-conscious – and continuously changing – image of the self (see Shukla 2015: 3–5).

But let us consider how wearing traditional attire has had an impact on Emberá identity. As I argued above there is no single original to be imitated, only an imagined dress code, a simplification of many different past dress practices. The indigenous attire, reconstituted for tourist presentations, represents an attempt to visualise the Emberá past in terms of a fairly undifferentiated – 'imagined' in Benedict Anderson's (1983) terms – community: a model according to which the Emberá can reconstitute themselves in imitation of themselves. The continuous, performative reenactment of such a collective identity is undoubtedly constitutive of newly embodied experiences (Bruner 2005): the Emberá dress in traditional attire to represent a primordial Emberá-ness, an 'indigenous essentialism' (Howe 2009). Through repetitive practice, however, they have begun increasingly to identify with the undifferentiated vision of Emberá-ness they embody in daily performance. They now say that they feel more comfortable wearing Emberá clothes – more comfortable than before they started wearing Emberá attire for tourism. In the ethnography presented in this book I referred to this newly acquired confidence as representational self-awareness.

Miller (2005a, 2005b) is right to stress that clothes, through their mere existence and materiality, shape identities. For example, the availability of traditional Emberá items of clothes in the communities that perform for tourists has resulted in new dress practices, mixed (indigenous/non-indigenous) dress codes or spontaneous dress combinations (see Chapter 7). If we assume that the Emberá in these communities have developed a new clothed *habitus* – in Bourdieusian terms – their shifting dress codes have given rise to a potentially 'infinite number of practices that are relatively unpredictable', yet 'limited in their diversity' (Bourdieu 1990: 55). Possibilities and limitations here are predicated on the material characteristics of the clothes in question: their condition, availability and possible combinations. Taken together, these material qualities and their repetitive embodiment (during or after the tourist encounter) play a role in constituting – to paraphrase Bruner (1993) – the new Emberá creatively clothed persona.

Take for example the resourceful combinations of the *paruma*-skirt with a variety of 'modern' tops. Matched with 'modern' tops – t-shirts, vest tops, tank tops and cropped tops – the *parumas* provide a wide array of dress combinations, indigenous and modern at the same time. Their simple shape – they are literally three-yard-long square pieces of cloth wrapped around the hips – makes them easy to wear for a variety of daily jobs. Their light synthetic fabric drapes effortlessly over the lower body – a distinctively comfortable and soft *paruma* feel (Banerjee and Miller 2003; Kuchler 2005). Meanwhile, their colourful patterns present opportunities for a wide palette of colour combinations with modern tops – for example, with a single-coloured top – which provides women (who only have a small number of clothes) with flexible dress choices.

Worn without a top, and combined with an *ubarí* or other necklace, the *parumas* are used as a constituent of the 'traditional' Emberá attire. But this formal use may be misleading: when matched with a modern top the *parumas* provide a very contemporary look, an indigenous-*and*-modern style of dress. Throughout Eastern Panama the presence of an indigenous fashion is ubiquitous: the *paruma*-skirts, emblems of Emberá (and Wounaan) identity, are gaining popularity, as the monthly introduction of new *paruma*-cloth – made in Asia, in new patterns and designs – excites the desire of younger and older women to acquire the latest *paruma* (see Chapter 8). At the beginning of the second decade of the twenty-first century, young Emberá women, wearing a modern black top – the colour most favoured by young Emberá at the time – matched with a recent (if not the latest) *paruma*, were visible in non-indigenous public spaces[2] more frequently than in previous years. An Emberá woman who wears the *paruma* on a daily basis – in her community, or for a short visit to a non-indigenous town – is not just a person wearing a *paruma* (see Miller 2005b): the fashionable character and indigenous associations of the *paruma* engender a particular (contemporary) identity, which can be seen as simultaneously modern-*and*-indigenous.

Disemia: indigenous-*and*-modern

Many times throughout this book, I connected the terms *indigenous* and *modern* as if they were one inseparable adjective: indigenous-*and*-modern. The two terms seem at first sight to be a pair of opposites, but this, as I am about to argue, is a rather misleading view. Indigeneity is not, strictly speaking, a substitute for tradition. Tradition – if we assume that tradition is modernity's relational opposite – does not encompass the racialised implications that the term *indigenous* conveys in Latin America (see Wade 1997). In Panama, for example, indigeneity is conceived in both ethnic and racial terms and it is attributed exclusively to specific groups that are 'indigenous' to the Americas – for example, the Emberá, the Wounaan, the Guna, the Ngäbe, the Buglé, the Teribe. Membership to these groups does not preclude one from being a *modern* person – in fact, Panamanian national education aims to inculcate exactly this subjectivity: to educate indigenous students as modern citizens of Panama.

It is in such terms that the Emberá feel – as many other people in Latin America do (see Conklin 2007) – simultaneously indigenous *and* modern. These are undoubtedly relational concepts, with countless local (and more specific) referents: Western modernity, in its reified sense, is substantiated by non-Western, marginal Others (Trouillot 1991, 2002; Comaroff and Comaroff 1991, 1997) who in turn introduce their own 'alternatively modern' views by means of selective 'appropriation, opposition, and redefinition' of indigenous authenticities (Knauft 2002). Indigeneity, in turn, is constituted by histories of previous discrimination and peripheralisation constructed by the West, but it is also renegotiated locally, according to context-specific criteria and meaning (see Saugestad 2001; Ramos 2003; Kenrick and Lewis 2004; Barnard 2006).

Both terms, modernity and indigeneity, are framed by Western referents, which are continuously redefined, subverted and transformed in non-Western settings. In fact, from most indigenous points of view, I would dare to generalise, modernity and indigeneity – with all their permeable, ever-changing connotations – do not exist in isolation from each other. If we recognise that isolated or static indigenous worlds do not really exist, as taken today axiomatically by most anthropologists, only one additional logical step is required to acknowledge the simultaneity of modernity and indigeneity. These two reified and imprecise concepts may coexist in a cloud of contradictions: a denial of indigeneity's coevalness (Fabian 1983) or a constantly shifting view of modernity's contemporaneity (see Miller 1994; Freidman 2002). Yet these very contradictions, as I will explain below, inspire bottom-up responses that open up the possibility of being indigenous and modern in a critical or alternative manner (Knauft 2002b).

To elucidate the simultaneity of modernity and indigeneity, I introduced the concept of 'indigenous *disemia*'. This is an adaptation of Herzfeld's (2005) original *disemia*: the ambivalence between official self-representation and the unofficial recognition of a more fluid identity for the Self. An advantage of this particular conceptualisation of ambivalence is its fluidity, which evades the Goffmanesque separation between on-stage and off-stage representation or, in the case of tourism, the distinction between front- and back-regions of interaction (see MacCannell 1976). Instead, Herzfeld's *disemia* redirects attention to the continuous oscillation between official and unofficial representation and the contradictions that emerge from their partial overlap, which engender *social poetics*: the play through which local actors negotiate their creative presentation in contradistinction with (or in terms that partially overlap with) 'the formal image of a national or collective self' (Herzfeld 2005: x).

Indigenous *disemia* in particular captures a similar sense of oscillating ambivalence, this time between established, formal expectations about being either modern or indigenous, and everyday practices that are simultaneously modern and indigenous. Formal representation may focus on ideal types: for example, what constitutes a good indigenous citizen or who remains faithful to a distinctive ethnic identity – the sort of narratives promoted by non-indigenous politicians or indigenous leaders. In contrast, everyday practices involve a much more fluid identification with heterogeneous elements: commodities, aesthetics, narratives and processes. These may represent the latest fashionable trend or they may reproduce what is already well known and established, or even a mixture of the two. In other words, everyday practices may not yet be fully articulated as part of a coherent narrative about modernity or indigeneity; they often incorporate elements of both.

Unsurprisingly, local actors, led by pragmatic concerns, navigate between the conceptual boundaries of what may be seen locally as purely modern *or* indigenous. The resulting imprecision may be constitutive of indigenous *disemia*, an ambivalence that corrupts the normative precision of those 'indigenous essentialisms' (Howe 2009) set up by various authenticators – 'the authorities in indigenous communities and the experts beyond who determine what is deemed authentic at any one time' (Jackson and Warren 2005: 559). It is in this respect that indigenous *disemia* subverts typologies, definitions and expectations, as it directs attention to the ambiguities that engender complicated identities such as in the case I examine here, the desire of many Emberá men and women to be simultaneously modern *and* indigenous: that is, contemporary citizens of their nation, with access to the commodities and benefits provided by non-indigenous society, who are still free to accentuate the aspects of their distinctive ethnic identity that they choose to draw attention to (which differ from context to context).

In everyday life the Emberá hesitate over how to describe their various identifications with commodities, aesthetics, narratives or processes that may be seen as more or less indigenous or modern. This is because very often their ambivalence is predicated on more than one – parallel and simultaneous – understanding of what is, or what is to be, expected from authentic Emberá life. For example, the indigenous *disemia* of many Emberá who live in communities that entertain tourists is stimulated by a concern for authenticity – understood as living a representative Emberá life, which is often introduced by travel agents and indigenous leaders (who act as authenticators). Yet, in Parara Puru, and other Emberá communities in Chagres, more than one standard of Emberá representativeness frame what is authentic (see Chapter 6): the first measure of the authentic refers to the way of life of the grandfathers,[3] who lived in dispersed settlement scattered along riverine rainforest locations, and the second refers to life in homogenous and politically organised concentrated communities – that is, life as experienced by most other Emberá communities in contemporary Panama.

Having established the parameters of these two parallel local views of authenticity, I am tempted to ask one more time: Who are the most authentic Emberá? Those dressed in traditional attire or those in 'modern' clothes? The essentialist limitations of this question are in themselves indicative of the dilemmas set up by indigenous *disemia*. In their everyday lives, the Emberá of Chagres navigate between the conceptual boundaries of more than one measure of authenticity, which sometimes partially overlap. For example, they have become accustomed to hosting and entertaining tourists dressed in the traditional attire that corresponds to the formal dress code of their grandparents. Travel agents and indigenous leaders have promoted this type of dress as an official representation of 'tradition'. But when the tourists depart, the Emberá dress in either 'modern' clothes or 'mixed' clothing combinations, containing both indigenous and modern elements. Some of the latter are spontaneous adaptations to the practical requirements necessitated by certain tasks, and often involve leaving the top part of the body uncovered – very much like the informal dress codes of the old times (which relates to the first local referent of authenticity). Other dress choices, however, which involve either 'modern' or 'mixed' modern-*and*-indigenous elements – for example a *paruma*-skirt with a modern top – represent broader fashions and are representative of how the Emberá dress in most other communities in Eastern Panama (that is, they comply with the second local referent of authenticity).

Here we see that a second measure of what is a representative of Emberá life – that is, what most other Emberá do – provides an alternative view of how the Emberá of Chagres should dress. This second view of authenticity-as-representativeness is very important to the residents of communities that were founded relatively recently, such as Parara Puru. The older and middle-aged residents grew up in scattered locations close to non-indigenous settlements, without the sheltering protection of an ethnically homogenous and politically organised community. This experience informs their desire to accentuate that they too, as most other Emberá, live in concentrated communities, which are now integral parts of Panamanian indigenous political structures. The underlying argument here is that the Emberá communities at Chagres are as authentic as any other contemporary and modern Emberá community in Eastern Panama. It is a basis from which to establish political claims – for example, entitlement to land – or to counteract the suspicion of inauthenticity introduced by some tourists (who do not see 'touristy' communities as 'real' communities).

The two measures of authenticity outlined above reproduce *disemic* ambiguities that pose representational challenges for the Emberá of Parara Puru and the other communities at Chagres. An indicative example is the emerging concern about what is a representative Emberá house (a topic discussed in more detail in Chapter 6). Most Emberá families in Parara attempt to achieve a compromise between a conception of the Emberá house seen as indigenous-*and*-modern (indigenous-Emberá in structure, but with modern accessories and materials) and a representation of the Emberá house that is indicative of the times of the grandparents. Here, ambivalence between two different established views of representativeness – which only partially overlap – is resolved through everyday Emberá solutions, which are fluid, creative and, in many respects, incomplete: the Emberá house is

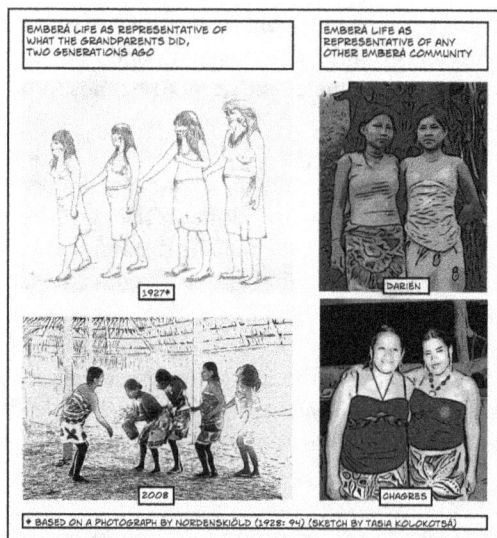

9.3 Two views of Emberá authenticity as representativeness

not a finished product, but a structure that is constantly modified, as it continually adapts to new challenges.

Interestingly, both views of Emberá representativeness – the authentic as either what the grandparents did or what most other Emberá nowadays do – are called into question during self-representation in tourism. As an Emberá friend in Parara Puru confided to me, if the Emberá strip their houses of everything that looks 'modern', the tourists would be equally dissatisfied! A normatively 'traditional' view of the Emberá house, sanitised of 'modern' features or appliances, may elicit suspicions of inauthenticity: a perception of Parara as uninhabited. Here the Emberá are confronted by contradictions that cannot be fully resolved. As we saw in Chapter 5, some other tourists search meticulously for various signs of modernity – television antennae, electrical equipment, modern clothing on the laundry line – and hasten to remark with imperialist nostalgia about the impending and inevitable loss that Emberá culture, like all other indigenous cultures, is bound to suffer. I referred to the contradictions that such comments generate as 'unintentional primitivisation', an ambivalent attitude about the intrinsic worth of Western civilisation, which does not challenge, nevertheless, the Western-civilisational project. It represents a position echoed by the tourist commentary, and disseminated to the community via the travel agents. Through their unintentional primitivisation, the tourists set for the Emberá new *disemic* dilemmas and representational challenges, which has inspired me to refer to the tourists as the exoticising spectres that haunt the Emberá present.

I will present one final example of the emerging overlap between established and negotiated practices that is so characteristic of indigenous *disemia*. In recent years, the practical solution of using a *paruma* to cover a woman's chest – a combination referred to as *paruma con paruma*, as the wearer uses another *paruma* as a skirt – has become quite established in Chagres among communities that entertain tourists. During the part of the day when tourists are present, the women avoid wearing modern tops in order to comply with the rules agreed at community level (see Chapter 7). They usually cover the upper part of their bodies with heavy *ubarí*-necklaces made of coins and beads, but enlarged to modestly cover their breasts. This practice follows the normative 'traditional' dress code, a publicly enacted standard of authenticity that alludes to Emberá life in the time of the grandparents.

On those occasions, however, when some women do not want to wear the heavy *ubarís* – for example, to perform a manual task – they protect their chest from the view of outsiders with a second *paruma*. This solution is regaining popularity, as it is practical and convenient, the women say. It represents an older solution to the problem of covering a woman's body from the view of outsiders, followed in the past by Emberá women visiting Afro-Darienita towns, as recorded by previous ethnographers in the 1960s (see Torres de Araúz 1966; Reverte Coma 2002; see Chapter 3). In this respect, the *paruma con paruma* combination represents a dress code with roots in the past, the 'authentic' era of the grandparents, when the Emberá relied much less on 'modern', non-indigenous clothes. It has become widespread once more now that the Emberá of Chagres – due to their involvement in tourism – avoid wearing Western clothes for a significant part of the day. Nowadays, however, the rather old-fashioned associations of this practice are made less visible by the popularity and colourful intensity of the contemporary *parumas*, which are fashionable – modern-*and*-indigenous – items of dress. The Emberá women cover themselves, in a traditional way, using modern-day indigenous clothes that follow the latest local fashions.

In the examples discussed here, and many others presented in the ethnography that supported this book, we see how fluid everyday choices about how to be indigenous-*and*-modern negotiate between more generally established conceptions of what it means to be representatively Emberá. In their self-representation to outsiders local Emberá actors choose to emphasise – in a *disemic* manner – the more established views of what constitutes indigenous Emberá life, in contrast to everyday practices that are simultaneously modern-*and*-indigenous. This ambivalence, however, is not discretely compartmentalised in social life – e.g. back- and front-regions, touristy or non-touristy performance – but permeates, to a greater or lesser degree, representational and non-representational contexts. Indigenous *disemia* is usually resolved with spontaneous and pragmatic decisions in the given present-time of social action, but has the propensity to return in the form of new dilemmas (or new versions of older ones) in the course of daily life, or in the next episode of transformative change in one's life.

Mirrors, caricatures and the recognition of the exotic in the Self

The *paruma* motif in figure 9.4 is rather unusual. It depicts a Chocó (Emberá-Wounaan) woman wearing a *paruma*. Here we see a *paruma* that mirrors its wearer: a simplified, exoticised imitation of a traditional self – a caricature. Although unusual in that it represents a human figure, the particular *paruma* is a variation on recent naturalistic *paruma* themes (e.g. leafs, flowers and birds; see Chapter 8). In this case, the woman depicted wearing a *paruma* is placed in a standard, naturalised frame with her chest uncovered, in a manner common to Chocó women until the 1960s – an evocative image of Emberá-Wounaan culture as it used to be, when the Chocó lived dispersed in the rainforest. Women's dress here stands as representative of 'tradition or authenticity' (Banerjee and Miller 2003: 235), and it is 'relatively more pronounced' than the dress of men (Knauft 2007: 103; see also C. Hendrickson 1995: 62; Veber 1996: 160), as is the case of other Panamanian ethnic groups (see Young 1971: 10–15; Taussig 1993: 141; Tice 1995: 28, 47, 81; Salvador 1997b: 151; Howe 1998: 17, 125, 178, 2009: 226–7).

The woman in the *paruma* design looks the viewer straight in the eye. She 'looks back to what Benjamin theorized as the "recently outmoded," the surrealist power of yesterday's fashion' (Taussig 1993: 231). Yesterday's fashion, in this case, is appropriated by today's *paruma* industry of indigenous fashion. The precise *paruma* design, like most others, was printed in different colours and made available in the Panamanian *paruma* market approximately seven years ago. At that point in time, yesterday's fashion was indeed the latest fashion: the *paruma* above was sold for

9.4 The self-mirroring *paruma*

a brief period of time at the highest price, until it was replaced in popularity by yet another different *paruma*. I acquired this particular *paruma* from an Emberá woman at Chagres, three years after it was released onto the market. She was happy to exchange it with one of the latest – at the time – and more expensive *parumas*.

Taussig has drawn attention to the dual-layered notion of imitation: the mimetic faculty generates 'a palpable, sensuous connection between the very body of the perceiver and the perceived', during which the representation – in our case, the design of the bare-breasted Chocó woman wearing a *paruma* – 'shares in or takes power from the represented' (Taussig 1993: 21–2). But what happens when this dynamic combination – the representation of the Chocó woman wearing a *paruma* – is bought and worn by the actual Emberá or Wounaan women for whom the particular cloth was manufactured? In the sketches of figure 9.5 we see the interplay of mirroring images – 'the image affecting what it is an image of' (Taussig 1993: 2) – that embody the intentionality of the wearer. An Emberá woman may wear the 'self-mirroring *paruma*' during tourist presentations to accentuate her connection with the Emberá past, laying emphasis on a representational continuity: 'We were once dressed like this; we can dress like this now.' An Emberá woman may choose to combine the 'self-mirroring *paruma*' with a modern top to go out of her community with a group of friends, and draw attention to her modern-*and*-indigenous subjectivity: 'We don't go in public with our chests uncovered anymore, but we are Emberá, as you see on my skirt [and by my wearing of a *paruma*-skirt], and proud to be indigenous.'

The design of the topless Chocó woman wearing a *paruma*, as depicted in figure 9.4, is an allusion to an older dress code, an exoticised, naturalised image of 'lost' indigenous innocence: the adolescent memory of an elderly woman – for example, of how she once dressed to dance in a shamanic ceremony or to attend a local celebration – or the expectation of a contemporary tourist or traveller, who strives to imagine, with a measure of imperialist nostalgia (Rosaldo 1989), a timeless yet disappearing indigenous past. Nevertheless, and more importantly, the image of the topless Chocó woman wearing a *paruma* (and also *jagua* designs on her arms, a crown of flowers, a necklace and bracelets) refers to a particular dress code – the component of the female Emberá attire, as it is nowadays reconstituted as a costume. In tourist presentations and advertisements it is matched with the complementary image of the generic Chocó man wearing a loincloth and similar adornments. As I highlighted in Chapter 2, this seems at first glance to represent a static, normative vision of Emberá dress based on standards of representativeness that confine indigenous authenticity to the past.

Due to an unexpected turn of circumstances, the Emberá attire, initially conceived – with a touch of structural nostalgia (Herzfeld 2005) – as an imitation of what was irrevocably lost, has now become an alternative *contemporary* code of dress. In the communities that specialise in tourism, the traditional attire outlines a set of clothing items that the Emberá wear for a large part of the day on any other day of their lives. And as with all contemporary cultural practices, the frequent use of the traditional costume – and the need to adapt to new representational challenges or practical circumstances – has prompted a small degree of change to the constituents of the costume itself. Some clothing items – such as *amburá*-belts or *ubarí*-necklaces – are now enlarged in line with contemporary standards of modesty. Other clothing items are now used even after the tourists have left, providing opportunities for all sorts of 'mixed' indigenous-*and*-modern combinations. As I stressed in Chapter 7, the transformations in Emberá clothing should not be conceived in terms of a unidirectional progression from the dress codes of the grandparents to the complete and irreversible adoption of Western clothes. Instead, they represent transformations based on previous transformations (Gow 2001a: 127) – changes that partly mirror and partly diverge from previous changes – that continue to unravel in uncharted directions as I write this book.

It is the dynamic and transformative nature of Emberá practices that Western observers – tourists, travellers, anthropologists[4] – disregard for the most part, trapped (very often) by their nostalgic expectations and the elusive search for indigenous authenticity unaffected by change. In a manner that so closely resembles the predilections of traveller-explorers Verrill and Marsh in the early-twentieth century (see Chapter 4), many contemporary tourists who visit the Emberá desire 'exclusive contact with Otherness', perpetuating (sometimes self-consciously) the illusion of 'discovering' an 'undiscovered' tribe – a secret world uncontaminated by Westernisation, a caricature of the noble-savage variety. The presence of other tourists or travellers, even that of an anthropologist, offends because the presence of other Westerners, like the Self, negates the illusion of discovery, the exclusivity of a transient encounter with alterity. From an ephemeral Western point of view, the indigenous Other is merely a mirror for self-contemplation, convenient to gaze back upon our Western selves (Ramos 1991: 157, 168) – that is, if we assume a Western subjectivity. But we need to remember that the images that emerge from such self-reflection are not immune to change (see Caiuby Novaes 1997: 43); self-caricatures can change as easily as any other caricatures.

For most tourists who visit the Emberá, it is not the content of the exotic that remains unchanged, but the desire to discover it – in an exclusive manner if possible, with some faith in a hidden authenticity and with a pinch of nostalgia. Their exoticising idealisation often turns to disappointment when they come across small pieces of 'evidence' of indigenous Westernisation. 'You can see cellular phones, antennae and Western pants', a North American tourist once said, 'even here, among the indigenous tribe!' The contradictory nature of the tourist expectations, as I described in Chapter 6, does not pass unnoticed by the indigenous

(a)

(b)

9.5a Wearing the 'self-mirroring'
paruma during tourist presentations

9.5b Wearing the 'self-mirroring' *paruma*
combined with modern top

hosts. It fuels new and old *disemic* dilemmas about social change and stimulates responses: new dress combinations, fluid cultural practices and emergent narratives about indigenous identity that counter-exoticise. The Emberá transform imperialist nostalgia (introduced by tourists) into structural nostalgia: a new, idealised vision of one's own past as tradition, which provides us with another example of nostalgia's transformative power (Angé and Berliner 2015: 9).

Howe (2009) has shown how the Guna, the neighbours of the Emberá, objectified their culture themselves by performing it for outsiders. By isolating particular elements and practices that they considered appropriate for presentation they started to treat such cultural elements and practices as distinct representational institutions (Ibid.: 181). This process entailed a focus on 'the ancient origin of cultural fundamentals', a type of primordialism to which Howe aptly refers as 'indigenous essentialism' (Ibid.: 233, 240). The Emberá have followed in the footsteps of the Guna, with a delay of two or three generations. In the last quarter of the twentieth century they negotiated their political reorganisation (see Herlihy 1986; Kane 1994) and later, at the turn of the twenty-first century, they became more actively concerned with how to communicate their cultural distinctiveness to outsiders.

As with the Guna, who started developing their representational narratives in dialogue with foreign ethnographers and supporters of indigenous affairs (Howe 2009), the Emberá are now responding to the exotic expectations of an international tourist audience. They selected certain elements of their culture that they saw as appropriate and visually compelling – in a sense, exotic enough – to attract the interest of foreign tourists-*cum*-sympathisers, and they started to articulate their own representation.

The emerging representational awareness of the Emberá addresses the expectations of Western visitors and answers back, by articulating bottom-up narratives about tradition, that attempt to correct, though not to openly challenge, the exoticising visions of their guests. It is in such terms that Emberá self-awareness invites a reversal of the exoticising gaze, the recognition of the exotic in the Self (see Kapferer and Theodossopoulos n.d.). Self-exoticisation may rely on referents of the exotic introduced by outsiders, but also entails the potential to generate some sense of control over the terms of representation, and a certain degree of self-reflection that emerges from increased representational confidence. The Emberá, for example, see the clothes of their grandparents in exotic terms. They discuss with critical introspection the self-exoticised figure of the odd 'old man with the *guayuco*' (*loincloth* in Spanish) who resisted change in the 1980s. But they also discuss with pride the success of 'the young tourism professional with the *andeá*' (*loincloth* in Emberá) who receives the admiration of visitors from the world's more powerful countries, and who 'teaches the foreigners', as some Emberá at Chagres say, what Emberá culture is. As I explained in Chapter 6, the men and women who present facets of their culture to outsiders become, in time, more confident and articulate in providing a narrative about indigeneity: they start guiding the tourists around their culture, instead of merely performing a spectacle.

Representational narratives, as they were introduced initially, may seem to typify Emberá culture in static terms, but they have now started to expand and become more pliable, permeated by new information, innovative ideas and experiential perspectives. Emberá cultural representation in tourism was originally packaged as an 'ethno-commodity', but it has acted itself out, in its short history, in unpredictable directions; for example, towards the re-fashioning of identity, the re-animation of cultural subjectivity, the recharging of a collective sentiment (Comaroff and Comaroff 2009: 20, 27–8). 'Every time heritage or tradition is enacted,' Bruner argues, 'it is given new life' (2005: 257). And every time the performers of heritage or tradition reposition themselves in front of different audiences, they relive the story they have chosen to tell about themselves: they mirror their Selves in front of their audience. The performative confidence that results from this reflexive exercise has encouraged a small degree of self-irony: self-conscious 'self-commodification' (Bunten 2008; see also Chapter 6), enacted in non-alienating, counter-exoticising terms.

This self-critical form of exoticisation entails a growing awareness of the view of the Other, a dynamic engagement with alterity that can lead to a reversal of the exoticising gaze: the Emberá look at Westerners dressed as Emberá and smile at each other with irony, humour and pride. 'The *gringos* want to become Emberá' – where

9.6 It is time to reunite – temporarily – my two authorial and nostalgic selves

Emberá is also translated as 'human being'; the humanity of the *gringos* is reconstituted by wearing Emberá clothes. I dare to predict that this gradual development of a bottom-up, critical approach to the exoticising stereotypes of Others, may even encourage a move away from the commercial orientation of state-endorsed multiculturalism that is so evident in the development of Panamanian tourism as a national project (Horton 2006; Guerrón-Montero 2006a; Velásquez Runk 2012). But it is too early to tell. The transformations engendered by the interplay of exoticisation and self-exoticisation in Emberá representation are still in an emerging and gradually developing stage. At this historical juncture, I can only verify that the patronising gaze of outsiders is received with counter-exoticising narratives that politely address Western stereotypes, de-exoticising Emberá culture via particularisation: the provision of corrective details about indigenous experience (see Chapter 5). Alterity is re-represented as particular and concrete.

Seen in this broader context, the practice of wearing Emberá attire – even merely for representational purposes – has contributed towards a renewed identification of the Emberá with their history and culture. Material objects, such as clothes, are not merely tools through which to negotiate identity; they also create identities (Miller 2005a, 2005b, 2010). As other Amerindian groups did before them, the Emberá have gained national and international visibility by exploiting the exotic referents of their costume (see Conklin 1997, 2007; Gow 2007; Ewart 2007; Santos-Granero 2009). Yet, the very act of gaining visibility while wearing their distinctive costume has encouraged, so far, a closer connection with the clothes themselves. In other words, the clothes that the Emberá wear are

9.7 A farewell

not simply mirrors for communicating messages, but become constitutive of the intended messages. By wearing indigenous, as well as modern, clothes the Emberá have reclaimed their place in their contemporary nation and the world. They have claimed coevalness (Fabian 1983) where coevalness was previously denied.

'We wear modern clothes, like anyone else', many Emberá at Chagres are now prepared to admit, 'but we are not embarrassed to be seen in our own [Emberá] clothes'; 'the *kampuniá* [all sorts of non-indigenous people] can see what we are.' Such words substantiate an inherently optimistic version of the story of Emberá clothing and, with respect to this optimism, one that conveys an empowering message: far from being a frozen museum exhibit, Emberá culture and identity are adapting to new challenges and circumstances in the twenty-first century. My younger anthropological Self – who prefers to focus, as many anthropologists before him, on underlying cultural patterns – is pleased at the thought that Emberá culture is as recognisable as before, and that more than one competing referent of Emberá authenticity find expression in revitalised practices: 'authentic discontinuities' (Kane 1994) that nowadays multiply exponentially, thanks to the international popularity of indigeneity. Yet, my older anthropological Self – who prefers to focus on intentionality and strategies – is content at the thought that the Emberá are taking advantage of new opportunities to renegotiate their representation.

I would have liked to write more than one book about the Emberá, to tell more than one story, and I hope that an older version of my self-as-author will have a chance to witness and to write about the next episodes in Emberá representation. And admittedly, to some great extent, my current ethnographic experience will inevitably predicate my future ethnographic nostalgia – and maybe that of my students: a testament of how a previous record of ethnographic experiences shapes the ethnographic outcome. Yet, as I am writing the final lines of this book, I am forced to recognise that my current insights about the limitations and virtues of ethnographic practice have emerged from the relentless deconstruction that this has previously made available. Ethnographic nostalgia – however irredeemable it may be – has given me the opportunity to recognise and contest the exotic 'beyond the normal registers of understanding' (Kapferer 2013); it has sent me – to paraphrase the poet Kavafis – on the 'marvellous' ethnographic journey! The most valuable insights I gained in my journey stem from the recognition of my errors and misperceptions as an ethnographer.

Notes

1 See 'Ithaca' by Konstantinos Kavafis (1863–1933).
2 For example, the streets of non-indigenous towns in Darién, non-indigenous settlements closer to Chagres or even Avenida Central in Panama City.
3 Who, in genealogical terms (and depending on one's age), were literally the grandparents or great-grandparents of the contemporary population.
4 I do not exempt myself from this fallacy. In an earlier article, I described in detail how I had previously fallen into the trap of an essentialist view of authenticity (Theodossopoulos 2013a).

References

Abram, Simone and Jacqueline Waldren. 1997. 'Introduction: identifying with people and places.' In *Tourists and Tourism: Identifying with People and Places*, eds. S. Abram, J. Waldren and D.V.L. Macleod, pp. 1–11. Oxford: Berg.

Allerton, Catherine. 2007. 'The Secret Life of Sarongs: Manggarai Textiles as Super-Skins.' *Journal of Material Culture* 12(1), 22–46.

Anderson, Benedict. 1983. *Imagined Communities: Reflections on the Origin and Spread of Nationalism*. London: Verso.

Angé, Olivia. 2015. 'Social and economic performativity of nostalgic narratives in Andean barter fairs.' In *Anthropology and Nostalgia*, eds. Olivia Angé and David Berliner, pp. 178–97. Oxford: Berghahn Books.

Angé, Olivia and David Berliner. 2015. 'Anthropology of nostalgia – anthropology as nostalgia.' In *Anthropology and Nostalgia*, eds. Olivia Angé and David Berliner, pp. 1–15. Oxford: Berghahn Books.

Appadurai, Arjun. 1986. *The Social Life of Things: Commodities in Cultural Perspective*. Cambridge: Cambridge University Press.

Appadurai, Arjun. 1996. *Modernity at Large: Cultural Dimensions of Globalization*. Minneapolis: University of Minnesota Press.

Argyrou, Vassos. 2002. *Anthropology and the Will to Meaning: A Postcolonial Critique*. London: Pluto.

Banerjee, Mukulika and Daniel Miller. 2003. *The Sari*. Oxford: Berg.

Banks, Marcus. 2013a. 'Post-Authenticity: Dilemmas of Identity in the 20th and 21st Centuries.' *Anthropological Quarterly* 86(2), 481–500.

Banks, Marcus. 2013b. 'True to life: authenticity and the photographic image.' In *Debating Authenticity: Concepts of Modernity in Anthropological Perspective*, eds. Thomas Fillitz and Jamie Saris, pp. 160–171. Oxford: Berghahn Books.

Barnard, Alan. 2006. 'Kalahari Revisionism, Vienna and the "Indigenous Peoples" Debate.' *Social Anthropology* 14(1), 1–16.

Barnes, Ruth and Joanne B. Eicher (eds.). 1992. *Dress and Gender: Making and Meaning in Cultural Contexts*. Oxford: Berg.

Barthes, Roland. 1985. *The Fashion System*. London: Jonathan Cape.

Bartoszko, Aleksandra. 2011. 'The Anthropological Comic Book: An Alternative Way of Reaching the Audience.' Accessed from http://www.antropologi.info/blog/anthropology/2011/anthropological-comic-book.

Bartoszko, Aleksandra, Birgitte Leseth and Marcin Ponomarew. 2011. 'Public Space, Information Accessibility, Technology, and Diversity at Oslo University College.' Accessed from http://anthrocomics.wordpress.com.

Battaglia, Debbora. 1995. 'On practical nostalgia: self-prospecting among urban Trobrianders'. In *Rhetorics of Self-Making*, ed. Debbora Battaglia, pp. 77–96. Berkeley: University of California Press.

Bendix, Regina. 1997. *In Search of Authenticity: The Formation of Folklore Studies*. Madison: University of Wisconsin Press.

Benjamin, Walter. 1992 (1936). *Illuminations*. London: Fontana.

Berkhofer, Robert F. 1978. *The White Man's Indian: Images of the American Indian from Columbus to the Present*. New York: Vintage Books.

Berliner, David. 2015. 'Are anthropologists nostalgist?' In *Anthropology and Nostalgia*, eds. Olivia Angé and David Berliner, pp. 17–34. Oxford: Berghahn Books.

Béteille, André. 1998. 'The Idea of Indigenous People'. *Current Anthropology* 39(2), 187–92.

Bissell, William C. 2005. 'Engaging Colonial Nostalgia'. *Cultural Anthropology* 20(2), 215–48.

Boissevain, Jeremy (ed.). 1996. *Coping with Tourists: European Reactions to Mass Tourism*. Oxford: Berghahn Books.

Bolton, Lissant. 2003. 'Gender, status and introduced clothing in Vanuatu'. In *Clothing the Pacific*, ed. Chloe Colchester, pp. 119–39. Oxford: Berg.

Bolton, Lissant. 2007. ' "Island dress that belongs to us all": mission dresses and the innovation of tradition in Vanuatu'. In *Body Arts and Modernity*, eds. Elizabeth Ewart and Michael O'Hanlon, pp. 165–82. Wantage: Sean Kingston.

Bourdieu, Pierre. 1984. *Distinction: A Social Critique of the Judgement of Taste*. London: Routledge and Kegan Paul.

Bourdieu, Pierre. 1990. *The Logic of Practice*. Cambridge: Polity.

Bourgois, Philippe. 1998. 'Conjugated Oppression: Class and Ethnicity among Guaymi and Kuna Banana Workers'. *American Ethnologist* 15(2), 328–48.

Bruner, Edward M. 1991. 'Transformation of Self in Tourism'. *Annals of Tourism Research* 18, 238–50.

Bruner, Edward M. 1993. 'Epilogue: creativity persona and the problem of authenticity'. In *Creativity/Anthropology*, eds. S. Lavie, K. Narayan and R. Rosaldo, pp. 321–34. Ithaca: Cornell University Press.

Bruner, Edward M. 1994. 'Abraham Lincoln as Authentic Reproduction: A Critique of Postmodernism'. *American Anthropologist* 96(2), 397–415.

Bruner, Edward M. 2001. 'The Maasai and the Lion King: Authenticity, Nationalism, and Globalization in African Tourism'. *American Ethnologist* 28(4), 881–908.

Bruner, Edward M. 2005. *Culture on Tour: Ethnographies of Travel*. Chicago: University of Chicago Press.

Bryant, Rebecca. 2015. 'Nostalgia and the discovery of loss: essentializing the Turkish Cypriot past'. In *Anthropology and Nostalgia*, eds. Olivia Angé and David Berliner, pp. 155–77. Oxford: Berghahn Books.

Bunten, Alexis. 2008. 'Sharing Culture or Selling Out? Developing the Commodified Persona in the Heritage Industry'. *American Ethnologist* 35(3), 380–95.

Bunten, Alexis. 2011. 'The paradox of gaze and resistance in Native American cultural tourism: an Alaskan case study'. In *Great Expectations: Imagination and Anticipation in the Anthropology of Tourism*, eds. J. Skinner and D. Theodossopoulos, pp. 61–81. Oxford: Berghahn Books.

Caballero Barahona, R. E. and B. Carpio Conquista. 2008. 'La comunidad de Emberá Querá, como fuente de recursos naturales y culturales para el desarrollo del ecoturismo'. Colón, Universidad de Panamá. Licenciatura thesis.

Caballero, Vicente and Bolivar Araúz. 1962. 'Inmigración de indios Chocoes en Río Pequeni y algunos aspectos de su cultura'. *Hombre y Cultura* 1(1), 44–61.

Cable, Eric and Richard Handler. 1996. 'After Authenticity at an American Heritage Site.' *American Anthropologist* 98(3), 568–78.

Caiuby Novaes, Sylvia. 1997. *Play of Mirrors: The Representation of Self as Mirrored in the Other*. Austin: University of Texas Press.

Callaghan, Margo M. 2002. *Darien Rainforest Basketry: Baskets of the Wounaan and Emberá Indians from the Darién Rainforest in Panamá*. Arizona: HPL Enterprises.

Candanedo, Indra, Ernesto Ponce and Lenín Riquelme. 2003. *Plan de conservación de área para el Alto Chagres. The Nature Conservancy (TNC) y Asociación Nacional para la Conservación de la Naturaleza (ANCON)*. Panamá, República de Panamá.

Carrier, James and Donald Macleod. 2005. 'Bursting the Bubble: The Socio-Cultural Context of Ecotourism.' *Journal of the Royal Anthropological Institute* 11(2), 315–34.

Clastres, Pierre. 1977. *Society Against the State*. New York: Urizen Books.

Clifford, James. 1986. 'On ethnographic allegory.' In *Writing Culture: The Poetics and Politics of Ethnography*, eds. J. Clifford and G.E. Marcus, pp. 98–121. Berkeley: University of California Press.

Clifford, James. 1988. *The Predicament of Culture: Twentieth-Century Ethnography, Literature, and Art*. Cambridge: Harvard University Press.

Clifford, James. 1997. *Routes: Travel and Translation in the Late Twentieth Century*. Cambridge: Harvard University Press.

Cohen, Erik. 1988. 'Authenticity and Commoditization in Tourism.' *Annals of Tourism Research* 15, 371–86.

Colchester, Chloe. 2003. 'Introduction.' In *Clothing the Pacific*, ed. Chloe Colchester, pp. 1–22. Oxford: Berg.

Coleman, Simon and Mike Crang (eds.). 2002. *Tourism: Between Place and Performance*. Oxford: Berghahn Books.

Colin, France-Lise. 2010. '"Nosotros no solamente podemos vivir de cultura": Identity, Nature, and Power in the Comarca Emberá of Eastern Panama.' Ph.D. dissertation, Carleton University.

Colin, France-Lise. 2013. 'Commodification of Indigenous Crafts and Reconfiguration of Gender Identities Among the Emberá of Eastern Panama.' *Gender, Place & Culture* 20(4), 487–509.

Comaroff, Jean and John Comaroff. 1991. *Of Revelation and Revolution: Christianity, Colonialism, and Consciousness in South Africa; Volume One*. Chicago: University of Chicago Press.

Comaroff, Jean and John L. Comaroff. 1993. 'Introduction.' In *Modernity and its Malcontents: Ritual and Power in Postcolonial Africa*, eds. J. Comaroff and J. L.Comaroff, pp. xi–xxxvii. Chicago: University of Chicago Press.

Comaroff, Jean and John L. Comaroff. 1997. *Of Revelation and Revolution II: the Dialectics of Modernity on a South African Frontier*. Chicago: University of Chicago Press.

Comaroff, John L. and Jean Comaroff. 2009. *Ethnicity, Inc.* Chicago: University of Chicago Press.

Conklin, Beth A. 1997. 'Body Paint, Feathers, and VCRs: Aesthetics and Authenticity in Amazonian Activism.' *American Ethnologist* 24(4), 711–37.

Conklin, Beth A. 2007. 'Ski masks, veils, nose-rings and feathers: identity on the frontlines of modernity.' In *Body Arts and Modernity*, eds. E. Ewart and M. O'Hanlon, pp. 18–35. Wantage: Sean Kington Publishing.

Conklin, Beth A. and Laura R. Graham. 1995. 'The Shifting Middle Ground: Amazonian Indians and Eco-Politics.' *American Anthropologist* 97(4), 695–710.

Cummings, William. 2003. 'Orientalism's Corporeal Dimension.' *Journal of Colonialism and Colonial History* 4(2). Accessed from http://muse.jhu.edu.chain.kent.ac.uk/journals/journal_of_colonialism_and_colonial_history/v004/4.2cummings.html.

Craik, Jennifer. 1994. *The Face of Fashion: Cultural Studies in Fashion*. London: Routledge.

Delaney, Carol. 2004. *Investigating Culture: An Experimental Introduction to Anthropology.* Oxford: Blackwell.

Detrich, Richard. 2009. 'Panama's Indigenous Peoples.' Accessed from http://richarddetrich.com/cruising-travel/panama-more-than-a-canal/indigenous/.

Dutton, Denis. 2003. 'Authenticity in art.' In *The Oxford Handbook of Aesthetics,* ed. Jerrold Levinson, pp. 258–74. New York: Oxford University Press.

Edensor, Tim. 1998. *Tourists at the Taj: Performance and Meaning at a Symbolic Site.* London: Routledge.

Eicher, Joanne B. 2010. 'Clothing, costume, and dress.' In *The Berg Companion to Fashion,* ed. Valerie Steele, pp. 151–2. New York: Berg.

Eicher, Joanne B. and Mary Ellen Roach-Higgins. 1992. 'Definition and classification of dress.' In *Dress and Gender: Making and Meaning in Cultural Contexts,* eds. Ruth Barnes and Joanne B. Eicher, pp. 8–28. Oxford: Berg.

Ellen, Roy. 1986. 'What Black Elk Left Unsaid: On the Illusory Images of Green Primitivism.' *Anthropology Today* **2**(6), 8–12.

Englund, Harri and James Leach. 2000. 'Ethnography and the Meta-Narratives of Modernity.' *Current Anthropology* 41(2), 225–48.

Ewart, Elisabeth. 2007. 'Black paint, red paint and a wristwatch: the aesthetics of modernity among the Panará in central Brazil.' In *Body Arts and Modernity,* eds. Elisabeth Ewart and Michael O'Hanlon, pp. 36–52. Wantage: Sean Kington Publishing.

Ewart, Elisabeth. 2013. *Space and Society in Central Brazil: A Panará Ethnography.* London: Bloomsbury.

Fabian, Johannes. 1983. *Time and the Other: How Anthropology Makes Its Object.* New York: Columbia University Press.

Faris, James C. 1972. *Nuba Personal Art.* London: Duckworth.

Faris, James C. 1988. 'Significance of difference in the male and female personal art of the southeast Nuba.' In *Marks of Civilization: Artistic Transformations of the Human Body,* ed. Arnold Rubin, pp. 29–40. Los Angeles: Museum of Cultural History.

Faris, James C. 2007. 'Body art and modernity: south-east Nuba.' In *Body Arts and Modernity,* eds. Elizabeth Ewart and Michael O'Hanlon, pp. 72–87. Wantage: Sean Kingston.

Faron, Louis C. 1961. 'A Reinterpretation of Choco Society.' *Southwestern Journal of Anthropology* 17(1), 94–102.

Faron, Louis C. 1962. 'Marriage, Residence, and Domestic Group Among the Panamanian Choco.' *Ethnology* 1(1), 13–38.

Field, Les. 2009. 'Four Kinds of Authenticity? Regarding Nicaraguan Pottery in Scandinavian Museums, 2006–08.' *American Ethnologist* 36(3), 507–20.

Fillitz, Thomas and A. Jamie Saris. 2013. 'Introduction.' In *Debating Authenticity: Concepts of Modernity in Anthropological Perspective,* eds. T. Fillitz and A. J. Saris, pp. 1–24. Oxford: Berghahn Books.

Fjellman, Stephen M. 1992. *Vinyl Leaves: Walt Disney World and America.* Boulder: Westview Press.

Fortis, Paolo. 2010. 'The Birth of Design: A Kuna Theory of Body and Personhood.' *Journal of the Royal Anthropological Institute* 16 (3), 480–95.

Fortis, Paolo. 2012a. *Kuna Art and Shamanism: An Ethnographic Approach.* Austin: University of Texas Press.

Fortis, Paolo. 2012b. 'Images of Person in an Amerindian Society: An Ethnographic Account of Kuna Woodcarving.' *Journal de la Société des Américanistes* 98(1), 7–37.

Franklin, Adrian. 2003. *Tourism: An Introduction.* London: Sage.

Frenkel, Stephen. 1996. 'Jungle Stories: North American Representations of Tropical Panama.' *The Geographical Review* 86(3), 317–33.

Friedman, Jonathan. 1994. *Cultural Identity and Global Process*. London: Sage.

Friedman, Jonathan. 2002. 'Modernity and other traditions.' In *Critically Modern: Alternatives, Alterities, Anthropologies*, ed. Bruce M. Knauft, pp. 287–313. Bloomington: Indiana University Press.

Gable, Eric and Richard Handler. 1996. 'After Authenticity at an American Heritage Site.' *American Anthropologist* 98(3), 568–78.

Gallup-Díaz, Ignacio. 2002. 'The Spanish Attempt to Tribalize the Darién, 1735–50.' *Ethnohistory* 49(2), 281–317.

García Casares, Joaquín. 2008. *Historia del Darién: Cuevas, Cunas, Españoles, Afros, presencia y actualidad de los Chocoes*. Panama: Editorial Universitaria, Carlos Manuel Gasteazoro.

Geertz, Clifford. 1973. *The Interpretation of Cultures: Selected Essays*. New York: Basic Books.

Geertz, Clifford. 1988. *Works and Lives: The Anthropologist as Author*. Stanford: Stanford University Press.

Gell, Alfred. 1975. *Metamorphosis of the Cassowaries: Umeda Society, Language and Ritual*. London: Athlone.

Gell, Alfred. 1993. *Wrapping in Images: Tattooing in Polynesia*. Oxford: Clarendon Press.

Goddard, Victoria A., Josep R. Llobera and Cris Shore (eds.). 1994. *Anthropology of Europe: Identities and Boundaries in Conflict*. Oxford: Berg.

Goffman, Erving. 1959. *The Presentation of the Self in Everyday Life*. Harmondsworth: Penguin Books.

Gow, Peter. 1999. 'Piro Designs: Painting as Meaningful Action in an Amazonian Lived World.' *Journal of the Royal Anthropological Institute* 5, 229–46.

Gow, Peter. 2001. *An Amazonian Myth and its History*. Oxford: Oxford University Press.

Gow, Peter. 2007. 'Clothing as acculturation in Peruvian Amazonia.' In *Body Arts and Modernity*, eds. Elizabeth Ewart and Michael O'Hanlon, pp. 53–71. Wantage: Sean Kingston.

Graburn, Nelson H. H. (ed.). 1976. *Ethnic and Tourist Arts: Cultural Expressions from the Fourth World*. Berkeley: University of California Press.

Graburn, Nelson H. H. 2004. 'Authentic Inuit Art: Creation and Exclusion in the Canadian North.' *Journal of Material Culture* 9(2), 141–59.

Graham, Laura R. 2002. 'How should an Indian speak? Amazonian Indians and the symbolic politics of language in the global public sphere.' In *Indigenous Movements, Self-representation, and the State in Latin America*, eds. K. B. Warren and J. E. Jackson, pp. 181–228. Austin: University of Texas Press.

Guerrón-Montero, Carla. 2006a. 'Tourism and Afro-Antillean Identity in Panama.' *Journal of Tourism and Cultural Change* 4(2), 65–84.

Guerrón-Montero, Carla. 2006b. 'Can't Beat Me Own Drum in Me Own Native Land: Calypso Music and Tourism in the Panamanian Atlantic Coast.' *Anthropological Quarterly* 79(4), 633–63.

Gunn, Wendy and Jared Donovan. 2012. 'Design anthropology: an introduction.' In *Design and Anthropology*, eds. Wendy Gunn and Jared Donovan, pp. 1–16. Farnham: Ashgate.

Guzman, Gonzalez R. 1966. 'Las migraciones Chocoes a la Provincia de Panama.' Facultad de Filosofia, Letras, y Educacion. Panama, Universidad de Panamá. Licenciatura thesis.

Hale, Charles R. 2002. 'Does Multiculturalism Menace? Governance, Cultural Rights and the Politics of Identity in Guatemala.' *Journal of Latin American Studies* 34(3), 485–524.

Hale, Charles R. 2005. 'Neoliberal Multiculturalism: The Remaking of Cultural Rights and Racial Dominance in Central America.' *Political and Legal Anthropology Review* 28(1), 10–19.

Hale, Charles R. 2006. 'Activist Research v. Cultural Critique: Indigenous Land Rights and the Contradictions of Politically Engaged Anthropology.' *Cultural Anthropology* 21(1), 96–120.

Hallam, Elizabeth and Tim Ingold. 2007. 'Creativity and cultural improvisation: an introduction.' In *Creativity and Cultural Improvisation*, eds. Elizabeth Hallam and Tim Ingold, pp. 1–24. Oxford: Berg.

Handler, Richard. 1986. 'Authenticity.' *Anthropology Today* 2(1), 2–4.

Handler, Richard. 2001. 'Authenticity, anthropology of.' In *International Encyclopedia of the Social and Behavioral Sciences, eds.* Neil J. Smelser and Paul B. Baltes, pp. 963–7. Oxford: Elsevier.

Handler, Richard and Jocelyn Linnekin. 1984. 'Tradition, Genuine or Spurious.' *The Journal of American Folklore* 97(385), 273–90.

Handler, Richard and William Saxton. 1988. 'Dyssimulation: Reflexivity, Narrative, and the Quest for Authenticity in "Living History."' *Cultural Anthropology* 3(3), 242–60.

Hansen, Karen Tranberg. 2004. 'The World in Dress: Anthropological Perspectives on Clothing, Fashion, and Culture.' *Annual Review of Anthropology* 33, 369–92.

Hanson, Allan. 1989. 'The Making of the Maori: Culture Invention and Its Logic.' *American Anthropologist* 91, 890–902.

Hendrickson, Carol. 1995. *Weaving Identities: Construction of Dress and Self in a Highland Guatemalan Town*. Austin: University of Texas Press.

Hendrickson, Hildi (ed.). 1996. *Clothing and Difference: Embodied Identities in Colonial and Post-Colonial Africa*. Durham: Duke University Press.

Herlihy, Peter H. 1985a. 'Settlement and Subsistence Change among the Chocó Indians of the Darién Province, Eastern Panama: An Overview.' *Yearbook, Conference of Latin Americanist Geographers* 11, 11–16.

Herlihy, Peter H. 1985b. 'Chocó Indian Relocation in Darién, Panama.' *Cultural Survival Quarterly* 9 (2), no page numbers.

Herlihy, Peter H. 1986. 'A Cultural Geography of the Emberá and Wounaan (Choco) Indians of Darien, Panama, with Emphasis on Recent Village Formation and Economic Diversification.' Ph.D. dissertation, Louisiana State University.

Herlihy, Peter H. 1988. 'Panama's Quiet Revolution: Comarca Homelands and Indian Rights.' *Cultural Survival Quarterly* 13(3), no page numbers.

Herlihy, Peter H. 1989. 'Opening Panama's Darién Gap.' *Journal of Cultural Geography* 9(2), 42–59.

Herlihy, Peter H. 2003. 'Participatory Research: Mapping of Indigenous Lands in Darien, Panama.' *Human Organisation* 62, 315–31.

Herrera, Francisco. 1972. 'Politizacioón de la población indígena en Panamá.' In *Actas del II Simposium Nacional de Antropología, Arqueología y Etnohistoria de Panamá, abril de 1971* (Panama, 1972), pp. 291–305. Panama: Universidad de Panamá.

Herzfeld, Michael. 1982. 'The Etymology of Excuses: Aspects of Rhetorical Performance in Greece.' *American Ethnologist* 9, 644–63.

Herzfeld, Michael. 1985. *The Poetics of Manhood: Contest and Identity in a Cretan Mountain Village*. Princeton: Princeton University Press.

Herzfeld, Michael. 1986. *Ours Once More: Folklore, Ideology, and the Making of Modern Greece*. New York: Pella Publishing Company.

Herzfeld, Michael. 1987. *Anthropology Through the Looking-Glass: Critical Ethnography in the Margins of Europe*. Cambridge: Cambridge University Press.

Herzfeld, Michael. 1992. *The Social Production of Indifference: Exploring the Symbolic Roots of Western Bureaucracy*. Chicago: University of Chicago Press.

Herzfeld, Michael. 2005 (1997). *Cultural Intimacy: Social Poetics in the Nation-State*. New York: Routledge.

Hirsch, Eric and Charles Stewart. 2005. 'Introduction: Ethnographies of Historicity.' *History and Anthropology* 16(3), 261–74.

Hirschfeld, Lawrence A. 1977a. 'Art in Cunaland: Ideology and Cultural Adaption.' *Man* 12 (1), 104–23.

Hirschfeld, Lawrence A. 1977b. 'Cuna Aesthetics: A Quantitative Analysis.' *Ethnology* 16 (2), 147–66.

Hobsbawm, Eric. 1992. 'Introduction: inventing traditions.' In *The Invention of Tradition*, eds. Eric Hobsbawm and Terence Ranger, pp. 1–14. Cambridge: Cambridge University Press.

Hollander, Anne. 1993. *Seeing Through Clothes*. Berkeley: University of California Press.

Holloman, Regina E. 1969. 'Developmental Change in San Blas.' Ph.D. dissertation, Northwestern University.

Holloman, Regina E. 1976. 'Cuna household types and the domestic cycle.' In *Frontier Adaptation in Lower South America*, eds. Mary Helms and Franklin Loveland, 131–49. Philadelphia: Institute for the Study of Human Issues.

Holtorf, Cornelius. 2005. *From Stonehenge to Las Vegas: Archaeology as Popular Culture*. Walnut Creek: Altamira Press.

Holtorf, Cornelius and Tim Schadla-Hall. 1999. 'Age as Artefact: On Arcaheological Authenticity.' *European Journal of Archaeology* 2(2), 229–47.

Horton, Lynn. 2006. 'Contesting State Multiculturalisms: Indigenous Land Struggles in Eastern Panama.' *Journal of Latin American Studies* 38, 829–58.

Howe, James. 1986. *The Kuna Gathering: Contemporary Village Politics in Panama*. Austin: University of Texas Press.

Howe, James. 1998. *A People Who Would Not Kneel: Panama, the United States and the San Blas Kuna*. Washington: Smithsonian Institution Press.

Howe, James. 2009. *Chiefs, Scribes, and Ethnographers: Kuna Culture from Inside and Out*. Austin: University of Texas Press.

Hugh-Jones, Stephen. 1992. 'Yesterday's luxuries, tomorrow's necessities: business and barter in northwest Amazonia.' In *Barter, Exchange and Value: An Anthropological Approach*, eds. C. Humphrey and S. Hugh-Jones, pp. 42–74. Cambridge: Cambridge University Press.

Ingold, Tim. 2000. *The Perception of the Environment*. London: Routledge.

Ingold, Tim. 2007. *Lines: A Brief History*. London: Routledge.

Ingold, Tim. 2011. 'Introduction.' In *Redrawing Anthropology: Materials, Movements, Lines*, ed. Tim Ingold, pp. 1–20. Farnham: Ashgate.

Ingold, Tim. 2012. 'Introduction: the perception of the user-producer.' In *Design and Anthropology*, eds. Wendy Gunn and Jared Donovan, pp. 19–33. Farnham: Ashgate.

Ingold, Tim. 2014. 'That's Enough About Ethnography!' *HAU: Journal of Ethnographic Theory* 4 (1), 383–95.

Isacsson, Sven-Erik. 1976. 'Emberá: territorio y régimen agrario de una tribu selvática bajo la dorninación española.' In *Tierra, tradición y poder en Colombia. Enfoques antropologicos.*, ed. N.S. de Friedemann, pp. 21–38. Bogotá: Biblioteca Básica Colombiana.

Isacsson, Sven-Erik. 1987. 'The egalitarian society in colonial retrospect: Emberá leadership and conflict management under the Spanish, 1660–1810.' In *Natives and Neighbours in South America*, eds. Harald O. Skar and Frank Salomon, pp. 97–129. Göteborg: Göteborgs Etnografiska Museum.

Isacsson, Sven-Erik. 1993. *Transformations of Eternity: On Man and Cosmos in Emberá Thought*. Göteborg: University of Göteborg.

Jackson, Jean E. 1995. 'Culture, Genuine and Spurious: The Politics of Indianess in the Vaupés, Colombia.' *American Ethnologist* 22(1), 3–27.

Jackson, Jean E. and Kay B. Warren. 2005. 'Indigenous Movements in Latin America, 1992–2004: Controversies, Ironies, New Directions.' *Annual Review of Anthropology* 34, 549–73.

Jones, Siân. 2010. 'Negotiating Authentic Objects and Authentic Selves.' *Journal of Material Culture* 15(2), 181–203.

Just, Roger. 2000. *A Greek Island Cosmos: Kinship & Community on Meganisi*. Oxford: James Currey.

Kalshoven, Petra Tjitske. 2012. *Crafting 'The Indian': Knowledge, Desire, and Play in Indianist Reenactment*. Oxford: Berghahn Books.

Kane, Stephanie. 1986. 'Emberá (Chocó) Village Formation: The Politics of Everyday Life in the Darién Forest.' Ph.D. Dissertation, The University of Texas at Austin.

Kane, Stephanie. 1992. 'Experience and Myth in a Colombian Chocó Case of Attempted Murder.' *Journal of Folklore Research* 29(3), 269–86.

Kane, Stephanie. 1994. *The Phantom Gringo Boat: Shamanic Discourse and Development in Panama*. Washington: Smithsonian Institution.

Kapferer, Bruce. 2013. 'How Anthropologists Think: Configurations of the Exotic.' *Journal of the Royal Anthropological Institute* 19 (4), 813–36.

Kapferer, Bruce and Dimitrios Theodossopoulos. In press. 'Introduction: Counter-Exoticization or the Exotic Regained.' *Social Analysis*.

Karkotis, Alexis. 2012. '"Now We Live Together": Village Formation Amongst the Ngöbe and How "Majority Rule is Still an Alien Concept to Most Guaymi".' Ph.D. Dissertation, University of Bristol.

Keane, Webb. 2005. 'Signs are not the garb of meaning: on the social analysis of material things.' In *Materiality*, ed. Daniel Miller, pp. 182-206. Durham: Duke University Press.

Kennedy, Elizabeth Lapovsky. 1972. 'The Waunan of the Siguirisua River: a Study of Individual Autonomy and Social Responsibility with Special Reference to the Economic Aspects.' Ph.D. dissertation, University of Cambridge.

Kenrick, Justin and Jerome Lewis. 2004. 'Indigenous Peoples' Rights and the Politics of the Term "Indigenous".' *Anthropology Today* 20(2), 4–9.

Kirtsoglou, Elisabeth and Dimitios Theodossopoulos. 2004. '"They are Taking Our Culture Away": Tourism and Culture Commodification in the Black Carib Community of Roatan.' *Critique of Anthropology* 24(2), 135–57.

Knauft, Bruce M. 1989. 'Bodily images in Melanesia: cultural substances and natural metaphors.' In *Fragments for a History of the Human Body: Part Three*, eds. M. Feher, R. Naddaff and N. Tazi, pp. 198–299. New York: Urzone.

Knauft, Bruce M. 1999. *From Primitive to Post Colonial in Melanesia and Anthropology*. Ann Arbor: University of Michigan Press.

Knauft, Bruce M. 2002a. *Exchanging the Past: A Rainforest World of Before and After*. Chicago: University of Chicago Press.

Knauft, Bruce M. 2002b. 'Critically modern: an introduction.' In *Critically Modern: Alternatives, alterities, anthropologies*, ed. Bruce M. Knauft, pp. 1–54. Bloomington: Indiana University Press.

Knauft, Bruce M. 2007. 'From self-decoration to self-fashioning: orientalism as backward progress among the Gebusi of Papua New Guinea.' In *Body Arts and Modernity*, eds. Elizabeth Ewart and Michael O'Hanlon, pp. 88–107. Wantage: Sean Kingston.

Knowles, Caroline. 2014. *Flip-Flop: A Journey Through Globalisation's Backroads*. London: Pluto.

Knudsen, Britta T. and Anne M. Waade (eds.). 2010. *Re-Investing Authenticity: Tourism, Place and Emotion*. Bristol: Channel View.

Koster, R. M. 2005. 'Master of Survival: Chief Antonio Zarco of the Choco Indians of Panama.' Accessed from http://www.escapeartist.com/efam/76/Zarco_Panama.html (Originally published in 1981 in *Quest Magazine*).

Krieger, Herbert W. 1926. '*Material culture of the people of southeastern Panama.*' In *United States National Museum Bulletin 134*. Washington: Smithsonian Institution.

Küchler, Susanne. 2003. 'The poncho and the quilt: material Christianity in the Cook Islands.' In *Clothing the Pacific*, ed. Chloe Colchester, pp. 97–116. Oxford: Berg.

Küchler, Susanne. 2005. 'Materiality and cognition: the changing face of things.' In *Materiality*, ed. Daniel Miller, pp. 206–30. Durham: Duke University Press.

Küchler, Susanne and Daniel Miller (eds.). 2005. *Clothing as Material Culture*. Oxford: Berg.

Küchler, Susanne and Graeme Were. 2005. *The Art of Clothing: A Pacific Experience*. London: UCL Press.

Kuper, Adam. 1988. *The Invention of Primitive Society: Transformations of an Illusion*. London: Routledge.

Kuper, Adam. 2003. 'The Return of the Native.' *Current Anthropology* 44(3), 389–402.

Leite, Naomi and Nelson Graburn. 2009. 'Anthropological interventions in tourism studies.' In *The Sage Handbook of Tourism Studies*, eds. M. Robinson and T. Jamal, pp. 35–64. London: Sage.

Levi-Strauss, Claude. 1963. *Structural Anthropology*. Translated from the French by Claire Jacobson and Brooke Grundfest Schoepf. New York: Basic Books.

Lindholm, Charles. 2001. *Culture and Identity: The History, Theory, and Practice of Psychological Anthropology*. Boston: McGraw-Hill.

Lindholm, Charles. 2002. "Authenticity, Anthropology, and the Sacred." *Anthropological Quarterly* 75(2), 331–9.

Lindholm, Charles. 2008. *Culture and Authenticity*. Oxford: Blackwell.

Lindholm, Charles. 2013. 'The Rise of Expressive Authenticity.' *Anthropological Quarterly* 86(2), 361–95.

Linnekin, Jocelyn. 1991. 'Cultural Invention and the Dilemma of Authenticity.' *American Anthropologist* 93(2), 446–9.

Linstroth, John. P. 1996. 'Book Review: Stephanie C. Kane, *The Phantom Gringo Boat: Shamanic Discourse and Development in Panama.*' *JASO: Journal of the Anthropological Society of Oxford*. XXVII(2), 184–6.

Loewen, Jacob A. 1963a. 'Choco I: Introduction and Bibliography.' *International Journal of American Linguistics* 29(3), 239–63.

Loewen, Jacob A. 1963b. 'Choco II: Phonological Problems.' *International Journal of American Linguistics* 29(4), 357–71.

Loewen, Jacob A. 1975. *Culture and Human Values: Christian Intervention in Anthropological Perspective*. Pasadena: William Carey Library.

Loewen, Jacob A. 1985. 'Developing moralnets: twenty-five years of culture and change among the Choco.' In *Missionaries, Anthropology, and Cultural Change (Part I)*, ed. Darrell L. Whiteman. Publication Number 25: 229–61.Williamsburg, Virginia: Department of Anthropology, College of William and Mary.

MacCannell, Dean. 1976. *The Tourist: A New Theory of the Leisure Class*. New York: Schocken Books.

Malinowski, Bronislaw. 1922. *Argonauts of the Western Pacific: An Account of Native Enterprise and Adventure in the Archipelagoes of Melanesian New Guinea*. London: Routledge & K. Paul.

Marcus, George E. 1998. *Ethnography Through Thick and Thin*. Princeton: Princeton University Press.

Margiotti, Margherita. 2013. 'Clothing Sociality: Materiality and the Everyday Among the Kuna of Panama.' *Journal of Material Culture* 18(4), 389–407.

Marsh, Richard Oglesby. 1934. *White Indians of Darien*. New York: Putnam.

Martínez Mauri, Mónica. 2003. *Médiation et développement. L'emergence des ONG et des passeurs culturels à Kuna Yala (Panama)*. Genève: Publications de l'Institut Universitaire d'Etudes du Développement.

Martínez Mauri, Mónica. 2008. 'De sociedades a ONGs: mediación cultural y organización política en Kuna Yala (Panamá).' *Societé Suisse des Américanistes* 70, 31–8.

Martínez Mauri, Mónica. 2011a. *La autonomía indígena en Panamá: La experiencia del Pueblo Kuna (siglos XVI-XXI)*. Panama: SENACYT.

Martínez Mauri, Mónica. 2011b. *Kuna Yala, tierra de mar: ecología y territorio indígena en Panamá*. Panama: SENACYT.

Martínez Mauri, Mónica. 2012. 'Molas, turismo y etnicidad entre los gunas de Panamá. Nuevos modos de relación con los emblemas identitarios.' In *El turismo es cosa de pobres? Patrimonio cultural, pueblos indígenas y nuevas formas de turismo en América Latina*, eds. Raúl H. Asensio and Beatriz Pérez Galán, pp. 15–33. El Sauzal, Tenerife: Asociación Canaria de Antropología.

Meléndez, Mariselle. 2005. 'Visualizing difference: the rhetoric of clothing in colonial Spanish America.' In *The Latin American Fashion Reader*, ed. Regina Root, pp. 17–30. Oxford: Berg.

Mendizábal, Tomás E. and Theodossopoulos, Dimitrios. 2012. 'The Emberá, Tourism and Indigenous Archaeology: "Rediscovering" the Past in Eastern Panama.' *Memorias* 18, 88–114.

Miller, Daniel. 1994. *Modernity: An Ethnographic Approach*. Oxford: Berg.

Miller, Daniel. 2005a. 'Introduction.' In *Clothing as Material Culture*, eds. Susanne Kuchler and Daniel Miller, pp. 1–19. Oxford: Berg.

Miller, Daniel. 2005b. 'Materiality: an introduction.' In *Materiality*, ed. Daniel Miller, pp. 1–50. Durham: Duke University Press.

Miller, Daniel. 2008. *The Comfort of Things*. Cambridge: Polity Press.

Miller, Daniel. 2010. *Stuff*. Cambridge: Polity Press.

Milton, Kay. 1996. *Environmentalism and Cultural Theory: Exploring the Role of Anthropology in Environmental Discourse*. London: Routledge.

Morris, Brian. 1981. 'Changing Views of Nature.' *The Ecologist* 11, 130–7.

Mortensen, Charles A. 1999. *A Reference Grammar of the Northern Emberá Languages*. Arlington: The University of Texas at Arlington.

Newman, Deena. 1998. 'Prophecies, Police Reports, Cartoons and other Ethnographic Rumours in Addis Ababa.' *Etnofoor* 11(2), 83–110.

Nordenskiold, Erland. 1927. 'The Chocó Indians of Colombia and Panama.' *Discovery* 8, 347–50.

Nordenskiold, Erland. 1928. *Indianerna pa Panamanaset*. Stockholm: Ahlén & Akerlunds Forlag.

Nugent, Stephen. 1990. *Big Mouth: The Amazon Speaks*. London: Fourth Estate.

Nugent, Stephen. 2007. *Scoping the Amazon: Image, Icon, Ethnography*. Walnut Creek: Left Coast Press.

O'Hanlon, Michael. 1989. *Reading the Skin: Adornment, Display and Society Among the Wahgi*. London: British Museum.

O'Hanlon, Michael. 1992. 'Unstable Images and Second Skins: Artifacts, Exegesis and Assessments in the New Guinea Highlands.' *Man* 27(3), 587–608.

O'Hanlon, Michael. 2007. 'Body arts and modernity: an introduction.' In *Body Arts and Modernity*, eds. Elizabeth Ewart and Michael O'Hanlon, pp. 1–17. Wantage: Sean Kingston.

Pereiro Pérez, Xerardo, Cebaldo de León, Monica Martínez-Mauri, Jorge Ventocilla and Yadixa del Valle. 2010. *Estudio estratégico del turismo en Kuna Yala: primera versión del informe de investigación 2008–2010*. Panama: SENACYT.

Phillips, David. 1997. *Exhibiting Authenticity*. Manchester: Manchester University Press.

Phillips, Ruth B. and Christopher B. Steiner. 1999. 'Art, authenticity, and the baggage of cultural encounter.' In *Unpacking Culture: Art and Commodity in Colonial and Postcolonial Worlds*, eds. Ruth B. Phillips and Christopher B. Steiner, pp. 3–19. Berkeley: University of California Press.

Pina-Cabral, Joao de. 1987. 'Paved Roads and Enchanted Mooresses: The Perception of the Past Among the Peasant Population of the Alto Minho.' *Man* 22 (4), 715–35.

Pineda, Roberto and Virginia Gutiérrez de Pineda. 1999. *Criaturas de Caragabí: indios Chocoes, Emberáes, Catíos, Chamíes y Noanamaes*. Medellín: Editorial Universidad de Antioquia.

Potvin, Catherine, Rogelio Cansari, Jane Hutton, Inocencio Caisamo and Bonarge Pacheco 2003. 'Preparation for Propagation: Understanding Germination of Giwa (Astrocaryum standleyanum), Wagara (Sabal mauritiiformis), and Eba (Socratea exorrhiza) for Future Cultivation.' *Biodiversity and Conservation* 12, 2161–71.

Price, Sally. 2007. 'Into the Mainstream: Shifting Authenticities in Art.' *American Ethnologist* 34(4), 603–20.

Ramos, Alcida R. 1991. 'A Hall of Mirrors: The Rhetoric of Indigenism in Brazil.' *Critique of Anthropology* 11(2), 155–69.

Ramos, Alcida R. 1998. *Indigenism: Ethnic Politics in Brazil*. Madison: University of Wisconsin Press.

Ramos, Alcida R. 2003. 'Comment on Kuper, The Return of the Native.' *Current Anthropology* **44**(3), 397-8.

Ramos, Alcida R. 2012. 'The Politics of Perspectivism.' *Annual Review of Anthropology* 41, 481–94.

Reichel-Dolmatoff, Gerardo. 1960. 'Notas etnográficas sobre los indios del Chocó.' *Revista Colombiana de Antropología* 9, 73–158.

Reichel-Dolmatoff, Gerardo. 1962. 'Contribuciones a la etnografía de los indios del Chocó.' *Revista Colombiana de Antropología* 11, 169–88.

Reisinger, Yvette. and Carol J. Steiner. 2006. 'Reconceptualizing Object Authenticity.' *Annals of Tourism Research* 33(1), 65–86.

Reverte Coma, José Manuel. 2002. *Tormenta en el Darien: vida de los Indios Chocoes en Panama*. Madrid: Museo Profesor Reverte Coma.

Roach-Higgins, Mary Ellen and Joanne B. Eicher. 1995. 'Dress and identity.' In *Dress and Identity*, eds. Mary Ellen Roach-Higgins, Joanne B. Eicher and Kim K. P. Johnson, pp. 7–18. New York: Fairchild Publications.

Robertson, Roland. 1992. *Globalization: Social Theory and Global Culture*. London: Sage.

Rosaldo, Renato. 1989. 'Imperialist Nostalgia.' *Representations* 26, 107–22.

Rosaldo, Renato. 1993. *Culture and Truth: The Remaking of Social Analysis*. London: Routledge.

Rudolf, Gloria. 1999. *Panama's Poor: Victims, Agents, and Historymakers*. Gainesville: University Press of Florida.

Sahlins, Marshall. 1999. 'Two or Three Things That I Know About Culture.' *The Journal of the Royal Anthropological Institute* 59(3), 399–421.

Sahlins, Marshall. 2000. ' "Sentimental pessimism" and ethnographic experience; or, why culture is not a disappearing "object".' In *Biographies of Scientific Objects*, ed. L. Daston, pp. 158–202. Chicago: University of Chicago Press.

Salazar, Noel. 2010. *Envisioning Eden: Mobilizing Imaginaries in Tourism and Beyond.* Oxford: Berghahn Books.

Salazar, Noel and Nelson Graburn. 2014. 'Toward an anthropology of tourism imaginaries.' In *Tourism Imaginaries: Through an Anthropological Lens,* eds. Nelson Graburn and Noel Salazar, pp. 1–28. Oxford: Berghahn Books.

Salvador, Mari Lyn. 1976. 'The clothing arts of the Cuna of San Blas, Panama.' In *Ethnic and Tourist Arts: Cultural Expression from the Fourth World,* ed. Nelson Graburn, pp. 165–82. Berkeley: University of California Press.

Salvador, Mari Lyn (ed.). 1997a. *The Art of Being Kuna: Layers of Meaning Among the Kuna of Panama.* Los Angeles: UCLA Fowler Museum of Cultural History.

Salvador, Mari Lyn. 1997b. 'Looking back: contemporary Kuna women's arts.' In *The Art of Being Kuna: Layers of Meaning Among the Kuna of Panama,* ed. Mari Lyn Salvador, pp. 151–211. Los Angeles: UCLA Fowler Museum of Cultural History.

Salvador, Mari Lyn and James Howe. 1997. 'Artful lives: the Kuna of Panama.' In *The Art of Being Kuna: Layers of Meaning Among the Kuna of Panama,* ed. Mari Lyn Salvador, pp. 29–51. Los Angeles: UCLA Fowler Museum of Cultural History.

Santos-Granero, Fernando. 2009. 'Hybrid Bodyscapes: A Visual History of Yanesha Patterns of Cultural Change.' *Current Anthropology* 50, 477–512.

Sarró, Ramon. 2009. *The Politics of Religious Change on the Upper Guinea Coast: Iconoclasm Done and Undone.* Edinburgh: Edinburgh University Press.

Saugestad, Sidsel. 2001. 'Contested images: "first peoples" or "marginalised minorities" in Africa?' In *Africa's Indigenous Peoples: 'First Peoples' or 'Marginalised?'* eds. A. Barnard and J. Kenrick, pp. 299–322. Edinburgh: Centre of African Studies.

Schildkrout, Enid. 2004. 'Inscribing the Body.' *Annual Review of Anthropology* 33, 319–44.

Schneider, Jane. 1987. 'The Anthropology of Cloth.' *Annual Review of Anthropology* 16, 409–48.

Schneider, Jane and Annette B. Weiner. 1989. 'Introduction.' In *Cloth and Human Experience,* eds. Annette B. Weiner and Jane Schneider, pp. 1–29. Washington: Smithsonian Institution Press.

Seeger, Anthony. 1975. 'The Meaning of Body Ornaments: A Suya Example.' *Ethnology* 14 (3), 211–24.

Selwyn, Tom (ed.). 1996. *The Tourist Image: Myths and Myth Making in Tourism.* Chichester: Wiley.

Sherzer, Dina and Joel Sherzer. 1976. 'Mormaknamaloe: the Cuna Mola.' In *Ritual and Symbol in Native Central America,* ed. James Howe, pp. 23–42. Oregon: University of Oregon Anthropological Papers No. 9.

Shukla, Pravina. 2015. *Costume: Performing Identities Through Dress.* Bloomington: Indiana University Press.

Sillitoe, Paul. 1988. 'From Head-Dresses to Head-Messages: The Art of Self-Decoration in the Highlands of Papua New Guinea.' *Man* 23(2), 298–318.

Sillitoe, Paul. 2015. 'The dialogue between indigenous studies and engaged anthropology: some first impressions.' In *Indigenous Studies and Engaged Anthropology: The Collaborative Moment,* ed. Paul Sillitoe, pp. 1–29. Surrey: Ashgate.

Skinner, Jonathan and Dimitrios Theodossopoulos. 2011. 'Introduction: the play of expectation in tourism.' In *Great Expectations: Imagination and Anticipation in Tourism,* eds. Jonathan Skinner and Dimitrios Theodossopoulos, pp. 1–26. Oxford: Berghahn Books.

Sligo, Frank and Elspeth Tilley. 2012. 'Cartoons as praxis: negotiating different needs in adult literacy research reporting.' In *Popularizing Research: Engaging New Genres, Media, and Audiences,* ed. Phillip Vannini, pp. 33–8. New York: Peter Lang.

Smith, Valene L. (ed.). 1989. *Hosts and Guests: The Anthropology of Tourism*. Philadelphia: University of Pennsylvania Press.

Spooner, Brian. 1986. 'Introduction: commodities and the politics of value.' In *The Social Life of Things: Commodities in Cultural Perspective*, ed. Arjun Appadurai, pp. 195–235. Cambridge: Cambridge University Press.

Stasch, Rupert. 2014. 'Toward symmetric treatment of imaginaries: nudity and payment in tourism to New Guinea's "treehouse people"'. In *Tourism Imaginaries: Through an Anthropological Lens,* eds. Nelson Graburn and Noel Salazar, pp. 9–56. Oxford: Berghahn Books.

Stewart, Charles. 2007. *Creolization: History, Ethnography, Theory*. Walnut Creek: Left Coast Press.

Stewart, Kathleen. 1988. 'Nostalgia–A Polemic.' *Cultural Anthropology* 3(3), 227–41.

Stout, David B. 1963. 'The Choco.' In *Handbook of South American Indians*, ed. J. H. Steward, pp. 269–76. New York: Cooper Square Publishers.

Strathern, Andrew. 1987. 'Dress, decoration, and art in New Guinea.' In *Man as Art: New Guinea Body Decoration*, ed. M. Kirk, pp. 15–36. London: Thames and Hudson.

Strathern, Andrew and Pamela J. Stewart. 2010. 'Shifting centers, tense peripheries: indigenous cosmopolitanisms'. In *United in Discontent: Local Responses to Cosmopolitanism and Globalization,* eds. D. Theodossopoulos and E. Kirtsoglou, pp. 20–44. Oxford: Berghahn Books.

Strathern, Marilyn. 1979. 'The Self in Self-Decoration.' *Oceania*, XLIX (4), 241–57.

Strathern, Marilyn. 1995. 'Nostalgia and the new genetics.' In *Rhetorics of Self-Making*, ed. Debbora Battaglia, pp. 97–120. Berkeley: University of California Press.

Strathern, Marilyn and Andrew Strathern. 1971. *Self-Decoration in Mount Hagen*. London: Duckworth.

Stronza, Amanda. 2001. 'Anthropology of Tourism: Forging New Ground for Ecotourism and Other Alternatives.' *Annual Review of Anthropology* 30, 261–83.

Sutton, David E. 1998. *Memories Cast in Stone: The Relevance of the Past in Everyday Life*. Oxford: Berg.

Swain, Margaret B. 1989. 'Gender roles in indigenous tourism: Kuna Mola, Kuna Yala and cultural survival.' In *Hosts and Guests: The Anthropology of Tourism*, ed. Valene L. Smith, pp. 83–104. Philadelphia: University of Pennsylvania Press.

Tarlo, Emma. 1996. *Clothing Matters: Dress and Identity in India*. London: Hurst.

Tarlo, Emma. 2010. *Visibly Muslim: Fashion, Politics, Faith*. Oxford: Berg.

Taussig, Michael T. 1987. *Shamanism, Colonialism, and the Wild Man: A Study in Terror and Healing*. Chicago: University of Chicago Press.

Taussig, Michael T. 1993. *Mimesis and Alterity: A Particular History of the Senses*. London: Routledge.

Taussig, Michael T. 2011. *I Swear I Saw This: Drawings in Fieldwork Notebooks, Namely My Own*. Chicago: University of Chicago Press.

Tayler, Donald. 1996. *Embarkations: Ethnography and Shamanism of the Chocó Indians of Colombia*. Oxford: Pitt Rivers Museum.

Taylor, John. 2001. 'Authenticity and Sincerity in Tourism.' *Annals of Tourism Research* 28(1), 7–26.

Theodossopoulos, Dimitrios. 2007. 'Encounters with Authentic Embera Culture in Panama.' *Journeys* 8(1), 43–65.

Theodossopoulos, Dimitrios. 2010a. 'Tourism and indigenous culture as resources: lessons from Emberá cultural tourism in Panama.' In *Tourism, Power and*

Culture: Anthropological Insights, eds. Donald V.L. Macleod and James G. Carrier, pp. 115–33. Bristol: Channel View.

Theodossopoulos, Dimitrios. 2010b. 'Introduction: united in discontent.' In *United in Discontent: Local Responses to Cosmopolitanism and Globalization*, eds. D. Theodossopoulos and E. Kirtsoglou, pp. 1–19. Oxford: Berghahn Books.

Theodossopoulos, Dimitrios. 2010c. 'With or Without *Gringos*: When Panamanians Talk About the United States and its Citizens.' *Social Analysis* 54 (1), 52–70.

Theodossopoulos, Dimitrios. 2011. 'Emberá indigenous tourism and the world of expectations.' In *Great Expectations: Imagination and Anticipation in Tourism*, eds. Jonathan Skinner and Dimitrios Theodossopoulos, pp. 40–60. Oxford: Berghahn Books.

Theodossopoulos, Dimitrios. 2012. 'Indigenous Attire, Exoticisation and Social Change: Dressing and Undressing Among the Emberá of Panama.' *Journal of the Royal Anthropological Institute*, 18(3), 591–612.

Theodossopoulos, Dimitrios. 2013a. 'Emberá Indigenous Tourism and the Trap of Authenticity: Beyond In-authenticity and Invention.' *Anthropological Quarterly* 86(2), 397–426.

Theodossopoulos, Dimitrios. 2013b. 'Laying Claim to Authenticity: Five Anthropological Dilemmas.' *Anthropological Quarterly* 86(2), 337–60.

Theodossopoulos, Dimitrios. 2013c. 'Dance, visibility, and representational self-awareness in an Embera community in Panama.' In *Dancing Cultures: Globalization, Tourism and Identity in the Anthropology of Dance*, eds. Hélène Neveu Kringelbach and Jonathan Skinner, pp. 121–40. Oxford: Berghahn Books.

Theodossopoulos, Dimitrios. 2014. 'Scorn or idealization? Tourism imaginaries, exoticisation and ambivalence in Emberá indigenous tourism.' In *Tourism Imaginaries: Through an Anthropological Lens,* eds. Nelson Graburn and Noel Salazar, pp. 57–79. Oxford: Berghahn Books.

Theodossopoulos, Dimitrios. 2015. 'Embera indigeneity and cultural representation: a view from engaged anthropology.' In *Indigenous Studies and Engaged Anthropology: The Collaborative Moment*, ed. Paul Sillitoe, pp. 33–54. Surrey: Ashgate.

Theodossopoulos Dimitrios. In press. 'On ethnographic nostalgia: exoticising and de-exoticising Emberá culture, for example.' *Social Analysis*.

Theodossopoulos, Dimitrios. n.d. 'Indigenous tourism as a transformative process: the case of the Emberá in Panama.' In *Cultural Tourism Movements: New Articulations of Indigenous Identity*, eds. Alexis Celeste Bunten, Jenny Chio and Nelson Graburn. Chicago: University of Chicago Press.

Theodossopoulos, Dimitrios and Elisabeth Kirtsoglou (eds.). 2010. *United in Discontent: Local Responses to Cosmopolitanism and Globalization*. Oxford: Berghahn Books.

Thomas, Nicholas. 2003. 'The case of the misplaced ponchos: speculations concerning the history of cloth in Polynesia.' In *Clothing the Pacific*, ed. Chloe Colchester, pp. 79–96. Oxford: Berg.

Tice, Karin E. 1995. *Kuna Crafts, Gender, and the Global Economy*. Austin: University of Texas Press.

Tilley, Elspeth, Frank Sligo, Fiona Shearer, Margie Comrie, Niki Murray, John Franklin, Franco Vaccarino and Bronwyn Watson. 2007. *Voices: First-Hand Experiences of Adult Literacy Learning and Employment in Wanganui*. Wellington: Department of Communication and Journalism, Massey University.

Tinajero, Araceli. 2005. 'Far eastern influences in Latin American fashions.' In *The Latin American Fashion Reader*, ed. Regina A. Root, pp. 66–75. Oxford: Berg.

Torres de Araúz, Reina. 1961. 'Etnografía: vestidos y adornos de los indios Chocoes." *Lotería* 6(73), 45–55.

Torres de Araúz, Reina. 1966. *La cultura Chocó: estudio ethnológico e historico.* Panama: Centro de Investigaciones Antropológicas, University of Panama.

Torres de Araúz, Reina. 1975. *Darién: etnología de una región histórica.* Panama: Instituto Nacional de Cultura.

Torres de Araúz, Reina. 1980. *Panama indigena.* Panama: Instituto Nacional de Cultura.

Trilling, Lionel. 1972. *Sincerity and Authenticity.* London: Oxford University Press.

Trouillot, Michel-Rolph. 1991. 'Anthropology and the savage slot.' In *Recapturing Anthropology: Working in the Present,* ed. R. Fox, pp. 17–44. Santa Fe: SAR Press.

Trouillot, Michel-Rolph. 2002. 'The otherwise modern: Caribbean lessons from the savage slot.' In *Critically Modern: Alternatives, Alterities, Anthropologies,* ed. Bruce M. Knauft, pp. 220–37. Bloomington: Indiana University Press.

Tucker, Hazel. 2011. 'Success and access to knowledge in the tourism-local encounter: confrontations with the unexpected in a Turkish community.' In *Great Expectations: Imagination and Anticipation in the Anthropology of Tourism,* eds. J. Skinner Jonathan and D. Theodossopoulos, pp. 27-39. Oxford: Berghahn Books.

Turner, Terence. 1969. 'Tchikrin: A Central Brazilian Tribe and its Symbolic Language of Bodily Adornment.' *Natural History* 78(8), 50–9.

Turner, Terence. 1980. 'The social skin.' In *Not Work Alone: A Cross-Cultural View of Activities Superfluous to Survival,* eds. Jeremy Cherfas and Roger Lewin, pp. 112–40. London: Temple Smith.

Turner, Terence. 1992a. 'Symbolic language of bodily adornment.' In *Kaiapó Amazonia: The Art of Body Decoration,* ed. Gustaaf Verswijver, pp. 27–35. Gent: Snoeck-Ducaju & Zoon.

Turner, Terence. 1992b. 'Representing, resisting, rethinking: historical transformations of Kayapó and anthropological consciousness.' In Colonial Situations, ed. *George Stocking,* pp. 285–313. Madison: University of Wisconsin Press.

Turner, Terence. 1992c. 'Defiant Images.' *Anthropology Today* 8(6), 5–15.

Turner, Terence. 2002. 'Representation, polyphony and the construction of power in a Kayapo video.' In *Indigenous Movements, Self-Representation, and the State in Latin America,* eds. K. B. Warren and J. E. Jackson, pp. 229–50. Austin: University of Texas Press.

Turner, Terence. 2006. 'Political Innovation and Inter-Ethnic Alliance.' *Anthropology Today* 22(5), 2–10.

Turner, Terence and Vanessa Fajans-Turner. 2006. 'Political Innovation and Inter-Ethnic Alliance: Kayapo Resistance to the Developmentalist State.' *Anthropology Today* 22(5), 3–10.

Turner, Victor. 1967. *The Forest of Symbols.* Ithaca: Cornell University Press.

Turner, Victor. 1969. *The Ritual Process: Structure and Anti-Structure.* Chicago: Aldine Pub.

Ulloa, Astrid. 1992. *Kipará: dibujo y pintura: dos formas embera de representar el mundo.* Bogotá: Universidad Nacional de Colombia.

Ulloa, Astrid. 2005. *The Ecological Native: Indigenous Peoples' Movements and Eco-Governmentality in Colombia.* London: Routledge.

Uribe Ángel, Manuel. 1885. *Geografía general y compendio historico del Estado de Antioquia en Colombia.* Paris: Talleres de Goupy et Jordan.

Urry, John. 1990. *The Tourist Gaze.* London: Sage.

Urry, John. 1995. *Consuming Places.* London: Routledge.

Van de Port, Mattijs. 2004. 'Registers of Incontestability: The Quest for Authenticity in Academia and Beyond.' *Etnofoor* XVII(1/2), 7–22.

Van de Port, Mattijs. 2005. 'Circulating Around the *Really Real*: Spirit Possession Ceremonies and the Search for Authenticity in Bahian Candomblé.' *Ethos* 33(2), 149–79.

Vargas, Patricia. 1993. *Los Emberá y los Cuna: impacto y reaccion ante la ocupacion Española, siglos XVI y XVII.* CEREC: Instituto Colombiano de Antropología.

Vasco Uribe, Luis Guillermo. 1985. *Jaibanás: los verdaderos hombres.* Bogotá: Biblioteca Banco popular.

Vasco Uribe, Luis Guillermo. 1987. *Semejantes a los dioses: Cerámica y cestería embera-chamí.* Bogotá: Universidad Nacional de Colombia.

Veber, Hanne. 1992. 'Why Indians Wear Clothes ... Managing Identity Across an Ethnic Boundary.' *Ethnos* 57(1–2), 51–60.

Veber, Hanne. 1996. 'External Inducement and non-Westernization in the Uses of the Ashéninka Cushma.' *Journal of Material Culture* 1, 155–82.

Velásquez Runk, Julie. 2001. 'Wounaan and Emberá Use and Management of the Fiber Palm Astrocaryum standleyanum (Arecaceae) for Basketry in Eastern Panama.' *Economic Botany* 55(1), 72–82.

Velásquez Runk, Julie. 2009. 'Social and River Networks for the Trees: Wounaan's Riverine Rhizomic Cosmos and Arboreal Conservation.' *American Anthropologist* 111(4), 456–67.

Velásquez Runk, Julie. 2012. 'Indigenous Land and Environmental Conflicts in Panama: Neoliberal Multiculturalism, Changing Legislation, and Human Rights.' *Journal of Latin American Geography* 11(2), 21–47.

Velásquez Runk, Julie. 2015. 'Creating Wild Darién: Centuries of Darién's Imaginative Geography and its Lasting Effects.' *Journal of Latin American Geography* 14(3), 127-56.

Velásquez Runk, Julie, Mónica Martínez Mauri, Blas Quintero Sánchez and Jorge Sarsaneda del Cid. 2011. *Pueblos indígenas en Panamá: una bibliografía.* Panamá: Acción Cultural Ngóbe (ACUN).

Verrill, Hyatt A. 1921. *Panama, Past and Present.* New York: Dodd, Mead & Co.

Verrill, Hyatt A. 1931. *Panama of Today.* New York: Dodd, Mead & Co.

Vidal, Lux and Gustaaf Verswijver. 1992. 'Body painting among the Kaiapó.' In *Kaiapó Amazonia: The Art of Body Decoration,* ed. Gustaaf Verswijver, pp. 37–47. Gent: Snoeck-Ducaju & Zoon.

Viveiros de Castro, Eduardo. 1998. 'Cosmological Deixis and Amerindian Perspectivism.' *The Journal of the Royal Anthropological Institute* 4(3), 469-88.

Wade, Peter. 1997. *Race and Ethnicity in Latin America.* London: Pluto.

Wali, Alaka. 1989. *Kilowatts and Crisis: Hydroelectric Power and Social Dislocation in Eastern Panama.* Boulder: Westview Press.

Wali, Alaka. 1993. 'The Transformation of a Frontier: State and Regional Relationships in Panama, 1972-1990.' *Human Organization* 52 (2), 115–29.

Walker, Harry. 2013. *Under a Watchful Eye: Self, Power, and Intimacy in Amazonia.* Berkeley: University of California Press.

Warren, Kay B. and Jean E. Jackson. 2002. 'Introduction: studying indigenous activism in Latin America.' In *Indigenous Movements, Self-Representation, and the State in Latin America,* eds. Kay B. Warren and Jean E. Jackson, pp. 1–46. Austin: University of Texas Press.

Wassén, Henry. 1935. 'Notes on Southern Groups of Chocó Indians in Colombia.' *Ethnologiska Studier* 1, 35–182.

Wassén, Henry. 1963. 'Ethnohistoria Chocoana y cinco cuentos Waunana apuntados en 1955.' *Ethnologiska Studier* 26, 9–78.

Weiner, Annette B. 1989. 'Why cloth?' In *Cloth and Human Experience*, eds. Annette B. Weiner and Jane Schneider, pp. 33–72. Washington: Smithsonian Institution Press.

Weiner, Annette B. 1992. *Inalienable Possessions: The Paradox of Keeping-While-Giving*. Berkeley: University of California Press.

Werbner, Pnina. In press. 'Between Triste Tropique and Cultural Creativity: Modern Times and the Vanishing Primitive.' *Social Analysis*.

West, Paige and James Carrier. 2004. 'Ecotourism and Authenticity: Getting Away from It All?' *Current Anthropology* 45(4), 483–98.

Wettstein, Marion. 2011. 'Small Notes on a Neglected Topic in Visual Anthropology.' Accessed from http://www.marionwettstein.ch/ethnographicdrawing.html.

Wickstrom, Stefanie. 2003. 'The Politics of Development in Indigenous Panama.' *Latin American Perspectives* 30(4), 43–68.

Williams, Caroline A. 2004. *Between Resistance and Adaptation: Indigenous Peoples and the Colonisation of the Chocó, 1510–1753*. Liverpool: Liverpool University Press.

Williams, Raymond. 1973. *The Country and the City*. Oxford: Oxford University Press.

Young, Philip D. 1971. *Ngawbe: Tradition and Change Among the Western Guaymí of Panama*. Urbana: University of Illinois Press.

Young, Philip D. and John R. Bort. 1999. 'Ngóbe adaptive responses to globalization in Panama.' In *Globalization and the Rural Poor in Latin America*, ed. W. Loker, pp. 111–36. Boulder: Lynne Rienner.

Index

EU authorised representative for GPSR:
Easy Access System Europe, Mustamäe tee 50,
10621 Tallinn, Estonia
gpsr.requests@easproject.com